About the Author

Dr. Rodney Schofield has a long and varied experience of the Christian Church. Brought up as a Methodist, he was ordained an Anglican priest in 1972, serving in English parishes and teaching in African seminaries, before becoming a Catholic priest in 2006. In this thought-provoking collection of talks and lectures he explores how the Christian faith expressed itself and developed over the years, highlighting the role of missionary pioneers as well as those deep thinkers who have faced the changing intellectual challenges. This is a book for clergy, churchgoers, and any who want to engage honestly with religious truth.

Dedication

This compilation is dedicated to:

my wife Sarah

the Christians of Wye

St John's College, Cambridge

in gratitude for all their support

Rodney Schofield

LEARNING CURVES

Pilgrims Pioneers Explorations
The Way Ahead

AUSTIN MACAULEY PUBLISHERS™

LONDON • CAMBRIDGE • NEW YORK • SHARJAH

A CIP catalogue record for this title is available from the British Library.

ISBN 978-1-78693-347-8 (Paperback)
ISBN 978-1-78693-348-5 (E-Book)

www.austinmacauley.com

First Published (2017)
Austin Macauley Publishers Ltd.™
25 Canada Square
Canary Wharf
London
E14 5LQ

OTHER PUBLICATIONS

Other publications

Jubilee Reflections
Rich and poor in Christian Perspective (Kachere Press, Malawi 2001)

Mystery or Magic
Biblical replies to the heterodox (Kachere Press, Malawi 2004)

Bordering on Faith
Developing orthopraxis in response to spiritual need (Melrose Press, UK 2009)

The Emerging Church
Christian communities in the earliest times (Melrose Press, UK 2012)

Malawi Mailings
Reflections of missionary life 2000-2003 (Mzuni Press, Malawi 2014)

Emerging Scriptures
Torah, Gospel and Qur'an in Christian perspective (Mzuni Press, Malawi 2015)

Learning Curves

Pilgrims

Pioneers

Explorations

The Way Ahead

Rodney Schofield

CONTENTS

A LARGE WOODEN NEEDLE

used by Mè Justina
at Lelapa la Jesu Seminary
(Roma, Lesotho)
to weave a rush fence
and the thatch on a rondavel

So too this book aims to weave
together a variety of talks
given to groups in Kent

about pilgrims on their journeys,
courageous witnesses to faith,
pioneers of Christian thought,
those who challenged the status quo
or explored our human destiny
within and beyond this universe,

and about the path of humility
followed by Jesus Christ.

It was at St Joseph's Mission Hospital in Roma that I anointed Justina's two week old nephew, who was expected to die very shortly. But God can surprise us. The following morning her sister appeared on our doorstep, having been discharged by the doctors – holding a lively baby.

INTRODUCTION

Over thirty years ago, when I was serving as an Anglican missionary priest in Lesotho, among the many visitors who stayed with us at Lelapa la Jesu Seminary were Dr Rowan Williams[1] and his wife Jane. They were on a lecture tour of Southern Africa, and in Roma we combined with the much longer established St Augustine's Catholic Seminary to hear each of them address us. It was actually Jane who made the greater impression upon our students – they had never previously seen or heard a woman speaking publicly on theological matters. I myself was particularly grateful for Rowan's words of wisdom, which in outline I still recall. He spoke of the teaching ministry of a priest: the task, he said, was to be 'a traveller across both time and space', and thus to help his flock keep in touch with their Christian heritage as well as the movements of God's spirit in the contemporary world.

This is a world which to many ordinary people sometimes seems to be overloaded with so much information that they can easily lose their way in exercising judgment and discrimination. Not least this can happen with religious teachings in a pluralist society, resulting in confusion about the deepest issues, uncertainty about what Christian faith itself stands for, and perhaps leaving some in a suspended state of agnosticism.

Some of these issues are explored here, along with varied accounts of the challenges faced by particular individuals or churches in past centuries. It is certainly not a comprehensive survey, but an exploration in some depth of topics relevant to different groups of churchgoers (and others) in the village of Wye, Kent desirous of finding out more both about their Christian ancestors and also how their faith expressed itself and developed over the years. (Wye, about 12 miles above Canterbury, lies in the Stour valley where the river has cut a gap between the North Downs.) The papers were given either as single talks or as a series of Lent lectures, mainly in St Ambrose' Catholic Church where clergy and members of other denominations joined us, but in other locations too

---

[1] He recently read some of this book, which he kindly said was 'really illuminating'. The rest may be less so, but I hope not riddled with too many errors or too many irrelevances.

(including the King's Head), and addressed to other village organisations (such as Wye Arts or the Historical Society).

My raison d'être for delving into these loosely-linked subjects has always been to act as a bridge between the academic world and the many others who appreciate St Anselm's famous phrase, *fides quaerens intellectum* ('faith seeking understanding'). For that reason there are hardly any footnotes, while references are chiefly confined to the Bible, a copy of which is still to be found in some households. Wye is indeed fortunate to have a good number of inquirers 'seeking understanding'; this tallies with the village's tradition of educational opportunity dating back to the 1440s when Cardinal John Kempe (who was of local stock) built and endowed a college here for priests; subsequently this became a grammar school and then, until recently, a renowned agricultural college. The topics do, however, all reflect something of a personal interest as well – places where I have lived or people who have influenced my own understanding, each of them affording experiences from which others will hopefully gain something:

• Thus, the opening trilogy ('Pilgrims') clearly relates to *Wye* itself, looking at its chequered past and an imagined scenario of its future (which has attracted quite a cult readership, especially in the United States), but starting with its location on ancient trackways and its convenience for medieval pilgrims. There are resonances here with my past involvement in guiding pilgrimages and religious 'tours'.

• *St Ambrose* (in 'Pioneers') is patron of our own Catholic Church, whose diamond jubilee in 2014 gave rise to a talk about his role in developing the Church's self-understanding. *Newman* like myself was a convert to Catholicism; his beatification in 2010 prompted this survey of teachings that eventually influenced the 2nd Vatican Council. The pioneers, *Livingstone and Colenso*, who broke new ground in Africa, each related to countries where I too served as a missionary: Magomero, the site chosen by Livingstone in 'Nyasaland', fell within my parish; while in Lesotho we came to know Natal quite well, staying in a Zulu rondavel more than once.

• 'Explorations' contains courses devised for Lent: *Change in the Church* along with *Joining the ranks of heaven* both originated in programmes that I taught in Africa, but also reflect later personal developments (not least the process of ageing). *God and the world* takes me further back, when my study of mathematics led to an interest in cosmology and time spent at the Royal Observatory.

- Yet for me 'The way ahead', the definitive guide to God's hopes and intentions for our future, lies in the person of *Jesus*, the focus of my lifelong faith, whether as a Methodist, an Anglican or a Catholic. My sympathies lie particularly with that motivating idea of *ressourcement* ('going back to the sources') that breathed new life into the Catholic Church and beyond at the time of Vatican 2.

Overall the collection is entitled *Learning Curves*. The illustrations included in the frontispiece and on the title page are a reminder that the process of learning is seldom straightforward. We learn by our mistakes and by discovering that some attractive ideas lead us down a blind alley – or worse, that they distort the truth and take us further from our goal.

If we sometimes 'spiral' back and forth (*see the frontispiece*) as if through a maze, we may learn the salutory lesson that in the end mere human beings can never hope to unravel fully the mystery of the spiralling cosmos or to reduce the ineffability of our Creator to any form of words. Even plausible mentors, like the 'wise' serpent of Eden who coils around the tree of the knowledge of good and evil (*see the title page*), can tempt us to claim too much for ourselves; but at least we may then discover our frailty and begin again the quest that takes us into eternity.

CAUTION

Work in progress

The goal of our searching is represented last of all (*see the end page*), a picture inspired by our grandson's reunion with his mother shortly after his fourth birthday: he was so delighted to be with her again that, holding her hands, he danced round and round her for sheer joy – a 'whirling dervish'! By comparison, the twenty-four elders envisioned by St John in his *Apocalypse* as sitting on thrones round 'him who is seated [in their midst], who lives for ever and ever' seem a little too stately – seemingly lacking in exuberance – even though from time to time they fall to the ground 'casting off their crowns' while singing a short acclamation of praise. So a carving from a craft centre in Malawi, sponsored by the White Fathers at Mua, is depicted here too. It suggests a more vibrant expression of heavenly ecstasy. The dancing figure is playing a pipe and a drum at the same time, possibly in rhythms differing from those of his dance – an African sophistication seldom matched elsewhere in the world. (I recall that, in 1988 when 'dancing' was permitted in the Zairean form of the Roman liturgy, the Congregation for the Doctrine of the Faith was insistent that it should be 'dignified'; their preferred description was 'a rhythmically ordered procession'.)

* * * * * * *

On the following pages there are (I hope encouraging) reminders of those who were faithful to their own calling in days gone by, despite the setbacks and obstacles that they encountered, together with some discussion of challenges that we continue to face today. It is common to hear of 'lessons to be learnt' from mistakes and tragedies inflicted upon our contemporaries, but some of our forebears still have much to teach us too: St Ambrose was one of the first Christians to reflect upon the Just War; Cardinal John Kempe strove to negotiate an end to the Hundred Years War; Blessed John Henry Newman insisted (as did St Paul) on the value attached to the individual's own insights; Dr David Livingstone raised awareness about the continuing scale of people trafficking; Bishop John William Colenso recognised the humanity and incipient faith of those who knew nothing of 'British values'. Supremely, Jesus himself still holds the key to human fulfilment despite his inversion of so many of our own natural assumptions.

Selected source documents

in order of occurrence in the text

The way to Canterbury
Diodorus Siculus: *Bibliotheca Historica* (1st century BC)
St Bede: *Ecclesiastical History of the English People* (early 8th century)
St Boniface: *Letter to Cuthbert, Archbishop of Canterbury* (early 8th century)
Julius Caesar: *De Bello Gallico* (1st century BC)
John Gillingham: *The King and his Castle* (2009)
Hilaire Belloc: *The Old Road* (1904)
St Cyril of Jerusalem: *Catechetical Lectures* (c.347)
Jonathan Sumption: *Pilgrimage* (1975)
St Jerome: *Against Vigilantius* (406)
Geoffrey Chaucer: *The Canterbury Tales* (late 14th century)
William Langland: *The Vision of Piers Plowman* (late 14th century)
John Bunyan: *The Pilgrim's Progress* (1678)

Catholics in Wye
St Gildas: *The Desolation of Britain* (c.540)
Peter Brown: *The Rise of Western Christianity* (1997)
Roger of Wendover: *Flores Historiarum* (early 13th century)
John Kempe: (*reported in*) *Court Proceedings* (1413)
Pope Gregory XIII: *Papal Letter to English Catholics* (1575)
Edwin Burton and Thomas Williams (eds): *The Douay Diaries* (1911)
Leonard Whatmore: *Recusancy in Kent* (1973)

A future fugitive from Wye
Russell Hoban: *Riddley Walker* (1980)
William Inge: *Romanes Lecture* (1920)
Anton Chekhov: *The Three Sisters* (1903)
Martin Esslin: *Absurd Drama* (1965)
Wilfred Owen: *The Parable of the Old Man and the Young* (1917)

Ambrose of Milan
Timothy Barnes: *Ambrose and the Basilicas of Milan* (2000)
St Ambrose: *Letters, Hymns, Sermons, De Officiis* (388)
Henry Chadwick: *Augustine* (1986)
Gary Wills: *Font of Life* (2012)
Peter Brown: *Through the Eye of a Needle* (2015)

John Henry Newman

John Henry Newman: *Writings as listed on page 132* (19th century)
Lytton Strachey: *Eminent Victorians* (1918)
Owen Chadwick: *Newman* (1983)
Ian Ker: *The Achievement of John Henry Newman* (1990)

Missionaries beyond the bounds

Congregation for the Defence of the Faith: *Mission Instruction* (1659)
David Livingstone: *Letters* (1840s and 1850s)
Owen Chadwick: *Mackenzie's Grave* (1959)
Alastair Hazell: *The Last Slave Market* (2011)
Thomas Pakenham: *The Scramble for Africa* (1990)
John William Colenso: *Ten Weeks in Natal* (1854), *First Steps* (1860), *Sermons* (1865), *Langalibalele and the Amahlube Tribe* (1871)

Change in the Church

Anon: *Acts of the Martyrdom of St Justin* (165)
Pliny the Younger: *Letter to Trajan* (early 2nd century)
Tertullian: *First Apology* (c.198)
Clement of Alexandria: *Paedogogus* (c.198)
St Justin Martyr: *First Apology* (mid 2nd century)
Hippolytus: *Apostolic Tradition* (early 3rd century)
Kenan Osborne: *Christian Sacraments in a Postmodern World* (1999)
St Augustine of Hippo: *Letter to Quodvultdeus* (428)
Robert Markus: *The End of Ancient Christianity* (1998)
Harold Drake: *The Church, Society and Political Power* (2007)
James Okoye: *The Eucharist in African Perspective* (2008)
W.A.Graham: *Beyond the Written Word* (1993)
John Barton: *Hulsean Lectures* (1990)
Josef Jungmann: *The Early Liturgy* (1959)
Vatican 2 Decrees: *Ad Gentes* (1965), *Nostra Aetate* (1965)
Aylward Shorter: *Towards a Theology of Inculturation* (1988)
Pope John XXIII: *Princeps Pastorum* (1959)
Pope Francis: *Evangelii Gaudium* (2013), *Laudato Si'* (2015), *Misericordiae Vultus* (2015), *Amoris Laetitia* (2016)
Yves Congar: *Vraie et Fausse Réforme dans l'Église* (1950)
Benezet Bujo: *The Ethical Dimension of Community* (1998)
Gustavo Gutiérrez: *A Theology of Liberation* (2001)
Paulo Freire: *The Pedagogy of the Oppressed* (1970)

God and the world

Vatican 2 Constitution: *Gaudium et Spes* (1965)
John Henry Newman: *Essays Critical and Historical* (1870), *Grammar of Assent* (1870), *Tamworth Reading Room* (1841), *The Dream of Gerontius* (1865)
Charles Darwin: *The Origin of Species* (1859), *The Descent of Man* (1871)
Adrian Desmond and James Moore: *Darwin's Sacred Cause* (2009)
Conway Morris: *Life's Solution* (2003)
Guy Consolmagno: *Article in The Tablet* (2016)

Stephen Hawking: *A Brief History of Time* (1988), *The Nature of Space and Time* (1996), *The Grand Design* (2010), *Reith Lectures* (2016)
Vlatko Vedral: *DecodingReality* (2010)
Ernest Nagel and James Newman: *Gödel's Proof* (1959)
Daniel Kahneman: *Thinking Fast and Slow* (2011)
St Augustine: *Confessions* (397)
Pierre-Simon Laplace: *A Philosophical Essay on Probabilities* (1814)

Joining the ranks of heaven
Pindar: *Olympian Odes* (c.470 BC)
Protagoras: *On the Gods* (5th century BC)
St Cyprian: *Letter to Antonianus* (c.250)
St Augustine: *Enchiridion* (422), *City of God* (426)
St Gregory of Tours: *De Virtutibus Sancti Martini* (c.587)
F.D.Maurice: *On Eternal Life and Eternal Death* (1853)
J.W.Colenso: *Commentary on Romans* (1861)
C.S.Lewis: *The Great Divorce* (1945)
Elizabeth von Arnim: *The Enchanted April* (1922)

PILGRIMS

Scallop shell

**A pilgrim's badge
gathered from the seashore
of the Holy Island of Lindisfarne
once home to St Cuthbert**

Medieval pilgrims to Santiago returned with local 'cockle' shells. Those who visited other shrines brought back similar mementos; but it was the scallop that became the main symbol of pilgrimage and has often been used in baptism, when one's lifelong pilgrimage of faith begins.

The way to Canterbury

JOURNEYING IN FAITH

Trackways old and new

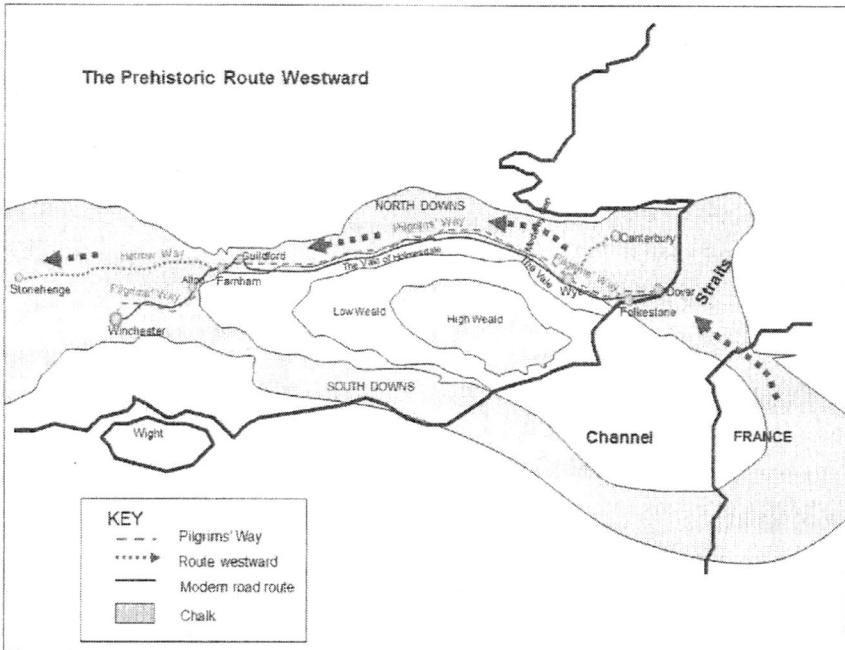

Before sea levels rose to create the 'English' Channel, it was possible for migrants and traders to reach Kent on foot from the continent, but by about 6000 BC this was no longer an option. No doubt this resulted in the inhabitants becoming relatively isolated, and their outside contacts more restricted – although trading across the waters certainly continued, as the Bronze Age boat discovered in Dover twenty years ago demonstrates.

Over a millennium later, in the 4th century BC, an explorer named Pytheas came here from the Greek colony of Massalia (later known as Marseilles) on the south coast of France. He was sent by merchants to find a route to the tin mines of southern Britain, which were an important source of that metal elsewhere in Europe. His report on a successful circumnavigation of Britain is cited subsequently by the historians Pliny and Diodorus. The latter's record begins as follows:

> Off the coast of Gaul, opposite the Hercynian Forest, are many islands in the Ocean of which the greatest is the so-called Pritain. In ancient times this had no communication with foreign powers, for we are not told that either Dionysus or Heracles or any other of the heroes invaded it. But in our day Julius Caesar was the first on record to subdue the island, and after defeating the Pritons he forced them to pay a fixed tribute. However, we shall write this up in detail at the proper time: now we will describe the island and the tin that is found there.
>
> In shape it is a triangle with unequal sides, something like Sicily. Lying obliquely off Europe, its point nearest the mainland, which they call *Kantion*, is said to be at a distance of 100 stades ...
>
> Pritain is said to be inhabited by aborigines who preserve the primitive ways of living. They use chariots for war, like the old Greek heroes we read of in the Trojan War, and their dwellings are mean, made for the most part of rushes or sticks: their harvest consists in cutting off the ears of corn and storing them in pits underground; from them they pluck each day the oldest ears and prepare them for food ...

The reference to Julius Caesar reminds us of his landing at Deal in 55 BC; he did not in fact 'subdue the island' – this was only achieved the following century, from 43 AD onwards, when a network of reliable roads was gradually established. Wye was then for centuries even better placed for travellers; those who followed the ancient trackway along the foot of the North Downs that led westwards were able at this point to ford the river Stour. And from Roman times a good road (seen here within a reconstruction of the network) just west of the Stour led conveniently to Canterbury. Unsurprisingly, excavations (still ongoing) in the Stour valley have revealed continuous settlement in or near Wye since at least Neolithic times, as illustrated by the following map.

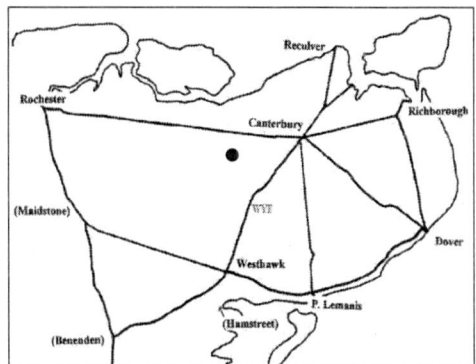

26

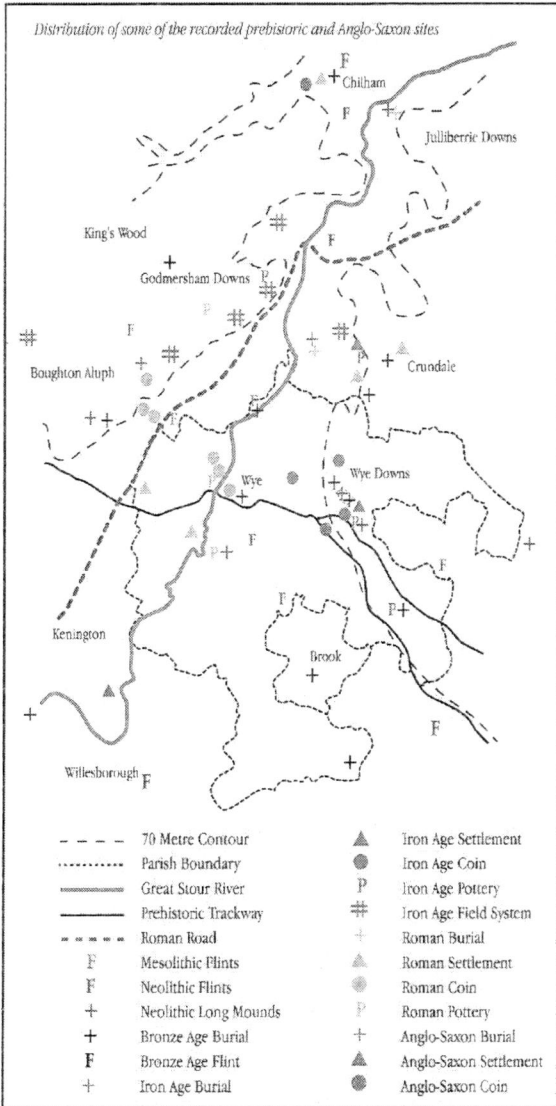

Distribution of some of the recorded prehistoric and Anglo-Saxon sites

- - - -	70 Metre Contour	▲	Iron Age Settlement
....	Parish Boundary	●	Iron Age Coin
~~	Great Stour River	P	Iron Age Pottery
——	Prehistoric Trackway	⌗	Iron Age Field System
- ·· - ·· -	Roman Road	+	Roman Burial
F	Mesolithic Flints	▲	Roman Settlement
F	Neolithic Flints	●	Roman Coin
+	Neolithic Long Mounds	P	Roman Pottery
+	Bronze Age Burial	+	Anglo-Saxon Burial
F	Bronze Age Flint	▲	Anglo-Saxon Settlement
+	Iron Age Burial	●	Anglo-Saxon Coin

Archaeological remains in the Stour valley

Yet even if Wye occupied such an advantageous site in East Kent, its relevance to wider traffic and commerce was always less secure. Those arriving from the continent might land at various points on the coast other than Dover (where the Romans built a lighthouse), depending (for

27

example) on weather conditions. Their onward route would inevitably depend upon the purpose of their visit and their ultimate destination, and the maps sketched here make no allowance for the many other roads and trackways that emerged over time. Similar observations apply to those travelling from different parts of England, giving rise to a host of questions: where did they begin their journey and where were they heading? were there other points of call? where would they find suitable hostelries? were there brigands to be avoided? how much depended on the time of year?

Some places – perhaps even in Kent? – were particularly fortunate during Edwin's extensive reign in the 620s. The Venerable Bede records:

> In those parts of Britain under King Edwin's jurisdiction, the proverb still runs that a woman could carry her new-born babe across the island from sea to sea without any fear of harm. And such was the king's concern for the welfare of his people, that in a number of places where he had noticed clear springs adjacent to the highway, he ordered posts to be erected with brass bowls hanging from them, so that travellers could drink and refresh themselves. And so great was the people's affection for him, and so great the awe in which he was held, that no one presumed to use these bowls for any other purpose.

Elsewhere (so Bede implies) women were in considerable danger of assault, and travellers might end up quenching their thirst with whatever brackish water they could find.

Soon after Bede's *History* was completed (*circa* 731), St Boniface wrote a long letter to Archbishop Cuthbert of Canterbury expressing his concerns about English women travelling abroad:

> There are only very few towns in Lombardy, in Francia or Gaul, in which there is not a woman who has broken her vows or a whore from among the race of Angles. And this is a nuisance and a shame for your whole Church.

He therefore pleaded that everything should be done to deter women from journeying too far afield and to forbid them making the pilgrimage to Rome. As yet pilgrimages within Britain were in their infancy, but Boniface's continental observations would no doubt have been equally true of lengthy journeys wherever they took place.

Although Canterbury became a leading shrine only after Thomas Becket's martyrdom in 1170, one should not forget that it had been an important centre from preRoman times, when it was already the headquarters of the Cantiaci tribe. Caesar noted in his *De Bello Gallico*:

> Of all these (British tribes), by far the most civilised are they who dwell in Kent, which is entirely a maritime region.

The Roman town that took shape a century later was a remodelling of the existing Celtic grid. Subsequently it became the capital of the Jutish kingdom and so for centuries saw many merchants and travellers. Wye itself could boast of a royal manor by Saxon times, which enhanced its own administrative importance and entailed much traffic with Canterbury. Wye Court (which burnt down in 1578) was later a substantial property where Edward I resided briefly, as did Edward II; Henry VI visited in 1429, and his Protector, Humphrey of Gloucester, was here in 1430 and 1431. Commerce came also from the opposite direction, especially from Battle Abbey which after the Norman Conquest became the overLord of Wye.

Perhaps the most significant royal visit to Wye occurred, however, in 1177 as John Gillingham has described in *The King and his Castle*:

> On Palm Sunday ... King Henry II was at Reading when he heard of Count Philip (of Flanders)'s intention of visiting Becket's tomb. King and count met at Canterbury on 21 April. The next day (Good Friday) he escorted Philip back to Dover and stayed there while the count made a night crossing. Next day Henry went to Wye, a manor near Ashford, where he celebrated Easter 'with his earls and barons'.

The provision of English highways in the 12th and 13th centuries can only be inferred from fragmentary pieces of evidence. But a map is extant showing a series of roads across the country in the middle of the 14th century. Some highways familiar to the compiler were omitted since he only included a route when he believed he knew the distances along it. There are three major roads independent of London which he included, one of which has no modern equivalent viz. from Southampton, through Havant, Chichester, Arundel, Bramber, Lewes, Winchelsea and Rye, to Appledore and onwards to Canterbury. The final stages of this road would surely have

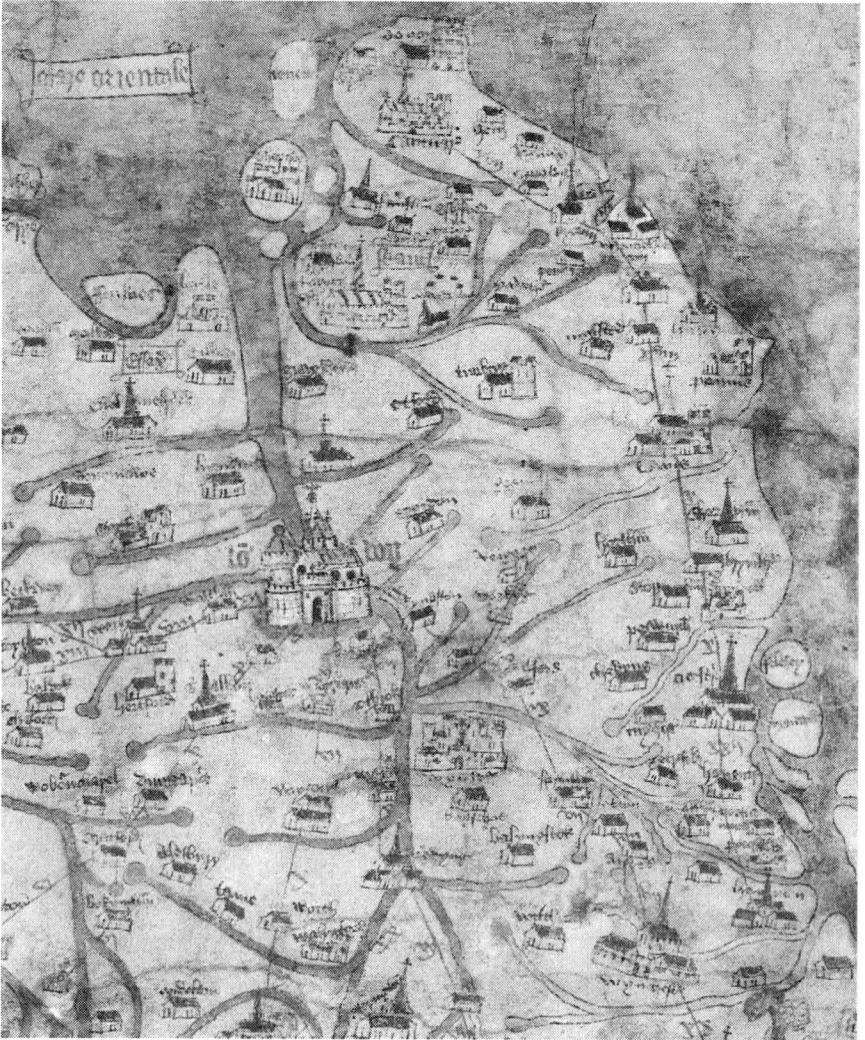

The Gough (or Bodleian) Map c.1360

The oldest surviving <u>route map</u> of Great Britain is named after <u>Richard Gough</u>, who gave it to the <u>Bodleian Library</u> in 1809. Apart from roads radiating from London, the above section shows a notional road (*a thin line on the RHS*), linking Southampton to Canterbury *(at the very top i.e. the east)*. It appears to cross the Stour at the limit of its navigability (a depth of roughly 50 cm) – presumably close to Wye? Nevertheless, unless tracks were well-constructed, they might easily disappear within a few generations: this is quite evident from the more abundant maps of later centuries.

This was convenient for the monks of Battle, and for the transport of wine barrels ('barriques') which came to the 13th century undercroft in the centre of Wye from the port of Winchelsea. The presence of this 'off-licence' suggests a flourishing trade (until interrupted by the hundred years' war with France?), which may have supplied some of the more affluent pilgrims.

Pilgrimage to Canterbury came to a virtual end after the Reformation. But in Victorian times there was a considerable revival of interest in 'the Pilgrims Way' (as it was called), and indeed in the Becket heritage itself. Restoration work on the medieval glass of Canterbury cathedral took

place, and from the early 1900s (and onwards) a lot more of it was apparently being reclaimed by Samuel Caldwell Jr. It was in a sympathetic style, and continued to impress the public until the 1970s when his works were exposed as well-disguised forgeries, of which two examples are illustrated here.

Thomas Becket   **Medieval pilgrims**

Again, it was in 1892 that Grant Allen published his *Science of Arcady*, in which he claimed that there was 'a very old trackway known as the Pilgrims Way, because it was followed in later times by medieval wayfarers from Somerset and Dorset to the shrine of St Thomas a Becket at Canterbury' – yet dated back to 'the Bronze Age for the transport of tin from the mines in Cornwall to the port of Sandwich.' His theory has since been discredited. The most influential writing came from the better known pen of Hilaire Belloc, who published *The Old Road* in 1904. He argued in favour of a particular track favoured by travellers, following the edge of the North Downs all the way from Dover to Salisbury Plain and Stonehenge, later supplanted by Winchester as their main destination. It could of course be traversed in the opposite direction too, and in time, he suggested, its end point here became Canterbury rather than Dover. In this he was following the slightly earlier publication of Julia Cartwright entitled *The Pilgrims Way – from Winchester to Canterbury*. Belloc's route is shown above (on the map on page 20) where it is labelled 'The Pilgrims Way', although in his terms it was either 'The Road' or 'The Way'.

Leaving aside the learned articles that continued to be published in the wake of Belloc's book, it was Kent County Council who announced their intention to reclaim and signpost some 62 miles of such a route in time for the 1951 Festival of Britain. Although signposts were erected, there was

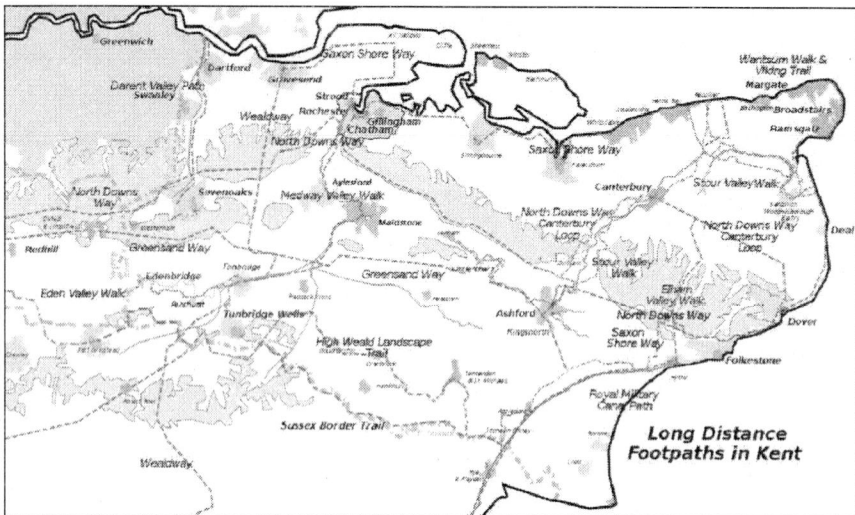

Long Distance Footpaths in Kent

considerable disagreement about the actual route, which some considered 'phoney'. In 1963 the name 'North Downs Way' was thought to be preferable. After an extensive survey, it was agreed that a route on 'a line which offers the best scenic qualities for the walker' along the ridge of the North Downs, rather than the Pilgrims Way (which even in the 1960s was predominantly metalled), was preferred. The North Downs Way was finally completed in 1978, covering roughly 150 miles, including 36 miles of newly created public rights of way. East of Boughton Lees, the path splits in two, the northern route taking in Canterbury and the southern passing through Wye (where it was inaugurated by the Archbishop of Canterbury), prior to meeting up again at Dover. The name 'Pilgrims Way Trackway' is still found as a separate route on Ordnance Survey 1:25000 maps, for example near the village of Brook, running below the Downs not far beyond Wye.

Although Wye has none itself at present, 'Pilgrims Way' road signs can be found in Hastingleigh (to the east), in Chilham (to the north) and in Boughton Lees (to the west). These are all historically plausible routes, although it should be remembered that there were many different ways of reaching Canterbury: obviously too, as the pilgrim drew closer to his goal, his path was likely to converge with those from elsewhere. A comparison may be drawn with pilgrim routes to Santiago: even if today there are dedicated hostels on one particular route, the historical reality was more of a 'corridor' crossing Northern Spain through which most foot travellers would pass one way or another. In recent years pilgrimages undertaken the authentic way -- on foot -- have regained popularity, and there has been a revival of the route from Winchester to Canterbury.

Its website http://www.pilgrimswaycanterbury.org/ has some alternative possibilities, including those for pilgrims who start their journey in London. Displaying as it does convenient places of refreshment and accommodation (including religious houses and retreat centres), together with nearby churches, shrines and other historic sites, it also allows (as was surely the case with medieval pilgrims, particularly those who sought healing for their ailments and diseases) for deviations to satisfy particular needs, both physical and spiritual. Wye is listed as a place with much to offer.

Early shrines

We turn our attention now to the developing tradition of Christian pilgrimage, and its slightly later arrival in Britain. The idea of pilgrimage is embedded in the Bible, exemplified by Abraham's journey of faith 'to the land which I will show you' [Gen 12.1]; by Jesus himself heading for Jerusalem, 'walking ahead' of his disciples [Mk 10.32] as he initiates the way of the Cross; and by the subsequent exhortation to Christians to 'run with perseverance the race that is set before us' [Heb 12.1]. Revelatory journeys are also recorded in the New Testament – of the Magi [Mt 2.1-12], of two disciples heading for Emmaus [Lk 24.13-35], of Philip and the Ethiopian eunuch likewise exploring the scriptures as they travel [Acts8.26-39], and then of Saul converted on the Damascus road [Acts 9.1ff]. The last example mentions specifically that, before the name Christian was given to Jesus' followers, they were known as those 'belonging to the Way'.

'Pilgrimage' has therefore been an image of the Christian life from its inception, with a characteristically *spiritual* meaning attached to it. So, in the language of the reforming 2nd Vatican Council, the Church itself can rightly be called 'the pilgrim people of God'. *Physical* pilgrimages were necessarily a development occurring later, being dependent upon individual circumstances and certainly upon the broader political situation. It was under Constantine in the early 4th century that the latter changed, and gradually pilgrimages to the holy places of Jerusalem began, as did visits to the martyred remains of Peter, Paul and many other saints in Rome. It was, however, the sites associated with Jesus that ranked highest in sanctity and Cyril of Jerusalem actively encouraged pilgrims from far afield:

Others merely hear; we can see and touch.

Jerome, who spent many years living in Bethlehem, also highlighted the privilege of close contact, although he did warn Paulinus of Nola about noisy crowds and peripheral riff-raff. What truly mattered for him was to get away from urban bustle 'so as to draw down upon myself the mercy of Christ in the solitude of the country'. As Jonathan Sumption puts it:

How he lived was more important than where, and even the sites of the Crucifixion and Resurrection were of no intrinsic spiritual value unless the pilgrim was ready to carry the cross of the Lord and be resurrected with him.

Gregory of Nyssa agreed that too much emphasis upon 'place' smacked of paganism and Judaism: was not the Christian God equally accessible anywhere, so that 'change of place does not effect any closer drawing nearer unto God'. Indeed, Gregory observed caustically that ascending the Mount of Olives would bear no fruit for anyone filled with pride, lust or envy. It was above all the appalling behaviour of many who went on pilgrimage that led him to reject the practice. These observations also informed the wandering Irish hermits of the 6th and 7th centuries; pilgrimage for such as St Columban was not *to* any particular place, but rather *away* from the distractions of ordinary life. Jerome's teaching on the matter continued to be read by equally serious pilgrims for a millennium after his death.

Yet the popularity of particular holy places and the rapidly expanding number of shrines indicate that the ascetism of the desert saints was not for everyone. To 'see and touch' has always been important for some at least. Already in the 3rd century there was a cult of relics, with the associated expectation that the power of God once manifest in a saint's life could only be more abundant when in death he or she came closer to the very source of blessings. In the *Acts of Thomas* is recorded the apocryphal legend of the healing power of dust from the saintly Thomas' tomb; at Cyprian's martyrdom the crowd threw a little pile of clothes to catch his blood; Eusebius mentions veneration of St James' hair, as well as miraculous oil from the time of Narcissus, bishop of Jerusalem a hundred years before him. To these may be added martyrs' clothes, cultic images, altar requisites and sacred codices, even priestly vestments – collectively termed *eulogiae*. Objects associated with a saint might also be transferred elsewhere, and in the 4th century the practice of creating new shrines to house them made less arduous pilgrimages possible apart from those to Jerusalem or Rome. Towards the end of the 4th century the pagan emperor Julian was famously to observe that the world was being filled with tombs and sepulchres. He characterised Christians as 'those who turn from the gods to the dead and their relics'.

Of course, with such rapidly growing interest, deceptions and abuses were not unknown. Martin of Tours unmasked the tomb of a supposed martyr as the burial site of a robber, while the saintly Pachomius, fearing exploitation after his death, demanded for himself an unmarked grave. Athanasius issued critical comments on veneration offered to those whose saintly identities were unclear, fearing that 'the urgency to find ever more saints to sanctify towns inspired preposterous relic inventions'. Again, Augustine of Hippo knew of imposters dressed as monks who sold spurious relics. When St Martin himself died in 397, the rival cities of Tours and Poitiers were prepared to fight in order to gain possession of his body, but the people of Tours won by stealth. They erected a shrine with the inscription:

Here lies Martin the bishop, of holy memory, whose soul is in the hand of God; but he is fully here, present and made plain in miracles of every kind.

His monastic cell at Marmoutier became the focus of pilgrimage almost immediately, and 'visitors would lie on his bed or seek to position themselves in his customary place of prayer'. Not all, however, were convinced that it was right to have close contact with the dead: the Jewish tradition taught that defilement would result; and in most Mediterranean cultures, including Roman, it was the custom for cemeteries to be quite separate from places of habitation. In the late 4th century *Apostolic Constitutions,* therefore, it was felt necessary to defend the novel Christian approach and 'to gather without fear in the cemeteries'.

Slightly later, Jerome answered criticisms from one Vigilantius. The latter had disparagingly referred to 'what is virtually a pagan rite', in which vast numbers of people light 'cheap little candles' and then 'kiss and worship a little bit of dust, wrapped in a linen cloth inside an expensive little container'. Jerome replied, 'You madman – who has ever worshipped the martyrs?' Veneration was his preferred term, 'the better to adore him whose martyrs they are'. Yet certainly there were excesses in the cult of martyrs. It troubled Augustine of Hippo that superstitious Christians could take veneration almost to the point of worshipping the saints. He preferred to draw attention to the love by which they were motivated and in which they may yet be imitated. Nor, he urged, was there any magical efficacy in relics, for Christian hope always remained with God himself.

The earliest confirmed record of any shrine in England is dated to 429, not long before Augustine of Hippo died. This was the occasion of St Germanus' first visit, occasioned by the need to counter the growing tide of Pelagian ideas in the country. He visited the shrine of St Alban, which had been erected not far from the important Roman city of Verulamium. It is also recorded that he brought with him relics of 'all the apostles and various martyrs', to enhance the holiness of the churches and thus those who worshipped in them. St Gildas, writing in the mid 6th century when the Christian presence had been severely weakened by invading forces, mentions that shrines had been made elsewhere too in the aftermath of the Diocletian persecution (during the first decade of the 4th century); however, this remains unsupported by other evidence. There is a slight possibility that the Roman mausoleum near Faversham (on which the medieval Stone Chapel later came to be built) housed an early Christian shrine, given the existence of comparable structures for that purpose on the continent. A text known as the *Obsecratio Augustini* suggests that, not

too distant from Canterbury, there was also a local cult of 'Sixtus', since St Gregory the Great (the document's supposed author) writes that, in response to Augustine of Canterbury's request, he is sending relics of the martyred Pope Sixtus II to replace those at the shrine.

The Stone Chapel in Kent

Knowledge of other cults may well have been lost – or ignored? Augustine's heroic missionary work from 597 led after his death in Canterbury (in 604) to his own veneration there.

In the following centuries there was significant growth in both the number of shrines and the spread of relics, increasingly displayed in sumptuous reliquaries as a fitting tribute to their spiritual importance. St Bede notes Augustine's entombment at Canterbury, which by then (a hundred years later) was a recognised place of pilgrimage. In addition there are two documents from about the 11th century that inform us of various Anglo-Saxon shrines. *Secgan – 'The Tale of God's saints who first rested in England'* – is a list of fifty places which had shrines and remains of Anglo-Saxon saints. In Kent, it mentions St Paulinus' shrine at Rochester, together with St Dunstan and 'other saints' at Canterbury, in addition to St Augustine. The other compilation, possibly intended as a local supplement to the *Secgan*, is known as *The Kentish Royal Legend*, a diverse group of texts which describe a wide circle of members of the royal family of Kent in the 7th and 8th centuries, quite a few of whom were regarded as saints. Altogether some twenty-seven Kentish saints have been identified from Saxon times. Not all were buried locally but, for those who were, Folkestone and Minster-in-Thanet (where there were 7th Century convents) are mentioned as burial sites alongside Canterbury.

What is quite clear though is that, long before Becket's time, Canterbury held an impressive number of shrines in the cathedral and especially at St Augustine's Abbey. The abbey itself was spared by the invading Danes and was later a beneficiary of King Cnut's new-found faith. In 1023 he ordered the remains of the martyred St Alphege to be transferred to Canterbury from London, and then in 1027 those of St Mildred from Minster-in-Thanet. Belief in the miraculous powers of the latter had already spread throughout Europe, and it brought many pilgrims (and their gifts) from afar.

Site of St Augustine's grave

Saxon Remains of St Pancras chapel in Canterbury

Site of Thomas Becket's martyrdom

Stones from St Augustine's Abbey were re-used by Sir Edward Hales in building his new mansion at Hales Court in 1758. This became a convent in the mid 19th century before serving as St Mary's (Jesuit) College until 1928. Sr Mary Hales, owner of the convent, was the donor of two Becket relics (ex Gubbio) to St Thomas', Canterbury. N.B: Mary's great uncle, also Edward, married Lucy Darrell of Calehill (see pp 56ff) in 1789 but died without issue.

There were also imported relics held both in Canterbury (including fragments of the True Cross and Aaron's Rod) and elsewhere in Kent. Indeed, when Mellitus came in 601 to assist Augustine's mission, he was equipped by Pope Gregory with what has been described as 'a starter pack' of relics, intended to be placed in the altars of (Roman-style) new churches. (Compare St Ambrose' late 4th century dedication of a church in Milan that included relics of St Peter and St Paul brought from Rome.) In the years that followed, the cross-channel import of relics has been reckoned worth more than any other commercial trading commodity. Some idea of this can be gleaned from the fact that seventy years after its foundation in 1121 Reading Abbey boasted 242 relics, 'including 29 of our Lord, 6 of the Virgin, 19 of the patriarchs and prophets, 14 of apostles, 73 of martyrs, 51 of confessors, and 49 of virgins'.

So there was clearly plenty of competition for Canterbury – not forgetting the eminent shrine of Walsingham which developed after the Holy House was built in the 1060s in obedience to a vision of the Virgin Mary. In a sense, therefore, the martyrdom of Thomas Becket in 1170 was not entirely unwelcome to the monks of Canterbury.

From an English Psalter c.1250.

The new shrine at Canterbury

The last major boost to the cult of saints at Canterbury had been in the 1090s when the Romanesque reconstruction of St Augustine's Abbey was being completed. The final stage was the repositioning of the tombs of the first six archbishops, with St Augustine's own tomb being the most renowned. It was in September 1091 that his body was laid open to view, still clad in his full pontificals. A detailed account is provided by Goscelin, an eye-witness who subsequently wrote in his *Historia translationis Sancti Augustini,* 'He looked as though he were still alive, only touch revealing his condition.' News travelled fast, and large crowds were attracted by a miraculous odour which spread through the city, and indeed much further afield. The feast of his translation was thereafter kept annually on 13th September, ensuring that the memory of his wondrous holiness (and of his successors) was kept alive. Religious fashion can, however, be somewhat fickle and to maintain any shrine prominently on the pilgrimage map in the face of up-and-coming rivals was never easy; the tendency of the laity was to visit the saint whose cult was most recently in the news.

Thomas Becket had of course been a close colleague of Henry II from 1155 as his Lord Chancellor, recommended for this post by the then archbishop Theobald, whom Becket served in his capacity as Archdeacon of Canterbury. In 1162 he succeeded Theobald himself (after first being ordained priest), with the king no doubt anticipating to increase his control of the English church. It was not to be, since Becket now transferred his loyalty to 'the king of kings' and resisted any encroachments on the rights of the Church. Exiled in France as a result from 1164, disagreements with the king continued after his return in November 1170 and the outcome was his murder in Canterbury cathedral on 29th December 1170. When the monks prepared his body for burial, it was discovered (according to some sources) that he had worn a hairshirt complete with lice under his garments, a sign of penance. The story continues (in Sumption's words) as follows:

> His cult was established within a fortnight of his death and was propagated with exceptional skill by the monks of Christ Church, Canterbury. William of Canterbury, who was the author of a great deal of this propaganda, reflects that all saints have their period of miracle-working when they command the veneration of Christians; then they withdraw gracefully and leave [it] to saints of more recent creation …

Becket was very much a political figure, who became a hero for standing so firmly against a king attempting to exceed his powers – and his martyrdom may have inspired others in the struggle that led to the signing of *Magna Carta*. Whether his sometimes abrupt character was invariably that of a Christian saint has been questioned, but his death was certainly an act of faith. Any doubts about him were swiftly dispelled by the miracles that followed; each one, so far as possible, was annotated and verified by William of Canterbury. They vindicated both Becket's sanctity and the justice of his cause, as in the following debate about him held in the University of Paris:

[Master Roger] swore that he had deserved to die (though not to die in such a manner), and judged the constancy of the blessed saint to be mere obstinacy. Master Peter on the other hand asserted that he was a worthy martyr of Christ, since he had died for the liberty of the Church. But the Saviour himself resolved their debate when he glorified him with many wonderful miracles.

The tide of veneration that swept across Europe in his favour was very soon a further political problem for Henry II. Becket was rapidly canonised (in 1173), and a year later the king visited Canterbury himself in an act of public penance – and perhaps with some sorrow for a former friend whom he had never fully understood. His penitential walk on 12th July began at the Hospital for Lepers (built in 1084) at Harbledown, west of the city; when he reached St Dunstan's church he continued barefoot until he reached Becket's tomb. One contemporary described this as an *imitatio Christi*, in that Henry allowed himself to be beaten with scourges, 'save that Christ did this for the remission of our sins, whereas Henry did it for the remission of his own'.

Only two months later a fire broke out at the east end of the cathedral, which led to its reconstruction in the Gothic style and to modifications, including the Trinity Chapel and the Corona, which enabled large numbers of pilgrims to have much better access. It was not, however, until 7th July 1220 that the relics were relocated to the lofty gold-plated, bejewelled shrine that then became the focus of devotion until 1538 when it was destroyed on orders from Henry VIII. The translation (which helped to revive the numbers of visiting pilgrims, especially as its annual feast day effected a popular shift from winter to the summer) was 'one of the great symbolic events in the life of the medieval English Church' and was attended by Henry III, the papal legate, the archbishop Stephen Langton and large numbers of dignitaries.

The evolution of Canterbury cathedral after the Norman Conquest

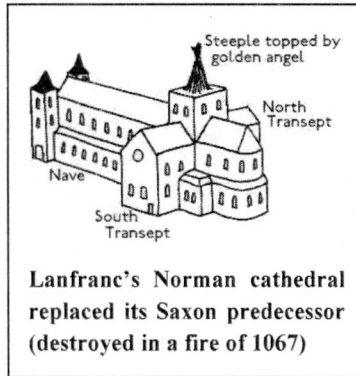

Lanfranc's Norman cathedral replaced its Saxon predecessor (destroyed in a fire of 1067)

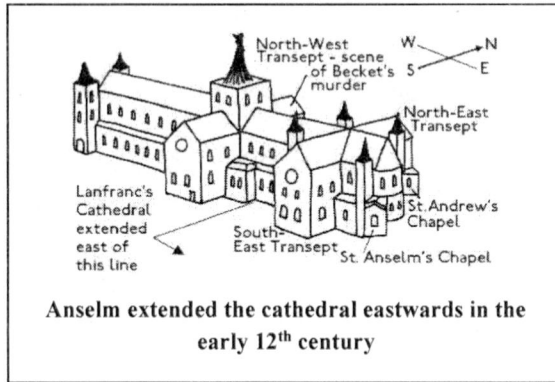

Anselm extended the cathedral eastwards in the early 12th century

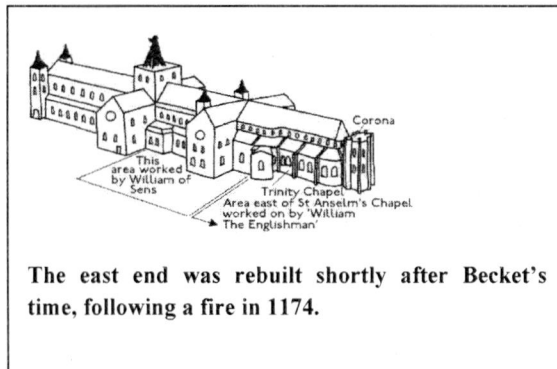

The east end was rebuilt shortly after Becket's time, following a fire in 1174.

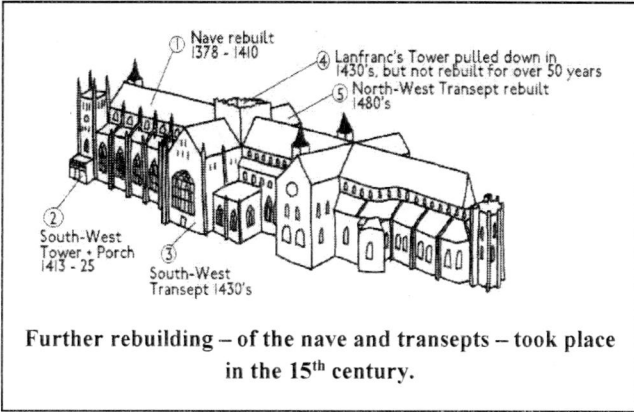

Further rebuilding – of the nave and transepts – took place in the 15th century.

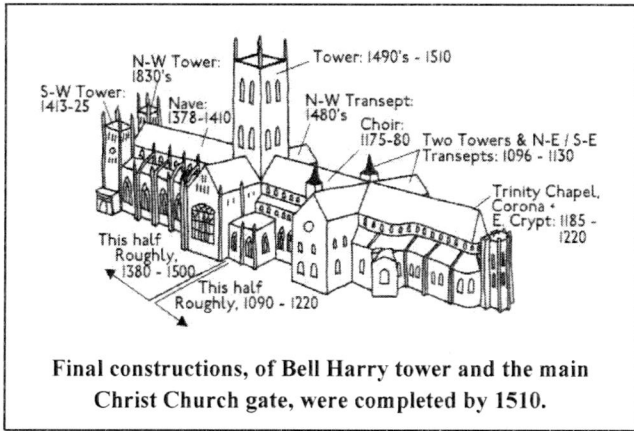

Final constructions, of Bell Harry tower and the main Christ Church gate, were completed by 1510.

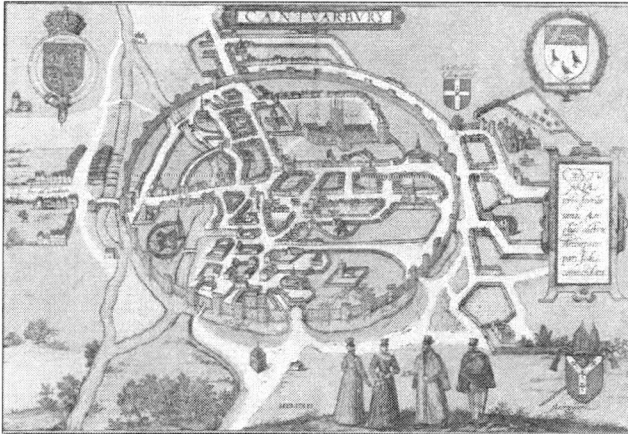

Canterbury in late Elizabethan times

When the jewels and precious metals that had accumulated at the shrine over the following centuries were finally confiscated, they filled two coffers and twenty-six carts. A Venetian diplomat who visited not long before the Dissolution remarked:

> Finest of all is a ruby, no larger than a man's thumbnail, which is set into the altar at the right-hand side, and which … I believe, was the gift of the King of France (Louis VII in 1179, when praying for the recovery of his only son).

The pavement where the shrine stood (beyond the present high altar) is now marked by a lit candle (with its 800th anniversary coming soon in 2020).

Apart from these lavish gifts, most pilgrims made cash donations which were sometimes in thanksgiving for their cure, or in the hope of securing future healing; alternatively they might be in fulfilment of a vow, or to gain some spiritual benefit. Annual figures fluctuated considerably over the years. Initially about a third of the pilgrims seem to have been noblemen, but the proportion was less at other times: the majority would probably have been smallholders, burgesses, freemen, or priests, whereas cottars, slaves and villeins would be tied to the manor where they belonged. Forty years on (in the early 13th century) when Becket's novelty had worn off and rival saints were reckoned to be more potent than St Thomas, there were distinctly fewer visitors for a time: pilgrimage income dropped to an average of £426 per year – still quite a sizeable amount – but in 1220, the year of St Thomas' translation, the sum recovered by a factor of three. The Jubilee years of the 14th and 15th centuries which offered ever-popular indulgences boosted the number of pilgrims; but since they were often of lesser social status, the overall profits were much reduced despite a short-lived rise in income. A directive of 1473 even attempted to prohibit 'those reliant on alms' from going on pilgrimage at all. By the time of the Dissolution receipts had sunk to a negligible £36 each year – just one seventh of the amount then being received at Walsingham. The lower returns may to a limited extent reflect also the fact that in these later years the proportion of men making the pilgrimage declined.

Other offerings left at the medieval shrine had little monetary value, but carried much spiritual significance. These were the *ex voto* models (or other symbols) of whatever parts of the body that had been miraculously healed. Typically they were made of wax, but might be a bodily specimen like the lock of hair left by Isabel of Longueville in gratitude for her restored hearing, or Henry of Maldon's actual tapeworm after its emergence. The guardian of the shrine was disappointed when a visiting archdeacon whose nose had been blocked by a cherry stone took it home with him once St Thomas had facilitated its extraction. On the other hand, a shepherd from Durham left his withered finger on the altar in the hope that another would grow in its place.

Although over the years some continental pilgrims would also have reached Canterbury, which was classified in the 13th century as a 'major' shrine along with Rome, Santiago and Cologne: since Jerusalem remained the prime goal, numbers crossing the channel were never too considerable. For a number of them, as for some English pilgrims, pilgrimage was a punishment, perhaps for criminal offences, for causing scandal (especially in the case of clerics or the nobility) or for propagating heresy.

For most penitential pilgrims after the 11th century their destination would have been specified. Among those sent to Canterbury were Robert Urry, who in 1308 molested a priest in the diocese of Winchester and was required to abstain from wine at least on his outward journey, and a priest named Simon de Buntingford who in 1332 was found guilty of adultery by the bishop of Rochester. The same bishop only once imposed a continental pilgrimage: this was in 1325 when John Mayde was sent to Santiago for the heinous offence of adultery with his godmother. In each case satisfactory evidence would have been required that the penance had been fulfilled.

A reverse corroboration was sometimes sought regarding supposed miracles: the monk responsible for recording these would require confirmation that there had been no subsequent relapse, and that any witnesses were of reliable character. Sumption notes that 'a madwoman of Rouen recovered her sanity at Canterbury but lost it when she returned home', that 'a monk of Poitiers found that his leprosy returned after he left', that 'a Fleming called Gerard was only temporarily relieved of his ulcer'. Relapses were explained in various ways: a failure to express gratitude to the saint; an insufficient thank-offering to the shrine; a pilgrimage vow left uncompleted; a hidden and undeclared sin; perhaps even a premature immersion in hard manual labour. There were times too when recovery occurred without much miraculous intervention: at Canterbury cathedral there was a considerable library of medical books and some monks were fully conversant with a range of herbal and other remedies; hence some visitors to the shrine might learn of therapies they could try for themselves. Nevertheless, a good number of supposed cures were undoubtedly fabrications, or mere variations of pious legends; church authorities were often timid about debunking them for fear of a subsequent drop in income.

Of course, pilgrims were frequently reminded by the clergy that the true purpose of pilgrimage was not to find a miraculous cure for their illness nor simply to gain pardon for their offences, but to be reformed in the image of Christ. It was said that this sentiment overtook many as they approached Becket's shrine – 'they promise to mend their ways as if rebaptised in the font of their own tears'. The atmosphere of devotion would perhaps have been at its height in Canterbury when the masses gathered at important vigils and on feast days. Yet it would not have been sustained too easily, given the motley composition of the crowd and their unruly background noise, alongside the rival attractions of fairs and drinking booths.

Most would, however, return from Canterbury with a physical reminder of their visit, potentially able to encourage their faith, to keep their hopes alive, and to share the blessings of the saint. This was the pilgrim's token worn around his neck, which at the shrine of St Thomas took the form of an *ampulla* (a small lead flask) filled with water containing a trace of the saint's own blood. According to a witness of Becket's murder, a monk present at the time used a basin to collect some of the spilt blood. This was subsequently transferred to a large cistern of water, which over the years was kept topped up – perhaps also with a little diluted red ochre added occasionally. The blend, 'the water of St Thomas', became a highly regarded medicine for a few decades at least: indeed, it was claimed that within a week of Becket's death a priest in London was cured by drinking the concoction.

Others might anoint ailing body parts with it, or give sips to their sick relatives – a reminder that, when a would-be pilgrim was too ill to make the journey, a husband, wife, or messenger might sometimes visit the shrine as their surrogate. With the passage of time penitential pilgrimages were also undertaken vicariously; funds might even be set aside in people's wills to gain posthumous indulgences by such means. It was clearly wise in ant case to make a will in advance of pilgrimage, 'should death befall' on the way.

Ampulla from shrine

Chaucer's Canterbury Tales

It was unusual for pilgrimages to be taken alone; as a rule, for reasons of personal safety, companions were sought. The experience of journeying together could be of much spiritual value. Hospitality was often provided by religious houses, some of which on the more popular routes had barns built specifically for pilgrims (such as Pilgrims Hall at Aylesford Priory). Otherwise inns, and sometimes private dwellings, might be available, and it was always meritorious to assist the poorest pilgrims without charge. Royal parties of course made quite different arrangements. Not too far from Wye they found the Archbishop's Palace at Charing as well as Leeds Castle (the king's own possession) to be convenient overnight resting places; Henry VIII made use of both of these when visiting Canterbury in 1520.

In Canterbury itself there was accommodation in the precincts. Distinguished ecclesiastics or nobility assigned to the prior found themselves near the most sacred part of the cathedral. The cellarer's buildings stood near the west end of the nave, whereas 'inferior' pilgrims and paupers were relegated to the north hall or almonry, just within the gate. Nearby was the Eastbridge Hospital of St Thomas the Martyr, constructed after 1198, which gave priority to the sick. If food was provided for the masses, it would seldom have been other than simple dairy products and cereals, washed down with ale. Wealthier pilgrims might find inns prepared to indulge their tastes better. Even there, though, sleeping accommodation might require the sharing of beds, and fleas were probably ubiquitous. Often rush- or straw-covered floors were all that was available. In modern terms, a comparison might be made with the conditions experienced by refugees and migrants. The cost of a pilgrimage could well vary with the season – around major feasts prices would probably rise sharply from (say) a basic 1d per night. The hire of horses for a journey was usually an expensive overhead.

When Chaucer wrote his *Canterbury Tales* in the late 1380s, he was living in Southwark and could observe pilgrims setting off on their journey. His thirty-strong company who gathered at the Tabard Inn was probably fairly representative of those who could afford to ride to Canterbury. It is instructive to note that he reckoned the season for pilgrimage began in spring – and that Canterbury indeed was still the principal shrine in England.

Whan that Aprille with shoures sote
The droghte of Marche hath perced to the rote …
Than longen folk to goon on pilgrimages
(And palmers for to seken straunge strondes)
To ferne halwes, couthe in sondry londes;
And specially, to Caunterbury they wende,
The holy blisful martir for to seke,
That hem hath holpen, whan that they were seke.

Outside the Tabard Inn
by E.H.Corbould (1815-1905)

We never get to hear all the tales that Chaucer had envisaged, as the work seems to have lapsed; nor do we actually reach Becket's shrine, although the author apparently did himself in the year 1388. It is quite clear though what a mixed company they are, from the devout to those who are plainly rogues – the latter including the prioress, the monk and the friar, in each of whom worldly interests predominate. The two church officials, the summoner (of parishioners to the archdeacon's court) and the pardoner (who peddles indulgences and probably fake relics) trade on people's credulity and are repulsively corrupt. Yet devout, sincere

Christians are also heading for Canterbury: the knight ('a verray parfit gentil knyght'); the clerk of Oxenford (who would much prefer 'at his beddes heed twenty books, clad in black or red' to any fine wardrobe); the 'poure persoun of a toun' (who preached Christ's message, 'but first he folwed it hymselve'); and there is the parson's brother the ploughman ('lyvynge in pees and parfit chaitee, God loved he best with al his hoole herte'). Whatever the virtues and the vices of his characters, however, Chaucer is ever charitable. He had his own sincere faith, and was prepared to allow that the pilgrimage would in the end bring out the best in them all.

Pilgrimages did not entirely die out with the Reformation, despite the fierce criticisms levied against them. William Langland, a contemporary of Geoffrey Chaucer, is famous for *The Vision of Piers Plowman* in which he challenged those who merely eased their consciences by visiting a shrine instead of reforming their lives more thoroughly. The one saint to be sought above others was 'St Truth, for he may save you all'.

Nevertheless, the idea of the Christian life as a pilgrimage persisted, and was famously described three hundred years after Chaucer's day in a work written in Bedford jail by John Bunyan, who was imprisoned for twelve years after the restoration of the monarchy for his refusal to desist from unlicensed preaching. Specious claims have sometimes been made that the landscapes described in *The Pilgrim's Progress* are based on different parts of the journey towards Canterbury, but the imagery is both personal to Bunyan and at the same time biblical. The road depicted in the 19th century illustration here is for convenience a spiral, yet it also conveys the truth that spiritual advances seldom come in leaps and bounds: our goal can seem still as far away as when we started, yet even so we may be 'progressing':

> These troubles and distresses that you go through in these waters are no sign that God hath forsaken you, but are sent to try you whether you will call to mind that which heretofore you have received of his goodness, and live upon him in your distress.

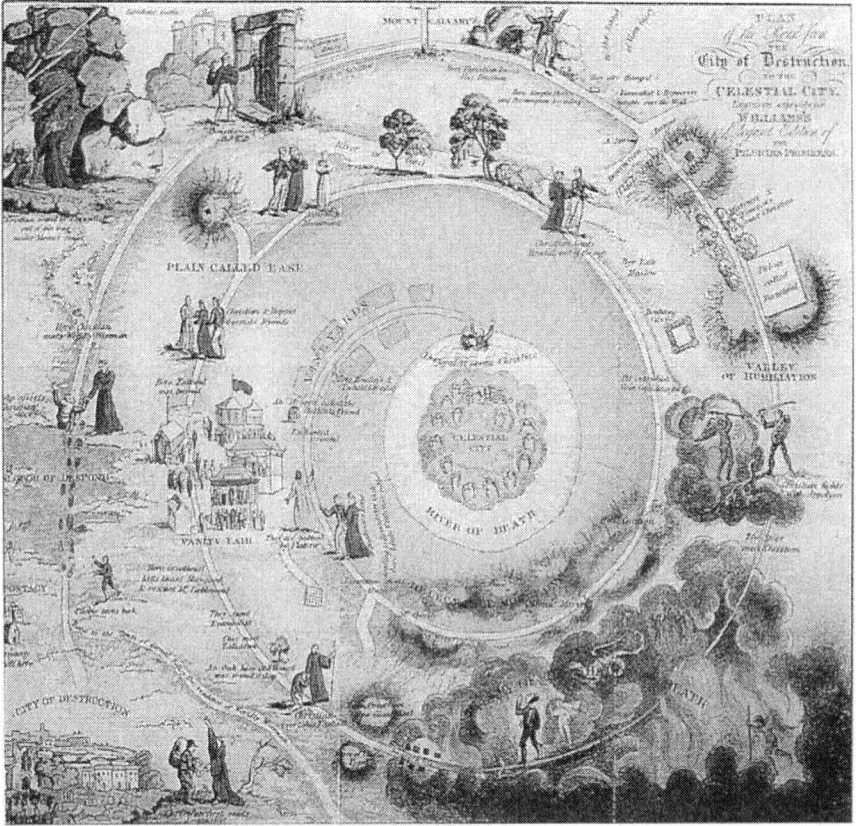

The Pilgrim's Progress
from the City of Destruction to the Celestial City

'And now were these two men, as 'twere, in
Heaven, before they came at it.'

Catholics in Wye

CHANGING TIMES AND SHIFTING FORTUNES

The early years

There were Christians in the south of England by the second half of the 2nd century. Whether there were any at that time living in or near Wye (whose name derives from an Old English word signifying a 'sacred' place) is unknown. North of the Thames there was the person of St Alban, who served in the Roman army but was martyred, perhaps in the year 209: he had received instruction from a local priest, and when the latter was being hunted down he arranged for his escape, subsequently refusing to renounce his own new-found faith. Just over a hundred years later, it is recorded that three English bishops (from London, York and Lincoln) were present at the Council of Arles held in 314 AD, following Constantine's Edict of Milan the previous year. Dating also from the (mid) 4th century is a treasured artefact held in the British Museum – a mosaic floor from a villa at Hinton St Mary in Dorset bearing as a central motif the head of Christ.

Christ wears a white pallium standing before a (Christian) Chi Rho symbol and two pomegranates. On each side there are forest and hunting scenes, mostly of a dog and a deer. In the corners are four quarter circles containing portrait busts, representing perhaps the winds or the seasons.

Another Chi Rho mosaic of the same period was found in the villa at Lullingstone in Kent. There was also a wall painting of six people, several of whom seem to be praying with outstretched arms. Although other panels seem to carry pagan overtones, this is typical of late Roman Christian art in the process of readjusting to new meanings and imagery.

***Orantes* at Lullingstone, suggestive of a house church**

After the Roman legions left Britain around 406-7, the country descended into the so-called Dark Ages. The heresy propagated by the British monk Pelagius was spreading in the country, and St Germanus came over from Gaul on two occasions (in 429 when he also visited the shrine of St Alban, and again around 447) in answer to appeals for help. Invasions from various continental tribes had then begun and lasted well into the 6th century. A plea for troops to repel the barbarians – who 'drive us into the sea, while the sea drives us back to the barbarians' – made to the consul Aetius in Gaul in the year 446 was refused. Already by about 456 some Britons had migrated westwards from Kent, but the incursions further south were resisted more strongly. A British bishop – '*Mansuetus episcopus Brittanorum*' – is listed among those attending a small council in Tours in 461, seemingly implying that he was ministering to those who had crossed the Channel into 'Brittany'.

St Gildas' account of the state of England a century later (perhaps the 540s) was justifiably entitled *The Desolation of Britain*, although this was composed partly as a prophetic judgment, pronouncing God's wrath upon Christian apostasy. Gildas was a renowned monk who died at Glastonbury, but had previously travelled widely, seeing at first hand ruined churches and encountering devastated communities along with panic-stricken refugees. Some people were enslaved, and twenty or so years after Gildas' death comes the famous story of Gregory seeing English slaves on sale in Rome: '*Non Angli sed angeli*' is the visionary comment attributed to him.

Early churches built on Roman foundations in Kent

☐ **Roman**

▨ **Later**

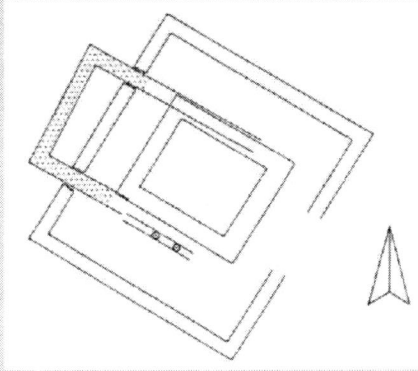

Lullingstone House Church

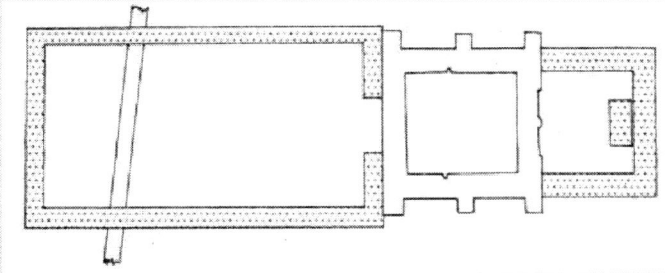

Stone Chapel, Faversham

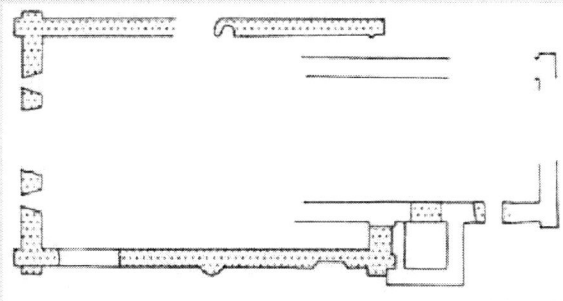

St Martin's Church, Canterbury

According to Bede: 'Having been granted his episcopal see in the royal capital... Augustine proceeded with the king's approval to repair a church (**Christ Church Cathedral**) which he was informed had been built long ago by Roman Christians.' Roman remains still lie under the present nave. *The Anglo-Saxon Chronicle* gives the cathedral's consecration as 9th June 603.

Soon afterwards he became Pope and was in a position to recruit Augustine, Prior of St Andrew's Monastery in Rome, along with a number of his God-fearing brother monks for the arduous mission of re-evangelising Britain. Initially they only reached Aix in Provence before losing heart and returning to Rome; but Gregory stiffened their resolve, and supplied Augustine with letters that would gain his party assistance as they travelled through France. This was provided by the Archbishop at Arles – and on reaching Tours they stopped at St Martin's tomb to pray for his help. Eventually (so Bede tells us) they reached England during Eastertide 597, landing at 'the large island of Thanet ... separated from the mainland by a channel some three furlongs broad ... and fordable in only two places'.

Augustine remained here for 'some days' while his Frankish interpreters announced his presence and the nature of his mission to King Ethelbert. Although Ethelbert was pagan, he was married to a member of the Frankish royal family – and Queen Bertha was a Christian whose parents had consented to her marriage only on condition that she be accompanied by her personal chaplain and be free to practise her faith without hindrance. Bertha had the use of a church built in earlier times in honour of St Martin which was just east of Canterbury, and this was made available to the missionaries.

Within a year Ethelbert was among those baptised by Augustine (although this may have had much to do with the king's intent to enhance his own standing on the Continent), and lent his support to the spread of churches within his realm. There is evidence that as many as four hundred churches were eventually built in Kent prior to the Norman invasion.

Mid-7th century Crundale buckle
Found in 1861 in a man's grave near Wye, now in the British Museum. Made of gilt-copper alloy with garnets. The *fish* was a Christian symbol – being hollow, it may have been a reliquary.

A church in Wye during Roman times is unlikely, since Christianity in Britain was then largely an urban phenomenon. It seems improbable too that there was any church in use here as early as Ethelbert's reign, despite Pope Gregory's advice sent to Mellitus who headed a second wave of missionaries in support of Augustine: namely, that existing pagan temples (one of which may have been located on or near Bolts Hill to the north of the present Bridge Street) were not to be destroyed, but consecrated with holy water and supplied with Christian altars enclosing sacred relics.

Our hope is that the people will continue indeed to use the buildings with which they are familiar, but with the realisation that it is no longer false gods that they worship but the one, true God.

In due course Saxon rule itself came under threat, after regional power struggles saw Wessex vying with Mercia for supremacy in the country. The last of the independent Kentish kings, Wihtred, died in 725, after which it seems that Wye began to emerge as a more significant centre with its own royal manor and a correspondingly notable church, located on the site of the present building. A key date in the annals is the year 762 when Ethelbert II issued a charter describing Wye as a Royal Vill. Wye Church, dedicated to St Gregory, may by then be described as a 'minster', responsible for eight other churches.

Christianisation, however (as Peter Brown comments here), did not proceed solely from the ministrations of bishops and priests, as Pope Gregory himself might have intended:

[It] often took place through somewhat anomalous persons ... a wide penumbra of half-participants mediated Christianity to their region.

For example, local warriors may have supported the Church in exchange for anticipated prowess in battle, with the promise of salvation in the world to come. Others perhaps hoped that church rituals would be more effective than pagan sacrifices in bestowing particular blessings on their crops, or on other features of daily life, or in emergencies. Pagan practices were not however wholly abandoned overnight, despite (for example) the imposition of penalties codified in *The Law od Wihtred* (c.695). 'Highly charged contact with the sacred' may have mattered more for some individuals than their regular practice of the Christian faith. Excavations of 8th century graves in East Kent have revealed that the quantity of 'grave goods' found in them did not diminish rapidly, but tended to 'dwindle' away little by little.

The later middle ages

Significant changes to the English Church came again in 1066 following William's victory in the battle of Hastings. The Abbey of St Martin was built on the site where fighting had taken place, in fulfilment of William's vow to do penance for the evil so incurred. Its endowment included the Royal Manor of Wye, and therefore it was Battle Abbey which was now in control of Wye Church. St Martin was subsequently joined with St Gregory in its dedication. The building itself remained as in Saxon times until its replacement around the end of the 13th century.

Spiritually, however, not all was quite as it should be. Here Wye's 'laxity' in the late 12th century was seen as by no means unique within the Christian world. The main issue was the breach of the commandment to 'keep the sabbath day holy', which collectively was believed to be a principal cause of the failure of the 3rd Crusade to recapture Jerusalem. When Innocent III became pope in 1198 he determined that a fresh attempt should be made. The chronicler Roger of Wendover, a monk of St Albans Abbey, compiled a work entitled *Flores Historiarum* ('Flowers of History', culled from many earlier sources). It dates from the early 1200s, and so may be presumed moderately accurate on events of recent origin, even though it is a somewhat colourful and no doubt overstated report. His writings were subsequently used by the more celebrated Matthew Paris as a basis for his own *Chronicles*. Roger recounts that it was in Jerusalem itself that a 'divine letter' appeared, castigating Christians for their heretical tendencies and poor Sunday observance – evidently the reason why God had not granted victory to the Crusaders. The letter came to the notice of the pope, who around the year 1200 'immediately ordained (i.e. commissioned) priests, who were to be sent out into every quarter of the world to preach the purport of the letter.'

Amongst these the abbot of Flaye (a Cistercian monastery in Normandy, St Germer de Fly, where the abbot was later entombed), Eustace by name, a religious and learned man, set out for England, and there shone forth in performing many miracles: he landed near the city of Dover and commenced the duty of his preaching in a town called Wi. In the neighbourhood of that place he bestowed his blessing on a certain spring which his merits so endowed with the Lord's favour, that, from the taste of it alone, the blind recovered sight, the lame their power of walking, the dumb their speech, and the deaf their hearing: and whatever sick person drank of it in faith, at once enjoyed restored health.

He goes on to tell of a woman with dropsy who drank the spring water: she at once vomited up two large black toads, which turned first into dogs, then into asses. However, a sprinkling of the water soon caused these monsters to disappear 'leaving behind them traces of their foulness', and the woman was henceforth completely recovered! The site of this spring at Withersdane can still be seen today, just one kilometre from the present St Ambrose' Catholic Church. When the latter was built in 1954, 'St Eustachius' was actually proposed as its patron, but he lost out to the more substantial historical figure of St Ambrose. Of course, Eustace's visit to Wye was only the start of his mission:

Afterwards going about from place to place, from province to province, from city to city, he by his preaching induced many to relax in usurious habits, admonished them to assume the Lord's cross, and turned the hearts of many to works of piety: he also forbade markets and traffic on Sundays.

His success, alas, was shortlived, since 'many returned to their old customs, like dogs to their vomit.' This relapse presumably included at least a few of Wye's parishioners. (In passing, it may be observed that military failure is seldom blamed today on Sunday trading back home, although our 'lax morals' may well count among the many factors behind terrorist aggression towards Western countries).

The next outstanding Christian associated with Wye also had significant links with foreign warfare. John Kempe (or Kemp) was born locally, probably at the family home at Olantigh (or Olanteigh) on the outskirts of the village, around the year 1380. His father Thomas was a Kentish gentleman whose family had held the seat since the reign of Edward I; his mother was Beatrice, daughter of Sir Thomas Lewknor; his elder brother Thomas fathered yet another Thomas who became bishop of London.

In 1395 Kempe's name first appears on the books of Merton College, Oxford, of which society he subsequently became a fellow. He ultimately proceeded doctor of laws, and practised as a lawyer in the ecclesiastical courts. In or after 1416 he became archdeacon of Durham. Henry V employed Kempe in several diplomatic negotiations. He attended the king on his invasion of Normandy, and in 1418 he was appointed, with two others, to hold the musters of the men-at-arms and archers at Bayeux. In the same year he became keeper of the privy seal, and in November was commissioned to treat with Yolande, queen of Sicily, and her son Louis, for a truce with Anjou and Maine. In January 1419 Kempe was elected bishop of Rochester. He remained, however, in Normandy discharging the king's business, and was probably consecrated bishop at Rouen. The following year he was one of an embassy empowered to treat for a truce or peace with France, after which he was made chancellor of Normandy, retaining that office until Henry V's death. In 1421 he was translated to the see of Chichester, but before performing any episcopal acts was further translated to London at the king's insistence.

Kempe was made a member of the new council appointed under Henry VI, and resigned the chancellorship of Normandy to reside in London. He continued to be employed on a variety of diplomatic missions. His prudence and moderation procured him the highest preferment in 1420, when he became successively chancellor and archbishop of York. In each case the appointment was the result of a compromise between rival factions in the country. Kempe remained chancellor till 1432 when he resigned the office on the pretence of bad health, although it was the internal struggles in the land that proved too much for him.

Deprived of office, Kempe continued an active member of the council. He now became a strenuous adherent of the new peace party in support of the efforts of Pope Eugenius IV to procure peace between France and England. In 1433 he was prominent in conducting negotiations with the French envoy in London. The pope's urgency at last forced the English to send ambassadors to the great European congress at Arras in 1435, and Kempe became head of the English embassy. The French were prepared to make concessions, but Kempe was hampered by his instructions and the unreasonable state of English public opinion. The negotiations were therefore destined to fail. Henceforth Kempe shared the unpopularity of all English statesmen who have sought an honourable end to a hopeless conflict. Negotiations were resumed in due course and in 1439 there were meetings in Calais which dragged on for three months, in the middle of which Kempe returned to England for further instructions. Henry, he learnt, would be content with Normandy and Guienne in full sovereignty, but without abandoning his claim to the French crown – a claim which Kempe had urged him to renounce. The conference therefore again proved abortive.

At the trial of Lord Cobham (accused of being a Lollard heretic), on the 25th September 1413, it is thus recorded: a **Doctour of Lawe**, called **Master Johan Kempe**, plucked out of his bosome a copye of (a) Byll ...

'My lord Cobham' (saythe this doctor) 'we must brefely know your mynde concernyng these four poynts here following.

The first of them is thys, And then he redde vpon the Byll. The Fayth and Determinacion of holy Church touching the Blessed Sacrement of the Alter is this, that after the sacramentall words be once spoken by a pryst in hys masse, the materyall bread that was before bread, is turned into Christes very blode. And so there remaineth in the sacrement of the Aulter from thens forth no materyall bread nor materyall wyne, which were there before the sacrementall words spoken; Sir, beluve ye not this?'

Then Lord Cobham sayed, 'This is not my Beleue; but my Faith is (as I sayed to you afore) that in the worshipful sacrament of the aulter, is very Christes body in fourme of bread.' Than said the Archbishop, 'Sir Johan, ye must saye otherwise.' Then Lord Cobham saide, 'Nay, that I shall not, if God be vpon my syde (as I trust he is) but that there is Christes bodye in fourm of bread, as the comon beleue is.'

Then redde the doctor again. 'The second Point is this : Holy Churche hath determined that euery Christen man lyuing here bodely vpon earth, ought to be shryen to a priest ordained by th' church, if he may come to him. Sir, What say ye to this?'

The Lord Cobham answered and said, 'A diseased or sore wounded man had nede to have a sure wyse chyrurgion, and a true; knowing both the ground and the danger of the same. Moost necessary were it therefore, to be fyrst shryuen vnto God which only knoweth our diseases and can help us. I deny not in this the going to a priest, if he be a man of good lyfe and learning: for the lawes of God are to be required of the Priest which is godly learned, But if he be an Ydiote, or a man of viciouse lyuing that is my curate, I ought rather to flee him than to seke vnto him. For souner might I catch yll of him that is nought, than any goodnesse towards my soule helth.'

Then redde the doctour againe, 'The third Point is this, Christe ordained Saint Peter ye Apostle to be his Vicar here in earth, whose see is the church of Rome. And he granted that the same power which he gave vnto Peter, should succeed to all Peter's successors, which we call now Popes of Rome. By whose special power in churches partycular he ordained prelates, archbishops, parsons, curates, and other degrees more; vnto whom christen men ought to obeye after the lawes of the church of Rome. This is the determination of Holy church ; Sir, belieue ye not this?'

To this he answered, and said, 'He that followeth Peter moost nighest in pure lyuing, is next vnto him in succession; but your Lordly ordre estemeth not greatly the lowly behauer of pore Peter; what soeuer ye prate of him: neither care you greatly for the humble maners of them that succeeded him tyll the lime of Sylvester, which for the most part were martirs, as I told ye afore. You can lett all their good condicions go by you, and not hurt your selues with them at all; all the world knows thys well enough by you, and ye can meke boast of Peter.'

Then redde the Doctor again: 'The fourth Pointe is this, holy Church hath determined, that it is meretorious to a chrysten manne to go on pilgrimage to holy places, and there specially to worship holy relicks and images of saintes, apostles, martirs, confessors, and all other saintes besides, approued by the Church of Rome; Sir, what say ye to this?'

Whereunto he answered: 'I owe them no seruice by any commandent of God, and therefore I minde not to seke them for your coueteovsness; It were best ye swept them fayre from cobwebs and duste.'

At the end of that year Pope Eugenius IV appointed Kempe as a cardinal, hoping that his exalted position would make him more influential in future peace negotiations. Henry VI declared that he was one of the wisest Lords of the land, and in thanking the pope for making him a cardinal, commended him for his 'holiness, purity of life, abundance of knowledge, ripeness of counsel, experience in business, wisdom, eloquence, gravity, and dignity of person.' It seems that he remained one of the king's chief confidants, since, despite being anxious for peace, he also upheld English interests.

Ten years later, in 1450, he was once again appointed chancellor, although by now he was old and infirm. Nevertheless, he dealt firmly with Jack Cade's Kentish rebellion in the following year. After Henry VI had fled from London to Kenilworth, Kempe remained behind and by sending pardons to the captain and his followers he effectively broke up the insurrection. As chancellor he continued to urge the necessity of putting down riots and defending the coasts from France, and hence was the mainstay of the king's party.

In 1452 he was translated from York to Canterbury. In London though, the growing tension between Lancastrians and Yorkists in the end proved too much for him and he died on 22nd March 1454. He was buried at Canterbury.

Although Kempe was not much of a bishop, and was generally unpopular in his dioceses, which he seldom visited, he was a godly man whose passion was for the peace and good order of the country. His chief act of beneficence ('to make recompense to God and to others to whom he was beholden') was the erection of a college of secular priests, or 'perpetual chantry', in conjunction with the parish church of Wye, for which he always showed a strong affection. He obtained a royal licence for this object in February 1432, and permission to add largely to its endowment in March 1439.

Kempe's tomb

But it was not until 1447 that the plans were finally completed. Kempe drew up elaborate statutes for the government of the master or provost and fellows of his college. It was to be run on scriptural lines emphasising sobriety in manner, conduct, and dress, with attendance required several times a day at services in church. He gave a preference to Merton men for the provostship.

WYE COLLEGE prior to later expansion

A grammar school was established in connection with the college, and one of the fellows was to act as curate of Wye. He also partially reconstructed Wye church, although his nephew Thomas was responsible for completing this programme and for continuing to support the new college.

Beyond the reformation

Wye College was of course eventually suppressed under Henry VIII. It became a private house in 1545, although the Grammar School continued for many years. A reformed church of a carefully regulated kind emerged in the reign of Elizabeth I. Disgust with the burnings under 'Bloody Mary' was a useful ideological buttress, and Foxe's book, by now universally called *The Book of Martyrs*, was bought for Wye Church in response to a general order. Like the English Bible, it was chained to a lectern for all comers to read. Then in 1559 Cranmer's 1552 Prayer Book was restored, with a few modifications. It was expected that everyone would attend Morning Prayer every Sunday and Holy Communion whenever it was celebrated, typically once a month. The churchwardens were ordered to impose fines of twelve pence on anyone who was absent without good reason. Defence of the spiritual primacy of the pope incurred forfeiture of goods and, if possessions were worth less than twenty pounds, imprisonment for a year. Serial offenders ran the risk of a traitor's death. For the first decade of Elizabeth's reign the letter of the law was not, however, rigidly enforced. Various factors lay behind this:

• Elizabeth was unsure of her own position, having been declared 'illegitimate' in 1536.
• There were signs of rapprochement on the continent between France and Spain, which might increase the possibility of military action being taken against England.
• The country had recently suffered the rule of Bloody Mary, and now had less enthusiasm for such violent reprisals.

The situation changed significantly as the 1560s progressed, with the threat posed by Mary Queen of Scots lurking in the background. She fled south in 1568, only to find herself held prisoner until her execution in 1587 – long awaited by some of Elizabeth's ministers who said of the more extreme Catholics, 'so long as there is life in her, there is hope (i.e. for the Catholic cause); so as they live in hope, we live in fear'. In 1569 there was an outbreak of unrest, the Catholic 'Rising of the North', whose aim was to depose the queen, which meant that state security had to be tightened.

Archdeacons throughout the country were then charged with keeping a vigilant eye at their regular parish visitations. At Archbishop Parker's Visitation of 1569 the twenty-nine Wye absentees[2] were probably all Catholic sympathisers, with the Kempe, Dryland and Clifton families prominent among them. William Clifton (noted as absent along with his wife Mary and – presumably his son – Thomas) was the schoolmaster, and was probably the William Clifton who graduated B.A. from Corpus Christi College, Cambridge in 1530, becoming Master of Faversham School in 1534. His father Richard had been schoolmaster in Wye before the Dissolution. A note was added to the Visitation report that 'we think [William] is not of sincere religion', with none of his household receiving communion during the past five years: '[he] doth stubbornly refuse to conform himself to unity and good religion, and cometh not to sermons accordingly.' Yet the forfeit required of each absentee was not apparently paid, and a blind eye continued to be turned in their direction. Four years later Mrs Clifton is still listed as a non-attender. It is noteworthy that the dissidents listed in 1569 appear to represent more than twenty different households, in other words, well over a quarter of the village of Wye: according to Matthew Parker's population statistics drawn up for the archdiocese of Canterbury in 1563 there were then 72 households.

Others named in the annals include the Rev Robert Serles, clearly more Catholic than Protestant, who had earlier preached (for example) that images of saints might be permitted in church without necessarily being regarded as idols; he retired to Wye, where he had wealthy family connections, when Elizabeth I acceded to the throne, and lived apparently undisturbed until his death in 1570. It was recorded too in the Archdeacon's Visitation of 1560 that Sir Thomas Southby, appointed Parochial Chaplain in 1540 before becoming a Perpetual Curate in 1545,

---

[2] 'These have not received:—Mr. Anthony Kemp, Mr. Richard Dryeland, Richard Hawke and his wife, William Clifton and his wife Mary Clifton, Thomas Clifton, George Younge, Thomas Barrow, William Hendelay and his wife, Francis Wheeler and his wife, Thomas Assan, Sampson Wells, John Morres servant to Mr. Serlys, John Alleyn, William Jekyn, Thomas Odyame, Nicholas Arden, William Tryton and his wife, Thomas Honye, William Rowland, John Russell, John Mylls, Mr. Blayston servant to Sir Thos. Kempe, William Glasyer servant to Sir Thomas Kempe, John Rooke, cowper.'

'useth his portres [breviary] every day when he cometh to church'. He was buried in Wye on 11th July 1560, too old to be disturbed any further.

Developments on the wider front in 1570 and 1571 had serious repercussions. First of all, Pope Pius V (rather unwisely) issued a bull, *Regnans in Excelsis*, dated 27th April 1570, which declared Elizabeth I a heretic and released her subjects from their allegiance to her. In response, Elizabeth, who had thus far tolerated Catholic worship in private, now actively started persecuting them for treason. A 1571 Act was passed, which among other things banned hallowed objects such as crucifixes and beads, and also made attendance at Holy Communion compulsory. This clause was vetoed by Elizabeth. It remained legal to proffer the excuse for non-attendance on the grounds of being 'out of charity with one's neighbours'. Even if Catholics did attend, they might well resort to blocking their ears, reading a book, scoffing the sermon afterwards – or sometimes wearing a hat when prayers were said for the queen. She herself put a stop to further debate with a message that 'concerninge rytes and ceremonyes she, beinge supreme hedd of the Church, wolde consider thereof as the case sholde require'. (It should be remembered that, in matters of authority, there were Catholic sovereigns in Europe who would also resist others encroaching on their rights, including not only parliaments but the pope himself if he overstepped the mark: for example, when the bull *In Coena Domini* condemning bull-fighting was issued at the end of 1567 it received short thrift in Spain!)

Elizabeth necessarily kept an eye on continental happenings, and the infamous St Bartholomew's Day massacre of 1572, in which Huguenots were killed by fanatical Catholic crowds in Paris, and later beyond, was taken as a dreadful warning. It reinforced in Protestant minds the conviction that Catholicism was 'a bloody and treacherous religion'. Yet retaliation against Catholics in England was limited. There had been no martyrdoms in the 1560s, and there were not more than a handful during the 1570s. It was later that executions mounted dramatically in number: 78 priests and 25 lay people met their death in the 1580s, with the total dropping a little in the remainder of Elizabeth's reign when 53 priests died along with 35 lay people. Under James I the gross figure in his entire reign was 25.

16th century anti Catholic cartoons

There were Catholics, though, who were respected by the queen as reliable subjects, some of whom held positions of responsibility under her. In particular, Viscount Montagu was well-known to be a Catholic, and yet was appointed in 1560 to be Elizabeth's ambassador to Spain and again in 1564 to represent her in the Low Countries. He also held an important military position as Lord Lieutenant of Sussex. Under Mary Tudor he had been one of three ambassadors charged with negotiating reconciliation between the Church of England and Rome. He was certainly the most politically important Catholic in Sussex, where he held Battle Abbey (along with Cowdray House and Montagu House), but he was no extremist and remained loyal to the Crown. In 1591, the year before he died, he entertained the queen for a week at Cowdray House (near Midhurst in West Sussex). It is recorded that on the Sunday when she arrived with her retinue, three oxen and a hundred and forty geese were consumed. The next day some thirty deer were rounded up and put in a paddock: the queen was given a crossbow and killed 'three or four' of them to the accompaniment of sweet music.

After her husband's death, Lady Magdalen (*whose own effigy is seen here*) resided at a reconstructed Battle Abbey, which must have been the nearest centre for Wye Catholics occasionally to attend mass without fear of reprisals. She maintained a household of eighty or more people, almost all of whom were Catholics. There were also three priests in

residence at Battle, which was known locally as Little Rome. One of these was the great-grandson of the martyr Thomas More. Lady Magdalen built a chapel at Battle, and on feast days as many as 120 Catholics attended. Along with Montagu House in Southwark, Battle Abbey became an important safe house for Catholic priests travelling to and from the continent. It was largely ignored by Sussex magistrates since many were at least crypto-Catholics themselves. For her part Lady Magdalen was always scrupulous in avoiding any accusation of treason: in 1597 her brother Francis Dacre, who was a conspirator, sent a messenger to Battle with (no doubt compromising) letters for the Earl of Essex – so she handed both the messenger and his letters to the nearest magistrate and personally informed the Lord Lieutenant, Lord Brockhurst (to whom she was related by her daughter's marriage). When in 1599 she came under suspicion, her London home was searched for weapons and for gunpowder, but in vain.

> My hope is in God. Here sleeps in the Lord, John Roper, Distinguished knight, Lord and Baron of Teynham, with Elizabeth his wife, who was the daughter of Sir Richard Park. She gave birth to Christopher Roper, distinguished knight, Elizabeth who married George Vaux and mother of Lord Edward Vaux Baron of Harrowdon, and Jane wife of Sir Robert Lovell, distinguished knight. He (John) cultivated all that was fair and good. **He was assuredly a very loyal servant to three monarchs, Mary, Elizabeth and James. He was very patriotic**, generous and kind to the poor and to his neighbours. Mindful of his own mortality, and in sure and certain hope of the resurrection in Christ, set up this monument while he was still living. He lived for 84 years, and died 30th August 1618.

John Roper of Lynsted (near Faversham)
Another 'loyal' Catholic.

Battle Abbey was not the only safe house this side of London. Scotney Castle near Lamberhurst was another such place, apparently provided with one of 'Little John' Owen's famous priest holes. Little John's actual name was Nicholas: he was an incomparable carpenter heavily involved with the Catholic 'underground' from about 1588. His hides were always different, so discovering any particular one would be of little help in finding others. Often ceilings and floors were raised or lowered, with hides concealed in roof spaces, behind panelling, in or below false fireplaces. Owen worked alone and despite his small stature he must have been a really powerful man since he had frequently to cut through walls, floors and wooden beams.

Scotney Castle

The owner of Scotney in his day was Thomas Darrell, who retained a Jesuit priest named Richard Blount in the castle from 1591 to 1598. When the authorities returned there for a more thorough search to arrest him, he fled over a wall into the moat and so escaped. Owen himself was a prize catch for the authorities and the fact that he died rather than reveal his secrets helped to elevate him to heroic status among his peers. He was canonised in 1970, having died under torture in the Tower of London in 1606. (The Darrells feature more locally when we reach the 18th century.)

Not all Catholics were as cautious as Lady Magdalen or as easily hidden as at Scotney Castle. Some were more readily suspected of possible sedition, many lacked influence in high places. Thomas Clifton, offspring of the staunch Catholic family in Wye already mentioned in connection with the school, was in his 20s during the increasingly tense 1570s. Two factors may have influenced his decision to seek ordination to the priesthood: (1) In the aftermath of the Council of Trent, the Catholic Church decided upon a policy of providing better priestly formation by opening a number of seminaries. One of these lay not far across the channel at Douay, which commenced its training in 1568. (2) In 1575 Pope Gregory XIII, who was largely responsible for implementing the Tridentine reforms, proclaimed a Jubilee Year. Thousands from across Europe visited Rome, but – realising this was largely impossible for Catholics in England – he offered them alternatives:

Hereupon, forasmuch as we understand that English people, faithful and Catholic Christians, as well in England as out of England, dispersed in divers countries, cannot come to Rome to enjoy the fruits of this year of Jubilee; some because they are not permitted to come out of the realm, and some in that they have lost their goods, and are banished persons for the Catholic faith, not able to bear the charge and travail of so long a journey, or otherwise having some just impediments : We therefore, as the duty and office of an Universal Pastor requireth, and of fatherly love towards all Christian people, desirous to provide for the health of their souls, do grant unto all the aforesaid Catholics of England, as well men as women, being truly penitent and confessed, who shall fifteen times religiously visit four churches, if there be so many, or if not, three, two, or one only church, where there are no more, and shall devoutly pray unto God, and perform all other things contained in our letter of indiction of this year of Jubilee; And to them also that be in England, wherein in no church, nor in any other place whatsoever, as we are informed, it is permitted that God after a Catholic manner be publicly honoured, being there detained by any lawful impediment, if they do and work after the prescribed order of a discreet confessor, regard being had to the state, condition, and calling of every person with the time and place, or if a ghostly Father cannot be gotten, then reciting devoutly fifteen times, with true contrition of heart, the Rosary or crown of our Blessed Lady, that they and every one of them have all, yea, plenary indulgence and remission of their sins, as fully as if they personally had visited this sacred city.

The Jubilee undoubtedly resulted in a more confident mood among Catholics, inclining many to a feeling of *Romanitas* (a term originally coined by Tertullian). This feeling was heightened when in 1578 the catacomb of Priscilla was uncovered in Rome and the murals found there testified to its ancient heritage of courageous faith. The fervour generated may have infected Thomas Clifton, inspiring him to offer for the priesthood. He certainly made a major decision and crossed over to France, where on 9th October 1579 he was given minor orders at Arras, before going on to study at Douay English College, recently (April 1578) relocated to Rheims. After relatively brief training as a Catholic priest he was ordained at Laon on 19th December, 1579. When he returned to England on 7th January, 1580, he was initially able to minister as a priest, but was arrested on 15th November.

His timing was unfortunate, in that the summer of 1580 had seen a Jesuit mission (led by Robert Parsons and Edmund Campion) launched in an attempt to restore the Catholic faith to England. Despite the fact that Gregory XIII had been persuaded to suspend the bull of excommunication against Elizabeth, and that Catholics were advised to obey the queen outwardly in all civil matters, the mission was seen as a hostile threat. This was hardly surprising, given that not long since some foreign troops had been equipped to back Catholic rebellion in Ireland. It was undoubtedly this mission that triggered the widespread arrests of priests in England, some one hundred of whom, like Thomas Clifton, had already entered the country in recent years. There were now also stronger repercussions for those who professed any signs of Catholicism: from 1581 the fine for non-attendance in the local parish church was increased to £20 per month, which mounted up over a year to something like the average income of many landed gentry. No longer could the latter afford to resort to their private chapels.

Thomas was charged under the statute of Praemunire for 'extolling the Pope's authority'. He was sentenced to forfeit all his possessions and to be imprisoned for life, news of which reached his parents in late 1581. The *Douay Diaries* record the following:

> Mr Clifton, priest... who has already for some months suffered so much from the heretics by cold, hunger and the load of his chains in a dungeon among fiends that his being yet alive seems a miracle. This man when of late he was led through the streets, loaded with heavy irons, to the bar, in the company of thieves, his companions sighing and almost all the people being moved to commiseration, he alone was cheerful and dragged his chains along with a smiling countenance. And when one asked him why he more than the rest should laugh, his case being so deplorable as it was, he answered, 'Because I look for greater gain than they from my sufferings; and it is just they should laugh that win.'

He then fell upon his knees, and, with hands and eyes uplifted, said 'Alleluia, alleluia'. He was never executed, but was confined initially in Newgate, and then in the King's Bench prison (located near the present-day Borough tube station). From 1586 to 1587 he was certainly in the Marshalsea prison, and next appears in Bridewell prison where in 1589 the Governors appealed to Sir Francis Walsingham for resources to relieve poor prisoners, including 'Thomas Clifton, priest', who were presumably having no help from family or friends. It was said that he fed on 'the bread of sorrow, having his hands, feet, and neck chained in such sort that he could neither sit down nor stir out of his place all the day, and every night was put down into a horrid and darksome dungeon'. A letter written in 1593 to a certain Fr Garnett reported that he had died in prison, so (in addition to the town's earlier Protestant martyrs) Wye has a Catholic martyr too, whose death was probably in 1592.

The position of Sir Thomas Kempe was ambiguous. As the local justice of the peace he played a prominent part in the disposal of redundant church vestments and ornaments, not only in Wye but also throughout the lathe of Shepway. In 1564 all the Kent justices of the peace were described by the archbishop of Canterbury as at least 'outwardly conformable' in religion. However, after his third marriage Kempe began to cause the ecclesiastical authorities anxiety. In 1578 he and his wife were noted by the ecclesiastical visitors as not having received communion, so Kempe was put off the commission of the peace. The Kempe family was, however, well placed to avoid too much interference since four of Thomas' five daughters married members of parliament. While the Kempes gave lodging to Mary Clifton, widowed by her husband William's death in 1577, they apparently did nothing for her son Thomas after his arrest and imprisonment a few years later. It seems that Sir Thomas dared not risk intervening on his behalf: he remained discreet in his own religious commitment, and proved his patriotic loyalty as a Commissioner for Coastal Defence (having previously served as High Sheriff in 1555 and 1564) by organising the system of armada beacons. He died on 7th March 1591, and was buried at Wye. His son and heir, also Thomas, served as High Sheriff in 1597.

Not all Catholic priests who were incarcerated fared as badly as Clifton. Others were released on condition of leaving the country: thus, Christopher Dryland, another young man from Wye who had become a Catholic priest, was imprisoned for some years, mainly in Wisbech Castle, but was then allowed to leave the country in 1603 and settled quietly in Rome. A third priest associated with Wye, according to *Lives of the English Martyrs*, was named John Stransham; he trained at Douay, and was in 'the service of Moyle Kempe Esq., third son of Sir Thomas Kempe of Wye, Kent'. The *Douay Diaries* mention too another Stransham (alias Potter), of the diocese of Canterbury, who was ordained priest in 1585. It is suggested that this George Stransham may have been John's brother, although Stransham was not in those days an unusual Kentish surname. It was of course common practice for Catholic priests returning from abroad to travel under a different name – thus, Edward Stransham of Oxford (not necessarily any relation) was martyred on 21st January 1586 as 'Edward Barber'. A stricter law had been passed in March 1585 making it a capital offence for priests ordained abroad after 1559 to be in the country: once the act came into force, any such were allowed 40 days to return to the continent. Two years later, further punitive measures were passed.

It was in the 1580s – a decade that ended with the defeat of the Spanish Armada, after Elizabeth had effectively declared war on Spain by sending the Earl of Leicester's expeditionary force to fight in the Low Countries – that parochial visitations noted once again the names of any suspected of harbouring Romish sympathies. In 1581 William Nightingale and his wife are accused of 'persuading certain to withdraw from the religion now established'. In 1583 Lady Mordaunt, who had married Sir Thomas Kempe, was named as an absentee along with her husband and 'divers of their families', along with 'my lady's gentlewoman' Mary Engham. In 1586 'the common fame and report' reckoned her ladyship had not received communion 'these ten years last past'. One Ingram Marten was listed as harbouring papists in his house, including for at least two months his own sister Clare, who 'hath openly said that she would not read the scriptures for that they make much contention'. The last mention of Ingram, along with his wife Anne, is in the 1590s. Richard Dryland, gentleman, and Gertrude his wife, are listed in 1590 too as 'favourers of the Romish religion' who 'have not received the communion these many years; but whether they do it of obstinacy or not, we know not'. The same entry occurs in 1597.

A general idea of religious loyalties in England in the mid 1580s may be gleaned from a letter sent on 13th August 1586 by Bernardino de Mendoza to Philip II of Spain. He reported the impressions gained by his agents up and down the country of the probable strength of Catholic support in each county. The north country as a whole was predominantly Catholic, but while some Catholics were to be found in Kent, he estimated that its 'whole population... is infested with heresy'. (This assessment may be compared with later estimates – whose reliability may obviously be questioned: in 1773, Kent was reckoned to be home to a mere 300 Catholics, rising to 600 in 1790 with five centres of regular worship, including Calehill, the Darrell home north-west of Ashford, as well as Hales Place and Nash Court, both near Canterbury; by 1814 the figure had risen sharply to 3317.)

As with all public surveys, the true position may have been somewhat different. Clearly in some areas there would have been considerable reluctance to admit Catholic sympathies of any sort. Some interesting revelations emerge from records in Canterbury of Wye recusants in the 1590s. In 1592, 'a whole posse of parishioners were taken before the Consistory Court at Canterbury, and fined for acts of recusancy, misbehaviour in church and other offences'. Another entry indicates that the authorities had little power of enforcement: 'There were diverse others that were appointed to compound, but they would not obey the order'. Towards the end of that decade, things were quite out of hand. Churchwardens' accounts for Wye (covering the years 1515 to 1663) indicate that they purchased 'a copy of the articles against the recusants to be read the first Sunday of every month' as a warning, yet the number of parishioners brought before the archdeacon's correctional court continued to mount up all through Elizabeth's reign, with sometimes as many as forty summoned to appear. In 1597 the churchwardens confessed to the archdeacon that they found it impossible to levy the prescribed forfeitures because the number of recusants was too great. It seems likely that the news of Thomas Clifton's death in prison played a part in this growing rebellion.

The revival of catholic worship

Soon after the Elizabethan era the Catholic minority in Wye vanishes from view. None were reported in the 'Compton Census' of 1676, but not long afterwards the Darrell family emerged as willing collaborators in James II's religious policies. Although they had largely conformed since the days of the Reformation, it proved to be their home at Calehill near Little Chart (7 miles due west of Wye) that in the 18th and 19th centuries provided a local chapel for Catholic worship. Here we may recall the aforementioned Thomas Darrell who resided at Scotney in the 1590s. The Darrells originated in Yorkshire, but a younger brother William had come south to Kent where he soon established himself among the landowning gentry. He acquired several estates by a combination of astute marriage alliances and successful purchases. In 1410 he bought the manor of Calehill (first mentioned in 839, when it was granted to the monks of Canterbury), and when he married for a second time in 1418 his new wife's settlement from her uncle – Archbishop Chichele – included Scotney Castle. The former property was inherited by Sir James Darrell in 1664. It pained him to discover that his own heir, a young distant cousin, had recently been admitted to Douay Seminary, as he put it, 'to pervert him in his principles of religion', yet it may have been this relative who later inclined the family to return to the old religion.

James II was of course deposed in the Glorious Revolution of 1688, but it was in that year that four 'vicars apostolic' (i.e. missionary bishops) were appointed to serve across the country. In the following century there was gradually more social acceptance of Catholics, and a somewhat higher profile was possible for the practice of Catholic worship. John Darrell, who succeeded to the estate on his father's death in 1693 was himself a Catholic and had several sons who became Jesuit priests; in time, his son James came back home to serve in the chapel dedicated to St Joseph at Calehill from 1769 to 1775, in effect becoming the first parish priest of an area which included Ashford and Wye. The responsible vicar apostolic at this time was the famous Richard Challoner who used as his quasi-cathedral the Sardinian Embassy Chapel in London.

Calehill House, before its demolition in 1952

In addition to the chapel at Calehill House which dates from around 1754 when the house was rebuilt, there was also an older Darrell chapel in the parish church at Little Chart. The above John died in 1739 and is buried in the vault, as are many of his descendants up until 1875. His father was the last one to be buried in the chapel itself, but sadly this no longer remains as a flying bomb destroyed it around Christmas 1944.

The Priest's House at Calehill, near the South Gate

There was a long succession of priests who served at Calehill from the mid 18th century until the 1850s when regular worship (which had actually become legal in 1791) began in Ashford itself. The *Catholic Directory* of 1844 gives what was probably typical of the mass schedule for the entire period:

Sundays and Holy Days Mass at 10am
Evening Prayers at 3pm
followed by Catechism on Sundays
Weekdays Mass at 9am

In 1847 a request was lodged for the registration of the chapel for marriages, and bore the signatures of 31 members of the congregation, 11 of whom (including 5 surnamed Darrell) were listed as 'inmates' of Calehill House itself. In 1856, Benediction was introduced on Sunday afternoons.

Earlier in the 19th century several important factors give a fillip to the Catholic presence in the country. In 1829 the Emancipation Act restored most of the rights already enjoyed by the majority of people. In the 1840s there was mass Irish immigration after their famine, with a number of converts from the Church of England, including the future Cardinals Manning and Newman. In 1850 the Catholic hierarchy was restored, giving Southwark its own Archbishop.

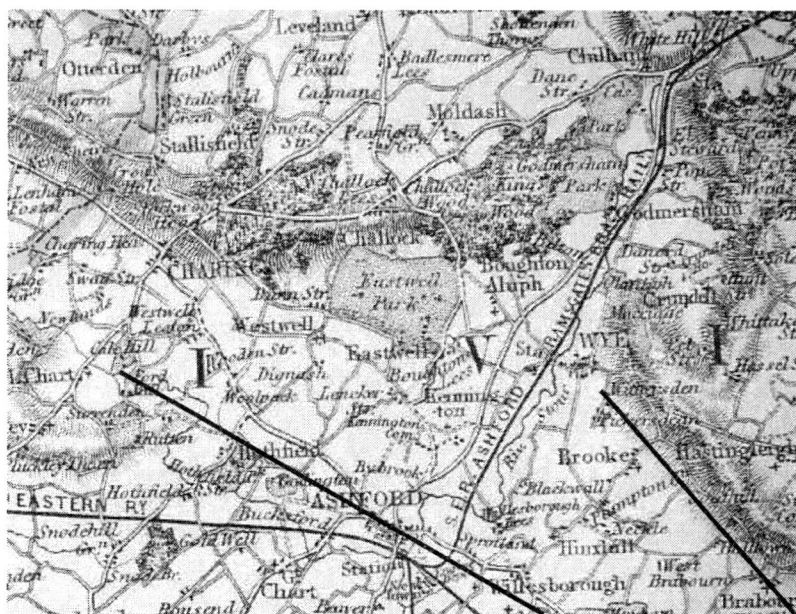

A map of 1863
Showing the relative positions of Calehill, Ashford and Wye

The shift from Calehill to Ashford itself took place in the 1850s in response to the rising numbers of Catholics. The first mention of church premises in Ashford occurs at the very end of 1854: baptisms are recorded *'in capella apud Ashford'*. Subsequently an advertisement appeared in the *Catholic Directory* of 1856 appealing for subscriptions in support of the new venture 'in this increasing town for the benefit of Catholics who are there, or of others who may come to the neighbourhood'. In 1857 Fr Edward Sheridan hired a room in New Street, Ashford for mass on Sundays; this was known as St Dunstan's (later it became a pub called 'Three Ones'), which in 1859 added Sunday vespers to its list of services, a practice which had earlier come into the country with French emigré priests. Then came the chapel dedicated to St Teresa, opened on 15th October 1862 under Fr Antonio Oromi, who shortly afterwards made Ashford rather than Calehill his base, leaving Fr Patrick Kelly to care for the older mission. St Teresa's chapel was on the present site of Barrow Hill, and by 1864 was supplying Calehill with a priest rather than vice versa. It remained in position until the nave roof of the new St Teresa's was finished. This was designed by Edward Welby Pugin (son of the better-known Pugin).

The church of St Teresa, Ashford from 1865 – 1989
opened on 22nd August 1865 by Bishop Grant,
with Cardinal Manning as the preacher.

Meanwhile Calehill chapel continued in use until about 1930, apart from the war years 1914-18. The property was sold by the Darrells just before the Great War and was bought by a wealthy American Catholic, Chester Beatty, undoubtedly the most famous person ever to be associated with Calehill. Calehill House was eventually demolished, and the estate sold, in the early 1950s, although other listed buildings still remain there.

Biblical Papyri

Chester Beatty's library (now in Dublin) is the finest private collection of manuscripts and books made in the 20th century. The discovery of the Chester Beatty was made public in 1931. Previously, the most important manuscripts of the Greek New Testament were codices from the 4th and 5th centuries, whereas his New Testament papyri are much earlier.

P45 (Gospels and Acts) dates from c. 250; P46 (Paul's Letters – illustrated here) is from c. 200.

A new beginning in Wye

Until the Second World War Catholics from Wye would have travelled to one of the neighbouring churches or chapels, for example, just occasionally to Battle Abbey in the late 16th century, later on to Calehill, and eventually into Ashford, although at times a priest might be discreetly available in a house more locally. There were opportunities in other directions too, not least in Canterbury where the present St Thomas Becket's Church was opened in 1875. But during WW2 the army's presence in Wye College, which would have included serving Catholics, brought a chaplain over regularly from Shorncliffe camp near Folkestone to offer mass. This took place every Sunday, either in the Old Lecture Theatre or in the dining room, with a dozen or more local people (and several children) joining in as well.

After the war, it was the initiative of a Mrs Whatmore, who purchased the Old Vicarage in Upper Bridge Street in 1946 for the sum of £900, to keep things going. At first, mass was held in one of her rooms, but it was realized fairly soon that this was too small and inconvenient. Attention moved to the adjacent stable, no longer occupied by any animal. Since one of Mrs Whatmore's sons was a Catholic priest, Fr Leonard,[3] who had been ordained in June 1941 for the diocese of Southwark, expert advice was readily available as to its necessary re-ordering. Mr O'Malley, who hailed originally from County Mayo but (like Mrs Whatmore) had come recently from Birmingham to Wye and lived in an adjacent cottage (now demolished), then helped to modify and furnish the stable.

The stable chapel:
'Mary was able to turn a stable into a
home for Jesus, with poor swaddling
clothes and an abundance of love'
(Pope Francis 2013)

---

[3] It may be of interest to record an extract from Fr Leonard's obituary notice as it appeared in *The Catholic Herald* on 16th April 1982:

Fr Leonard Whatmore, who for many years figured prominently in the now-defunct Catholic Priests' Association, has died at the age of 69. Born in Birmingham in 1912, Fr Whatmore studied for the priesthood at St John's seminary, Wonersh ...

Among his academic achievements was an MA degree in Classics and Fellowship of the Royal Historical Society. He worked for the cause of canonisation of the English Martyrs.

A little more can be added about his academic interests. Apart from occasional papers, his most significant writing, published in 1973, was *Highway to Walsingham* which gives an account of early pilgrimages to the shrine there. So his particular interest was in the medieval Catholic Church and its 16th century martyrs. I am grateful for the research detailed in his *Recusancy in Kent: Studies and Documents*, which has supplied several details about Ashford and Wye, especially during the years 1560-1860.

Inside the stable chapel

At first, starting in 1947, Mass was held about once a month, with Fr Leonard occasionally acting as the celebrant. More often, an Irish missioner came, although the time of Mass was variable. As many as twenty adults and children, some from nearby villages such as Brook and Hastingleigh, attended; one or two sometimes arrived on horseback. The service was occasionally enhanced by the braying of the donkey in the adjacent paddock. On Sundays when Mass was not being held in Wye some parishioners would catch the 6.30 am train into Ashford and go to the 8 am Mass at St Teresa's.

The Old Vicarage, Upper Bridge Street, Wye
(Mrs Whatmore's house, with its stable on the left)

Although the Whatmore residence became a retirement home for ladies in 1949, the new owner Mrs Canby was a Catholic who retained the chapel, which now had a regular Sunday Mass. She also ran a small church choir principally to sing at festivals, which she accompanied herself on the harmonium. A particular highlight was the Mass held in 1953 on Coronation Day – although Mrs Canby had by then moved. When her retirement home fell into debt Southwark Diocese purchased its grounds on favourable terms with a view to building a church there. The chapel came at this time under the pastoral care of Ashford Parish. There were also ideas – soon abandoned – of using Oxenturn House (almost opposite) as a convent when it came on the market for £2000. Fr Butler, the parish priest, was active in drawing up plans for the proposed church, insisting in particular that, since Wye would serve a wide geographical area, a hall and toilet facilities would be essential.

The present building

The first step towards erecting a purpose-built church on the 'Whatmore site' was to construct a hall with much greater capacity than the stable; the intention was to use it as a chapel until the church itself could be properly funded. Since Fr Butler's ill-health took him away from the parish, it was Fr Woods who implemented his plans. The cost of the hall (£600) was born by Mr Fitzpatrick, formerly of County Mayo. The two oak benches that are still in the sanctuary came from the private chapel at Calehill, near Little Chart. Other seats and pews, mostly considered rather 'plush', came from there too; being in much poorer condition, however, they were replaced in 1991 by the pine pews from the former St Teresa's Church, Ashford. The Christmas crib, still in use, was made by Mr Yeomans of Brook. Before the roof girders were covered in 1973, they also came into their own at Christmas, when they were festooned with children's decorations. The Blessed Sacrament has been reserved since that same year, the tabernacle being installed by the then-owner of the nearby Wife of Bath restaurant, Mr Michael Waterfield. He raised funds for these renovations (which included removing the stone dais from the sanctuary) by laying on a special dinner, although this was not popular with the ladies who had volunteered to run coffee mornings. The present organ, another local gift, stands where once the confessional was situated. There was no permanent font for many years, until Mrs Carolyn Hamley provided one in memory of her deceased parents.

**The procession on 14th November 1954
led by Archbishop Cyril Cowderoy
(just 100 years after St Dunstan's Chapel, Ashford was opened)**

Within a relatively short space of time the congregation grew from perhaps thirty or more to over one hundred (with many children); some even needed to stand at the back or occasionally outside. Numbers were swelled by the presence of visitors from Willsborough and Kennington and from outlying villages such as Godmersham. There were also several Poles and Germans living locally, who had remained after World War 2 as agricultural labourers. Sunday Mass was held at 9.30 am which has remained the same until the present day, as has the weekday celebration of Mass on a Tuesday evening, preceded by the recitation of the Rosary. The catchment area today is wider still, stretching as far as Chilham to the north and beyond the M20 to the south. The building has, however, remained substantially the same, apart from certain renovations (recently, as well as in 1973).

The foundation stone.

An early view of the chapel

St Ambrose Church today

The adjacent site, once earmarked for a much larger church, was sold in 1989 soon after the arrival of Fr Tom Cooper as parish priest for the housing development known as St Ambrose Green. The capital released helped towards the building of the new St Teresa's Church, of which St Ambrose remains a daughter church – a reversal of roles since Saxon days.

Why, however, was the chapel dedicated to St Ambrose? In 1954 there was a distinct coincidence in that the Catholic parish priest of Ashford was *Ambrose* Woods (since immortalised in Kennington by the street named after him, Canon Woods Way). At first I imagined, as did many in the original congregation, that our little church in Wye must have been so named as his own preference. I understand now that he was much embarrassed at the time by this assumption! The full dedication is actually 'St Ambrose of Milan', and was chosen by the Archbishop, most likely because of Ambrose' courageous witness in an era when the Christian faith was not always readily embraced: 'Hold fast to the rudder of faith, that you may not be shaken by the heavy storms of the world', he once wrote to a fellow-bishop. Elizabethan recusants certainly had a high regard for Ambrose for this very reason – and the same has remained true for later generations of Catholics.

The diamond jubilee of St Ambrose' Church was celebrated on 14th November 2014 with Archbishop Peter Smith of Southwark presiding. A choir led by Mark Deller sang Byrd's 4 part mass along with other motets – a fitting tribute to Byrd's Catholic contemporary, Fr Thomas Clifton. The occasion was also marked by the Archbishop's presentation of the *Bene Merenti* papal medal to one of our stalwart members John Joliffe, in recognition of his many years of outstanding service to the local church.

A Future Fugitive from Wye

THE INCIPIENT FAITH OF RIDDLEY WALKER

Is it possible to speak of 'progress' in the sense of an onward march of civilisation? Many generations in the past have obviously seen promising developments in their own day and age, and have sometimes envisaged that a Golden Age might be just around the corner. So greater food security, advances in treating illness and disease, improvements in transport and technology, artistic and cultural blossoming, the cessation of hostilities and the removal of external threats, have all from time to time helped induce a sense of human flourishing – which might well be termed 'progress'. On the other hand, there have been many surprises and setbacks, so perhaps the Golden Age has never quite materialised. As St Paul once vividly remarked: 'It is when people are saying, "How quiet and peaceful it is" that the worst suddenly happens'.

We often see the late Victorian age as an epoch when hopes were running high, and this is borne out to some extent by a study which counted the incidence of the word 'progress' in books published in the past century and a half. Although hopes apparently rose again after each of the World Wars, the graph is somewhat deceptive, since those were years when the idea of progress actually came under severe criticism. For example, the celebrated Dean Inge of St Paul's, lecturing on the subject in 1920, was distinctly sceptical.

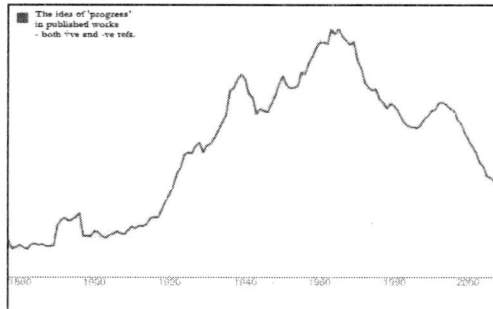

Note his comments here: 'Life is so chaotic, and development so sporadic and one-sided, that a brief and brilliant success may carry with it the seeds of its own early ruin... [Civilisation] has stumbled along blindly, falling into every possible pitfall'. We observe that the graph seems to confirm this perception in its generally downward direction over the past fifty years, suggesting that not so many now believe the world is necessarily 'progressing' at all. Indeed, unflattering cartoons are not uncommon.

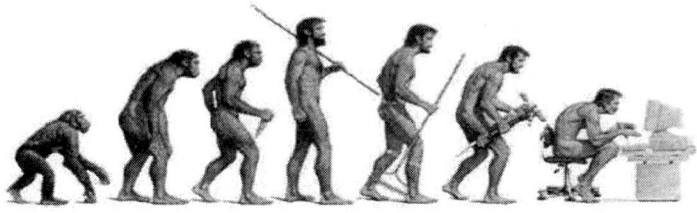

Inge's 1920 Romanes Lecture

So what will life be like a hundred years from now? Well, ours has been called an Age of Anxiety: we feel threatened in all sorts of ways, from terrorism to global warming, or from the spread of uncontrollable diseases to unmanageable population growth – and on top of these public worries we have our own personal fears about ill-health and money problems and the rest of the family.

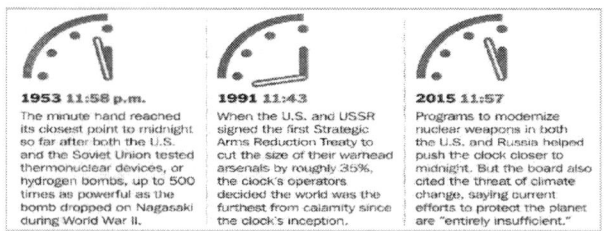

1953 11:58 p.m.
The minute hand reached its closest point to midnight so far after both the U.S. and the Soviet Union tested thermonuclear devices, or hydrogen bombs, up to 500 times as powerful as the bomb dropped on Nagasaki during World War II.

1991 11:43
When the U.S. and USSR signed the first Strategic Arms Reduction Treaty to cut the size of their warhead arsenals by roughly 35%, the clock's operators decided the world was the furthest from calamity since the clock's inception.

2015 11:57
Programs to modernize nuclear weapons in both the U.S. and Russia helped push the clock closer to midnight. But the board also cited the threat of climate change, saying current efforts to protect the planet are "entirely insufficient."

'Timeline' initiated by the Bulletin of Atomic Scientists in 1947
Its 'doomsday' clock is adjusted every few years
according to its perception of the international situation.

Authors, dramatists, artists and musicians have all played their part in addressing the changing scene. Let us observe their mood at the very beginning of the 20th century. 'When in Paris during the Exhibition of 1900,' wrote the composer Percy Grainger, 'I happened unexpectedly upon the statue of George Washington when strolling about the streets, and somehow or other this random occurrence galvanized in me a definite desire to typify the buoyant on-march of optimistic humanitarian democracy in a musical composition in which a forward-striding host of comradely affectionate athletic humanity might be heard *chanting the great pride of man in himself.'* The eventual outcome was a piece he entitled *Marching Song of Democracy.*

Not long after this experience (in 1903) the Russian playwright Anton Chekhov staged his longest drama *The Three Sisters.* It is set in a medium-sized town nearly a thousand miles east of Moscow, where troops have been temporarily stationed. There is no military campaign going on, so the officers have plenty of time to socialise, and the action takes place in the sisters' country villa. Two of the officers have gone there hoping for a samovar of tea and some playful conversation, but nothing much is doing. So, Vershinin the brigade commander (here on the right of the picture) says:

Vershinin :	If we can't have any tea, let's philosophize, at any rate.
Tuzenbach (a baron):	Yes, let's. About what?
Vershinin:	About what? Let us meditate... about life as it will be after our time; for example, in two or three hundred years.

Tuzenbach:	Well? After our time people will fly about in balloons, the cut of one's coat will change, perhaps they'll discover a sixth sense and develop it, but life will remain the same, laborious, mysterious, and happy. And in a thousand years' time, people will still be sighing: "Life is hard!"--and at the same time they'll be just as afraid of death, and unwilling to meet it, as we are.
Vershinin:	How can I put it? It seems to me that everything on earth must change, little by little, and is already changing under our very eyes. After two or three hundred years, after a thousand--the actual time doesn't matter--a new and happy age will begin.
Tuzenbach:	Not only after two or three centuries, but in a million years, life will still be as it was; life does not change, it remains for ever, following its own laws which do not concern us, or which, at any rate, you will never find out.

A couple of acts later, we discover the brigade is being posted hundreds of miles away to Poland; but Vershinin is still philosophizing as he makes his exit:

Vershinin:	It's time I went! Mankind used to be absorbed in wars, and all its existence was filled with campaigns, attacks, defeats, now we've outlived all that, leaving after us a great waste place, which there is nothing to fill with at present; but mankind is looking for something, and will certainly find it.

The irony is, of course, that revolution was already in the air for Russia, and less than fifteen years after the play was launched communism had taken hold of the country. And not only was internal conflict just round the corner: Russia was a major player in the long drawn out World War which changed everything, including the economies and social ordering of most European countries and the ensuing years of the Great Depression. It paved the way for the break-up of empires, and the unresolved political problems that led, seemingly inexorably, to the outbreak of the Second World War.

By this time the technology of weaponry and the industrial scale of destruction placed a vast question mark over what the future might look like.

If the majority of both soldiers and civilians had at the outset of WW1 been hugely naïve about its likely duration and its consequences, now in the 1940s few people could imagine anything approaching normality ever being quickly restored. It was during this time of bombing raids upon London that Henry Moore came to fame as an artist. The Blitz drove people to take shelter, and a number of Moore's paintings depict scenes in the London Underground to evoke their uncertainties and their fears: what would remain above ground when they emerged? would their homes and livelihoods have been destroyed? would their kith and kin still be alive? what kind of life would be possible in the future?

They were at least still free, whereas the composer Olivier Messiaen, 31 years old when France entered WW2, served in its army until being captured by the German army in June 1940 and was taken to a prisoner-of-war camp in Görlitz, Germany (now part of Poland). While in transit to the camp, Messiaen showed a fellow musician Henri Akoka sketches of a piece that would eventually be enlarged into his composition known as *Quatuor pour la Fin du Temps*. For him it seemed that the world was possibly coming to an end – observe his descending scale, an agonised plunge of two octaves:

Even though it was the war itself that ended, questions about the future direction of life on earth were still being asked. A picture painted by Henry Moore in 1948 bore the rather inscrutable title *Four Figures in a Setting*. It may have been influenced by that great poet of the First World War Wilfred Owen, who in 1917 entitled a poem *The Fates*. Moore's work incorporates here the three Greek Fates, 'the daughters of Necessity' who are described in Plato's Republic as Clotho who spins the thread of each person's life, Lachesis who measures its length, and Atropos who severs it. Atropos is on the right of the picture hidden behind a blood-soaked screen from the others: so the person sheltering on the far left has no means of telling what lies ahead, whether for him- or her-self or for the world in general.

'Four figures in a setting'

These and other works of Moore from this period were exhibited a couple of years ago at the Ashmolean museum in Oxford, when Moore was twinned with Francis Bacon. One of the most terrifying of Bacon's paintings reflects the emergence of the so-called Cold War, with its escalation of nuclear weapons and therefore the prospect of practically complete annihilation. *Man kneeling in Grass* dates from 1952: a nude figure is on all fours apparently eating grass. We are spying upon him, but there are lurking shadows which suggest that maybe there are unseen observers who in turn are watching us. The atmosphere is one of fear, and the trepidation that we shall all be reduced to primitive forms of survival.

Such fears remained with us, I believe, through the following three or four decades until at last the Berlin wall was breached and the Cold War petered out. I certainly encountered this sense of foreboding in Northamptonshire in the seventies, where I well remember my pastoral visits to a small boarding school which looked after girls in need of care. These girls were particularly vulnerable, but even so the possible outbreak of nuclear war was the number one anxiety for many of them. Or again, in

'Man kneeling in Grass'

Germany the future Nobel Laureate Günther Grass published his novel *Die Rättin* in 1986 which relates how, after Doomsday, rats took over the running of the world. A female rat describes people as mere 'has-beens, a remembered delusion'.

And there is a similar context for Russell Hoban's book Riddley Walker, written in the late 1970s and first published in 1980. It's a novel that speculates what the world might be like in the aftermath of a worldwide nuclear holocaust. Or, to be more precise, it sketches an imagined scenario here in the vicinity of Wye in East Kent. Although Hoban was an American writer – author of children's stories and some science fiction – he came to live in London, and he tells us that it was a visit to Canterbury in March 1974 that sparked his imagination:

It was my first visit to Canterbury; I'd given a talk at the Teachers' Centre the evening before, and next morning my host... showed me round the cathedral... The cathedral is what it is; as soon as we came into the nave I could feel the action of the place, and by the time we reached The Legend of St Eustace I was ready for something to happen.

Because the cathedral is so vast, with of course a strong focus upon St Thomas Becket, the 15th century wall painting which depicts scenes from the life of St Eustace is perhaps sometimes overlooked. It's in the north choir aisle and opposite its faint outlines is this more recent reconstruction of what it originally seems to have portrayed.

It is obviously a complex picture, not at all easy to decipher at a glance. The legend is a fictitious account of how in the time of the emperor Trajan a Roman general named Placidus was converted and baptised, and then (under his new name of Eustace) suffered severe losses rather like Job in the Old Testament: his wife is captured by pirates, his sons are taken off by respectively a wolf and a lion. Then at a later time of crisis for the Romans he re-emerges as Hadrian's victorious general, but afterwards refuses to sacrifice to the pagan gods; so, along with his family who have been miraculously restored to him, he is roasted to death in a brazen bull and then at last gets his true reward in heaven. These details and more appear in the mural, which tells (from the bottom upwards) what was evidently a very popular story in the middle ages, the earliest extant account being found in a martyrology of the 1270s entitled *The Golden Legend*. There is no explicit connection here with our own St Eustace (after whom the well next to the Withersdane cottages takes its name), who was actually a Cistercian abbot in Normandy charged by the Pope (in about 1200) to help reform the church in this country. He may perhaps have been named Eustace because of the growing popularity of the legend at that time?

What first caught Hoban's eye seems to have been the central figure of Eustace standing abandoned and alone in the middle of a river, hoping for better times. 'Seeing him for the first time that day in 1974,' he says, 'I had a strong fellow-feeling. People ask me how I got from St Eustace to *Riddley Walker* and all I can say is that it's a matter of being friends with your head. Things come into the mind and wait to hook up with other things; there are places that can heighten your responses, and if you let your head go its own way it might, with luck, make interesting connections. On March 14th 1974 I got lucky.'

Let me suggest just a few of the mural's features that seem to have taken hold of his imagination. There is certainly a sense of progression in Eustace's life: he is on a quest, or a pilgrimage, that takes him from being a successful general to being a martyr. What sparks this off is the

vision he saw when out hunting. Towards the bottom right hand corner of the mural is a large stag, and between his antlers is the figure of a crucified Christ – an image that may have been influenced by a pre-Christian Hungarian folk tale. In the legend he speaks to Eustace: 'You're hunting me, but now you need to know that I'm also hunting you.' And Hoban was not by any means the first to be haunted by this particular image: it resonated with many artists in the late medieval period, as the following selection of paintings may illustrate.

13ᵗʰ cent English ms.

Pisanello c.1440

The Elder Cranach (early 16ᵗʰ C)

Dürer (woodcut of 1501)

In Hoban's novel, Riddley Walker's very name evokes something of the progression in Eustace's life. Our hero is certainly a *walker*, on the move from one location to another. His first name too, if we retain just its initial syllable, summarises the outcome of his searches. Whereas he encounters other characters whose aim is to win power, his most profound discovery proves to be the 'thot' (that is, the 'thought' as spelt in the language he uses, which has been termed Riddleyspeak) that 'come to me', 'THE ONLYES POWER IS NO POWER'. So his quest proves to be about getting *rid* of false dreams and ambitions, together with a rejection of weaponry.

This essential truth discovered by Riddley is not, however, shared by the other main characters. The scene is set at least two and a half thousand years after the great nuclear devastation that virtually wiped out civilisation as it was known in the late twentieth century. Hoban appears to date it soon after 1997. Life since then has certainly regressed and technology, such as it is, is back to the Iron Age: ominously (as we learn later) there is charcoal production and a process of dyeing in which the potential to derive saltpetre from pig manure has been discovered. The semi-nomadic descendants of the few survivors shelter in small stockades, each fenced with some kind of elevated walkway used by lookouts in addition to its manned gatehouse. The inhabitants of any particular settlement are small in numbers; they live in simple thatched huts and often eat communally. Their diet is mainly one of meat, either from the goats or pigs they herd or from hunting in the woods. Sometimes it is made into 'sossages', and may be accompanied by locally grown 'pittaters and sweads' (the spelling is Riddley's – one of the very few who can read or write). Drinking 'tea' is mentioned more than once, but this appears to mean some local brew rather than any imported leaf. Smoking cannabis is a regular habit too.

It appears that, at the time of the story, pressure is being exerted from the 'Mincery' – the primitive but effective administration based in the Ram, which is the Island of Thanet – to increase the acreage of arable land which would of course place limits on local mobility. Security (as well as the Mincery's directives) is enforced in each locality by the Big Man and his half a dozen or more 'hevvys', tough guys who serve on rota from the Ram. A tax is collected by the sess men in midwinter on Shorsday (the shortest day). The Big 2 at the Ram are known as the Pry Mincer and his right-hand man the Wes Mincer (although he's subsequently labelled the 'shadder mincer' as he's intent upon seizing power for himself). At the start of the book those in office are Abel Goodparley – a smooth talker of course – and Erny Orfing, an earnest political 'orphan' with his own ideas.

Hoban's sketch map of east Kent

One notices from the map that sea levels have risen, with Romney Marsh again under water and Thanet separated as an island (Hoban obtained geological advice locally through Wye College, as it then was). There are dotted remnants of today's main roads; less well made tracks have long since disappeared. The place names are Hoban's provocative variations on those with which we're familiar: Horny Boy – Herne Bay; Widders Bel – Whitstable; Little Salting – Seasalter; Fathers Ham – Faversham; Good Mercy – Godmersham; Bernt Arse – Ashford; Widders Dump – Widdersdane; Mr Clever's Roaling Place – Devil's Kneading Trough; Brabbas Horn – Brabourne; Fork Stoan – Folkestone; Do It Over – Dover; Sams Itch – Sandwich; Dunk Your Arse – Dungeness. The River Sour is the Stour and Cambry is Canterbury. Not every location featured in the story is mapped here: in particular the Bundel (i.e. Crundale) Downs occur a number of times. Wye is fairly central, and is indeed Riddley's present home base; renamed because the question that attracts attention now is no longer Why? so much as How? – referring in particular to the overriding passion to rediscover the secret of the 1 Big 1

93

(the nuclear bomb) which exploded in Canterbury leaving only the pillars of the crypt still standing.

Mincery plans are not promulgated through paper or electronic media, which are non-existent, but through the occasional staging of Eusa shows. Halfway through the book Abel Goodparley explains the underlying thrust of his Eusa presentation: 'It ben Eusa wrote the *Eusa Story* he done it befor they stoaned him out of Cambry. After that he dint write nothing mor'. [The spelling is reminiscent of Nigel Molesworth – a boy much the same in age as Riddley – in *Down with Skool* and its sequels, of which *Whizz for Atomms: A Guide to Survival in the 20th Century* (1956) shows uncanny anticipations of Hoban's theme.] The *Eusa Story* to which Goodparley refers is portrayed as the sole surviving copy of the explanatory Legend found on the wall next to the St Eustace mural. It is revered as holding vital clues about the hidden meaning of the picture, even perhaps the very secret of bomb making – or so Goodparley hopes as he now explains (in terms that may strike us as quite comical) to Riddley:

You know who put me on to what this woal things about? ... 'It wer your oan dad it wer Brooder Walker the same... Orfing and me we done a special show then your dad come a long Nex Nite he done a connexion and a reveal the woal thing took lessen a minim. I wernt there to hear it but I heard of it. Dyou have that 1 in memberment?' I said, '0 yes I member that. "A littl salting and no saver." He said, 'Thats the 1. "A littl salting and no saver." Wel you know every now and agen youwl hear some thing it means what ever it means but youwl know theres mor in it as wel. Moren wer knowit by who ever said it. So that reveal stayd in my mynd.

'You see how it wer up to then I never thot this Legend ben anything moren a picter story about a bloak with a name near the same as Eusa. Nor I dint know nothing of chemistery nor fizzics then I hadnt payd no tension to it. Any how I wer reading over this here Legend like I use to do some times and I come to "the figure of the crucified Saviour". Number of the crucified Saviour and wunnering how that be come the Littl Shyning Man the Addom. Suddn it jumpt in to my mynd "A littl salting and no saver". I dint have no idear what crucified myt be nor up to then I hadnt give Saviour much thot I thot it myt mean some 1 as saves only that dint connect with nothing. Id never put it to gether with saver like in savery.

Not sweet. Salty. A salt crucified. I gone to the chemistery working I askit 1 Stoan Phist that wer Belnots dad what crucified myt be nor he wernt cern but he thot itwd be some thing you done in a cruciboal. 1st time Id heard the word. Thats a hard firet boal they use it doing a chemistery try out which you cud call that crucifrying or crucifying. Which that crucified Saviour or crucifryd salt thats our Littl Shyning Man him as got pult in 2 by Eusa. So "the figure of the crucified Saviour" is the number of the salt de vydit in 2 parts in the cruciboal and radiating the coming acrost on it. The salt and the saver. 1ce youve got that salt youre on your way to the woal chemistery and fizzics of it. Right up to your las try out which is the brazen bull which is to say your brazing boal and the chard coal. But thats all tecker knowledging realy you wunt hardly unner stan it nor I wont wear you out with it... Finely after the brazing boal you get your four souls which is your 4 salts gethert. Man and wife and littl childer coming back to gether for the las time thats your new clear family it aint the 1 you startit with its the finement of it in to shyning gethert to the 1 Big 1. Mynd you all this what Im saying its jus theary.'

Such a passage (indeed the whole narrative, which is Riddley's account of his transformative experiences during the week that followed his 'coming of age' when he turned 12) requires much comment. As well as a number of specific expressions that call for explanation, the very language needs to be understood as bearing various layers of meaning (a point expounded by Rowan Williams in his 2013 Gifford Lectures, '*The Edge of Words*'). In the epoch following WW2 that faced the prospect of nuclear extinction, writers struggled to find a way of communicating the prevalent uncertainties. Here are some reflections by the critic Martin Esslin as he introduces the new phenomenon known as the 'Theatre of the Absurd':

Becket's Endgame

Why should the emphasis in drama have shifted away from traditional forms towards images which, complex and suggestive as they may be, must necessarily lack the final clarity of definition, the neat resolutions we have been led to expect? Clearly because the playwrights concerned no longer believe in the possibility of such neatness of resolution.

They are indeed chiefly concerned with expressing a sense of wonder, of incomprehension, and at times of despair, at the lack of cohesion and meaning that they find in the world... There can be no doubt: for many intelligent and sensitive human beings the world of the mid twentieth century *has* lost its meaning and has simply ceased to make sense... What made sense at one moment has, at the next, become an obscure babble of voices in a foreign language. At once the comforting, familiar scene would

Ionesco's Rhinoceros

turn into one of nightmare and horror. With the loss of means of communication we should be compelled to view that world with the eyes of total outsiders as a succession of frightening images... [Thus] in its critique of language the Theatre of the Absurd closely reflects the preoccupation of contemporary philosophy.

Yet Esslin goes on to note that Absurd Drama (of which Samuel Becket's *Waiting for Godot* is perhaps the most familiar example) is not simply 'revolutionary novelty' but can 'best be understood as a new combination of a number of ancient, even archaic, traditions' – including 'miming and clowning', 'nonsense poetry', 'dream and nightmare literature', 'allegorical and symbolic drama', and 'the even more ancient tradition of ritual drama'.

Hoban's novel is not written for the stage, but it certainly includes many of these features, especially its emphasis upon the use of myths and puppet shows. The significance of these 'parables' (to use a biblical term) gradually emerges in the course of his book. The *Eusa Story* itself occupies the whole of chapter 6 and Riddley tells us that 'every body knows bits and peaces of it but the connexion men and the Eusa show men they all have the woal thing wrote down the same and they have to know all of it by hart'. They and the Mincery men are the only ones who can read anyway.

In summary it is a bowdlerised version of the Legend of St Eustace featuring Mr Clevver (a 'Big Man uv Inland' in the era preceding the nuclear holocaust) and Eusa (a 'noing man vere qwik he cud tern his han tu enne thing'). Eusa is the unconverted shadow side of Eustace, once a powerful military man. It is Mr Clevver who sets Eusa on his quest to put an end to 'aul thees Warrs' by doing just 1 Big 1. So like Eustace he finds himself in a dark wood where he comes across the 12 point stag with 'the Littl Shynin Man' between his antlers. He shoots the stag and then seizes the Littl Man, demanding of him that he reveal 'the No. uv the 1 Big 1' (that is, the formula which spells out the correct combination of elements). The Littl Man insists that this cannot be reduced to a form of words but is a secret accessible to everyone who reflects on life's mysterious dualities (dark and light, day and night, man and woman, plus and minus, big and little, all and nothing). But inevitably Eusa does not grasp his meaning, except to figure out that the secret is to do with *combining* elements together once again. What the Littl Man indicates, (as the reader eventually realises), is that the 1 Big 1 that will end 'aul thees Warrs' is the day of perfect harmony and reconciliation on earth, whose fulfilment lies indeed within each human heart. Despite this wise counsel Eusa's uncomprehending frustration mounts to rage and, demanding the 'all' just mentioned, he finds that he has stretched the Littl Man too far: 'He wuz ded. Pult in 2 lyk he wuz a chikken.'

But what follows from this 'splitting of the atom' (the Little Man is also termed the Addom which can be read both as 'atom' and as 'Adam')? 'Owt uv thay 2 peaces uv the Littl Shynin Man the Addom thayr cum shyningnes in wayvs in spredin circels.' Yes, what radiates from his splitting (his death) is described in the language of atomic physics: waves, circles, orbits – Hoban's whole book uses this kind of imagery, for example, in the ring of nine main settlements around Cambry, which has its own 'ring ditch' (perhaps modelled on the idea of a huge moat such as those built to defend centres of power, it also hints at much more recent particle accelerators); again, two of the characters mentioned in Goodparley's revelations to Riddley (from which I've already quoted) are named after nuclear scientists ('1 Stoan Phist' reads as Einstein Physicist, and his son 'Belnot' is a play on Nobel).

The rest of the *Eusa Story* corresponds to what happens to Eustace and his family in the original Legend, but concludes with a dialogue between Eusa and the Littl Man:

Yu let the Chaynjis out & now yuv got to go on thru them. Eusa sed, How menne Chaynjis ar thayr?... The Littl Man sed, As menne as reqwyrd. Eusa sed, reqwyrd by wut? The Littl Man sed, reqwyrd by the idear uv yu. Eusa sed, Wut is the idear uv me? The Littl Man sed, That we doan no til yuv gon thru aul yur Chaynjis.

As already indicated, this *Eusa Story* is re-enacted regularly by the Eusa Show men on behalf of the Mincery, although the first performance we encounter in the book is given in here in How (remember that's the new name for Wye) by Goodparley and Orfing themselves. They play the parts of Eusa, Mr Clevver, and the Littl Man using different puppet figures and improvising the dialogue as they go along. One of the props is a box which spews out numbers when its handle is cranked: it's an Iron Age computer, of course, which Eusa hopes will tell him the right formula to make his bomb. Personally it makes me think again of Molesworth whizzing for atomms! Yet Orfing is aware that Goodparley's presentation of the show is somewhat innovative, reflecting his own ideas. He admits that 'new things are happening and new chances every time', so that every Eusa show is going to be a bit different, but he complains that Goodparley's 'changit the story'. The seeds are sown of a later split between the two of them – in other words, a power struggle. That of course is really what prevents the Good Time, which is what they both hope for, ever arriving.

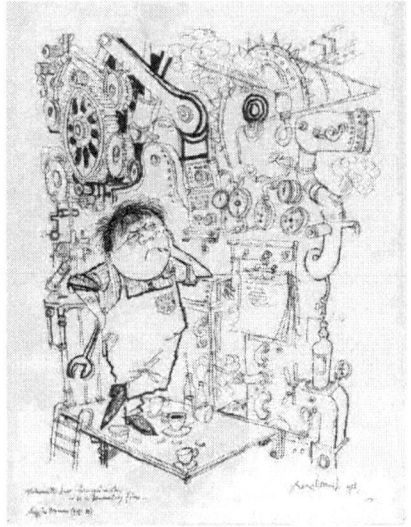

There is one other spin-off from the *Eusa Story* that we eventually discover to be more deeply disturbing than at first we realised. At the very beginning of the book Riddley recounts the tale known as the *Hart of the Wud* – a reference of course to the stag killed by Eusa, although the whole phrase also covers the trees in the wood and the true spirit of the wood. In brief, the story tells of three refugees (a man, a woman, and their child) who have fled from their town which has been devastated by explosions and are sheltering in a wood. They are met in their desperation by 'a clevver looking bloak' who strikes a deal with them. In exchange for using his cook pot and his knowledge of how to make a fire, they will provide the food: 'he wer looking at the chyld'. He eats the child's 'hart' and the couple eat the rest, after which they fall asleep by the fire. Having heaped it high to keep the blackness of the night at bay, it gets out of control – and they burn to death. So the quest for knowledge, power and security is self-destructive if divorced from our essential humanity.

Views of Punch

At the end of the book we find another story which forms an *inclusio* with this one. Earlier on Goodparley emptied Riddley's pockets and found a 'blackent hook nose hump back figger'. Riddley had been carrying this with him since he unearthed it at Widders Dump (Withersdane) from the muck: 'it wer a show figger like the 1s in the Eusa show. Woodin head and hans and the res of it clof ... the face had a big nose what hookit down and a big chin what hookit up and a smyling mouf. Some kynd of littl poyny hat on the head it curvit over with a wagger on the end of it.' It was Goodparley a few days later who recognised what it was – the figure of Mr Punch. When he was just a little younger than Riddley he'd been orphaned as a result of a raid from 'Outland' and effectively adopted by 'Granser' (as he called him) who, contrary to Mincery regulations, regularly carried out Punch and Pooty shows. 'Punch', he tells Riddley, is 'the oldes figger there is. He wer old time back way back long befor Eusa ever ben thot of.' A Punch show 'aint like a Eusa show its meant to stay the same all the time' – so, as a long-standing counter-narrative, it was obviously perceived as a potential political threat. But Goodparley's revelation also tells us where his own ideas started to take root, in his early bereavement and his subsequent subversive upbringing. And for Hoban, truth lies in bringing opposites together; the aspirations of the Eusa show certainly needs the earthy pathos of what happens in the Punch display that brings the story to a close. What that is can be revealed once the narrative has unfolded.

So at last, having set its context and suggested what are its main themes, the tale can be summarised as follows. It begins with Riddley on his naming day in How Fents when he reached 12, his coming of age, which he celebrated with the killing of his first 'wyld boar' – possibly the last surviving one on the Bundel (Crundale) Downs. He is further initiated by the local wise woman Lorna Elswint, who points him on his personal quest for meaning: 'You know Riddley theres some thing in us it dont have no name.' Although he probes further, she can only tell him that 'its all ways on the road'. He admits himself: 'Our woal life is a idear we dint think of nor we dont know what it is', but at least we can keep exploring what it is. Hence his daily journal that follows.

Three days later his father Brooder Walker came off the foraging rota

and was sent to Widders Dump to join the gang who were excavating old machinery that was buried in the ground: such was the source of iron that they had learnt to smelt for other uses. As the men hauled on the '16 man treadll crane with 2 weals' it slipped and his Dad (who was 33 years old) was crushed to death under 'that girt old black machine'.

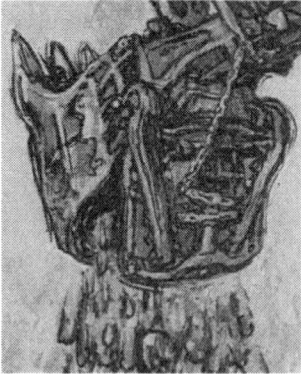

'Old machinery' by Hoban

So Riddley's now an orphan, having lost his mother who 'dyd of the coffing sickness when I wer 5.'

Ancient treadle crane

At the same time How has lost its 'connexion' man, the one who interprets (or 'reveals') the Eusa show afterwards for the local crowd. Who will succeed him? Inspired by the omen of an elderly 'leader' dog immolating himself on Riddley's spear, Lorna singles out Brooder's son as his successor. (We shall shortly discover a whole pack of dogs who accompany and protect Riddley on his travels: he has already learnt about their 'knowing' from Lorna.) When Goodparley and Orfing arrive soon afterwards they endorse the locals' choice and with Lorna's assistance perform the necessary initiation ritual which includes branding his belly. They leave after enacting their latest Eusa show (which as already mentioned gives rise to Orfing's complaint). So on the 'Nex Nite' Riddley attempts his first connexion 'reveal'. He records a previous Eusa show that led to his Dad's enigmatic pronouncement, 'a littl salting and no saver'; then (having confessed that he always thought he could do better) he himself utters an equally obscure saying, 'the shapes of Eusa head is dreaming us' – which

is certainly not well received. The following morning the gang ridicule him; 'Riddley Walker wernt no talker / Dint know what to say / Put his head up on a poal / And then it tol all day'.

The scene is set for Riddley's increasingly independent role. One of the hevvys at How, disillusioned with the 'cow shit shows and pontsing for the Ram', challenges him to exploit his undoubted charisma in opposition to the Mincery. Soon afterwards, when setting off for Widders Dump, he falls out with Durster Potter who mocks him over his father's death. In retaliation he strikes and wounds Durster. The next he sees of him is Durster holding an empty bow being savaged to death by two dogs: he wonders if the spent arrow was meant for one of the dogs – or for himself. Having taken Durster's body back to How Fents, it was a further day before he could make it to Widders Dump. This is then the occasion when he unearths the Punch figure, and is observed by 'that littl witey bloak Belnot Phist' (an albino whose inherited genes are presumably the end product of nuclear radiation). Since, contrary to regulations, he intends to keep this puppet for himself, he evades Phist's questionings, and then suddenly hurls Phist headfirst into the muck and makes a dash for it over the fents, down the bank and up out of the far ditch.

Here the 'black leader' of the dog pack is waiting for him and leads him away westwards, heading for Burnt Arse (Ashford). So his adventures begin. On the outskirts of this 'dead town', apparently unobserved by the lookouts, he stops on a small mound containing an underground shelter. Waiting by a trap door he hears a voice from below pleading for his help. After descending some steps and unbarring a lower door, he finds a strange 'figger': 'all he had for a face wer jus a bit pincht out for a nose and a cut for a mouf and that wer it. Dint have a woal pair of ears jus 2 littl blobs like they bin startit but not finisht'. This 'kid' was as tall as himself. As they make their exit, they hear a noise above: one of the hevvys from the Ram has spotted Riddley's presence, but is being torn to pices by the protective dogs. With no time to lose they head eastwards out of Burnt Arse, and a conversation begins between the two of them. It rapidly emerges that the 'kid' is the same age as Riddley and has just become the Ardship (Archbishop) of Canterbury, the latest in a long succession from Eusa himself. He is controlled by the Mincery since he represents a potential source of insight and revelation not otherwise accessible. He knows what is in store for himself, which is why he wants to escape from his expected future: 'Its sharna pax and get the poal innit. 1st the easy askings then its helping the qwirys then its Chops your Aunty [the Angel of Death] and your head on a poal.' In twelve years' time he will be thus brutally replaced: 'they do it for the knowing whats in us... to keep in memberment that cleverness what made us crookit. Savit a breeding stock in Cambry so therewd all ways be some of us [Eusa folk].' In fact, the Ardship is hoping to get back to Cambry 'to have a nother go at that Senter Power ... to try for deaper nor I ben.' His only technique is to be what he terms 'the Lissener' because that's how knowledge will come.

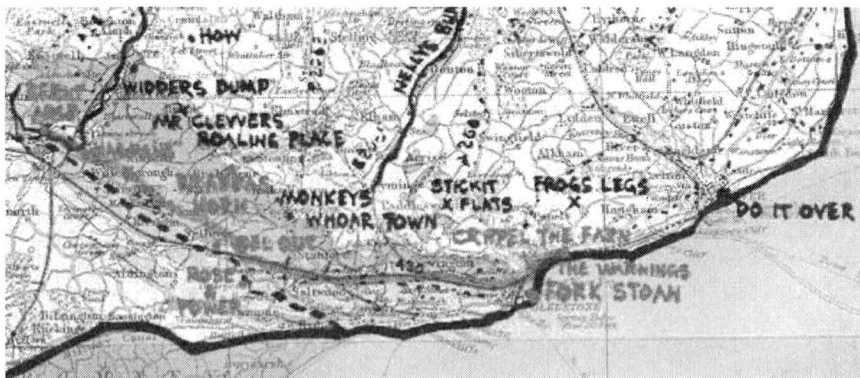

As Lissener he can find his way around by means of his 'fealys', some special 'stoans' he keeps in his pocket. But for the present Riddley keeps him company, and they decide to play safe by taking a route south-eastwards well clear of How and Widders Dump. This way, as they realise, they will actually 'Power roun a ring', 'keaping the circel which thatwl be axel rating the Inner G' (accelerating the energy). For part of the way to Fork Stoan they use 'the Iron Track tho there aint no iron to it' (the old railway line). While they walk Lissener (the Ardship) explains how the surviving Eusa folk are distributed:

> 45 counting me. Which they axel rate it roun the circel you see. Counting from Horny Boy its 1 in the 1st then 2 in the 2nd and so on til you have 9 in No. 9 which the pirntowt is 45. They all ways breed us up to moren a nuff and then they kul us down to that.

Carefully avoiding the 6 hevvys who were pre-occupied 'parbly changing the look out' – and still aided by their dogs – Lissener guides them to the shore where they find a boat 'knocking on stoan', '1/2 ful of water and hevvy'. Its mast has crashed down in a storm and killed its sailor, in whose pocket they find a 'littl bag of littl crummly stoans'. Lissener senses the Power in these stones (indeed, they are sulferous and so respond to the hand's heat by expanding, fracturing and crackling). He decides it is best to abandon their circling route (which would have taken them next to Do It Over). 'We bes get in to Cambry qwicks', he urges – the 'senter' that Riddley has never yet visited – despite the fact that, following the Ardship's escape, the Mincery has rounded up the other 44 Eusa folk and herded them all into Cambry under guard: 'Theres all ways 12 [hevvys] in Cambry plus theyve put on a exter 6.'

As they now head north, Riddley recalls what he overheard the hevvys at Fork Stoan discussing, which was a possible split in the Mincery with Belnot Phist using his inherited knowledge against Goodparley. Lissener then reckons that it might be worth their while to divide their newfound 'stoans' in half and to split up, in the hope that if Riddley finds Belnot Phist at Widders Dump and is 'Goodparleys nemminy' then 'he cud wel be our frend'. So he approaches from the Downs above Mr Clevvers Roaling Place, where he can 'see candl glimmers in the

gate house at Widders Dump'. The Roaling Place is so named because this is where Mr Clevver sometimes gets 'a larfing fit' and 'roals on the groun there'. Having then descended, Riddley approaches cautiously, 'cruising roun the primmeter ditch' which is waterlogged after heavy rain, then plunges through it, mounts the fence – and is suddenly grabbed from behind.

He is brought face to face with Goodparley, who is sitting with Belnot Phist. It rapidly emerges that ever since Riddley left Widders Dump in a hurry he has been tailed and kept under observation. Indeed, Goodparley asks him to hand over his 'stoans' – and accepts that he's telling the 'Truth' when he confesses that he has no idea as to what they are. Phist chimes in that Riddley isn't particularly 'clevver', but Goodparley reckons he's 'a mover and a happener' instead, and as such someone he'd prefer to have as his Shadder Mincer 'in stead of that dretful littl Orfing'. Now for the first time the stones are seen in daylight, and are 'yeller' – 'the yellerboy stoan the Salt 4' (the reference here is to the 'salt' in Brooder's cryptic reveal, but also to the SALT treaties current at the time of Hoban's writing). When Phist re-enters the conversation he pleads ignorance of these findings, but inadvertently uses the phrase 'colourt stoans or powders or what ever'. The word 'powders' arouses Goodparley's suspicion that he knows more than he's letting on, and he's dismissed to the gate house to 'have a nice cup of tea'.

There is then an interlude (reported in my preamble) in which Goodparley begins to explain his own musings on the *Eusa Story*, after which he finds Punch concealed in Riddley's pocket. This reminds him nostalgically of his own apprenticing as an orphan in the travelling shows with Mr Punch and induces a 'fit up' in which he re-enacts the show for Riddley's benefit. As he comes to, he recalls how his time with Granser ended: they had reached Good Mercy (Godmersham) and on his 12th naming day (when he became a man) he told Granser he'd be leaving him. Granser quickly arranged for him to be abused by '7 bloaks' and told him that this necessarily postponed his leaving for another year. So he stuck his knife into Granser and ran for it, falling in eventually with a Mincery crowd heading for the Ram.

Everything, he claims, 'wants to be whats in it to be'. His hands then clutch the 'yellerboy stoans', and Riddley intuits that what they want is to be 'the 1 Big 1'. As Goodparley continues pondering the *Eusa Story* he guesses that the 'yellerboy stoans' somehow help to put the 'Eusa family to gether, 4 souls in the blazing boal.' This brings Riddley to think of where Phist fits in to the picture. He rushes out to the gatehouse and finds Phist, not enjoying a cup of tea, but strung up with both arms stretched out like the Littl Shyning Man. He cuts him down, only to hear his final whispering: 'When the yeller boy / Fynds the pig shit / In the hart of the wood.' Riddley keeps these words to himself, and holding the 'yellerboy stoans' which Goodparley has returned to him, he sets off by himself for Cambry.

Riddley's route and Lissener's route to Cambry

104

His first encounter on the way is with Granser at Good Mercy (Godmersham), who appears very much alive and well despite his knifing by Goodparley many years earlier. He observes that Riddley is 'dog frendy' and larfs at his own joke about Riddley becoming 'Dog Pry Mincer'. This leaves both Riddley and the dogs feeling uneasy with him – as if some kind of horror may lie in wait – so they continue on their way.

Riddley reflects that he feels the same sort of apprehension with both 'the chard coal berners' and 'the dyers at the forms'. A scare crow at Pig Sweet Form (which seems to be somewhere near Pope Street) then intensifies the feeling. As he reaches the Ring Ditch he feels 'the Powr of the goast of the Power what ben ... the Power of the 2ness trying to tear the 1 a part'. This induces the sense that Goodparley and Granser could get what they want (the 1 Big 1) if he only turned around and handed them the yellerboy stoans. But the moment he makes a move in their direction the dogs growl 'low and deap', so he continues towards Cambry. As he reaches what remains of the cathedral the Power gets hold of him again, especially in the choir whose shape strikes him as 'like the woman dollys they hang over where a womans bearthing'. The dogs, however, run a little to the west of it and descend down 'old stoan steps' to a 'hoal' (the crypt) which he finds hard to describe: 'it were stoan trees growing unner the groun... the hart of the wood in the hart in the hart of the stoan in the woom of her what has her woom in Cambry'. He then describes the thoughts that came to him here:

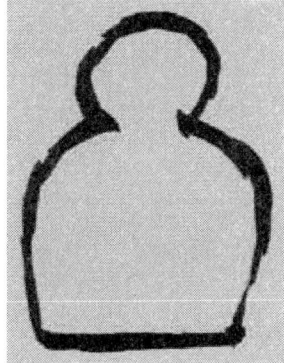

Them as made Canterbury (*sic*) musve put ther selfs right. only it dint stay right did it. Somers in be twean them stoan trees and the Power Ring they musve put ther selfs wrong. Now we dint have the 1 nor the other.

There is something in the stones that moves him profoundly. Perhaps most of all it was seeing a Green Man carved on one of the pillars that opened his eyes and changed his thinking: 'take away the vines and leaves and it myt be Punchs face or it even myt be Eusas face.' So he realised the universality of life in every creature, adding:

It wer every face. It wer the face of the boar I kilt and the dog that old leader. It wer the face of my father what ben kilt in the digging, It wer Belnot Phist hung up by his hans tyd behynt him and it wer the Little Shyning Man...

By going to the 'senter', therefore, Riddley has had the time and space – and the stimulus – to discover the essence (we might say, the 'hart') of his own understanding, which he then encapsulates in the key phrase that I cited earlier, 'THE ONLYES POWER IS NO POWER'. He has come to realise that he wants no part with 'the yeller boy and the pig shit in the hart of the wood' (the sulphur, the saltpetre, and the charcoal which combine to give the explosive force – and the power – of gunpowder).

At this point he is interrupted by the dogs, and realises that the whole pack is together once more. They first alert him to a wooden Greanvine buried down in the hoal; it has 'a broak off peg in the back of him', which reminds him of the collapse of life 'when the wite shadder stood up over Canterbury'. A second Greanvine also prompts him to think of his erstwhile partner Lissener, and he wonders how he has been faring. Seeing a recent graffiti of Goodparley his mind turns again to Fork Stoan as the place to look, so this is now his destination.

There he finds 'Goodparley hung up by his hans behynd him sames hed hung up Belnot Phist'. Orfing is there, and tells Riddley, 'I aint Orfing no more Im Goodparley now'. For the Ardship this is revenge for what Abel did recently to his father. But Riddley ignores them and lowers Abel to the ground where the Eusa crowd gather round and beat him up. This completes his demoralisation, and he begs to be set free with Riddley as his companion in the staging of Punch shows here and there, sufficient to earn his 'meat'. He has retained the old puppet that he took from Riddley, and (unknown to Erny) the yellerboy stoans. They make their escape by

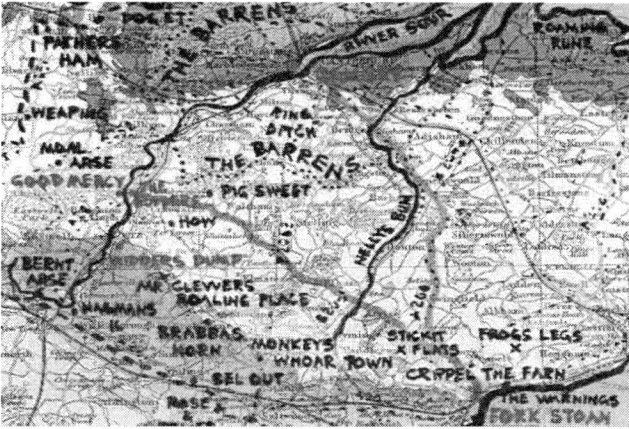

**Riddley's route to Fork Stoan
and then west with Goodparley**

night via the Bundel Downs, eventually in the morning reaching Good
Mercy where they find Granser. This is when Granser reveals the secret
symbolism of the Eusa body marks with which all three of them have
been branded. Abel sums it up: 'Thats the 3 of the 1 is it? The 3 of the 1
Littl 1 is yellerboy stoan and Saul & Peter and chard coal?' (The 'Saul &
Peter' is saltpeter, a mordant derived from pig manure by the dyers to fix
their colours; but we may recall how in the New Testament Saul is
blinded by divine light and Peter is named after the word 'rock' – hence in
combining saltpeter with sulphur and charcoal to make the explosive
power of gunpowder its description using such vivid biblical imagery is
not inappropriate.) Abel reveals that between them they now have all three
ingredients, and urges Granser to go ahead and put his knowledge to the
test (or otherwise Erny will beat them to it). The inevitable outcome is that
Granser and Abel are blown to pieces, leaving Riddley to make his exit
with the Punch outfit and head once again for Cambry.

The dogs are still keeping Riddley company, and it is they who find
Orfing in hiding there. He reports how it was the Ardship together with
the Eusa folk who were keen to exploit their possession of the other
yellerboy stoans. The Ardship would have waited for 'mor vansit theary',
but things got out of hand when the hevvys started mixing the various
ingredients in a pot and (of course) caused a huge explosion which killed
the Ardship and several others. So Orfing left in the hope of teaming up
again with Abel and Riddley, realising that the hevvys will sooner or later
acquire more sulphur from across the channel. He insists that in their
Punch show partnership Walker will have to speak the different voices,
and they are agreed in moving well away from the scenes of recent events,

aiming first for Weaping Form, the settlement that used to be known as Bad Mercy (Badlesmere).

On their arrival there is considerable reluctance to allow them entry, until Riddley breaks the deadlock with his Mr Punch's 'putcha, putcha, putcha' which makes the men on the gate laugh and relinquish their opposition. The show proceeds, until the crucial point when the baby is (as usual) about to be eaten by Punch. Then suddenly an outraged hevvy intervenes and grabs the puppet to stop this happening: it is unclear whether this is because it is all too near the bone for him, or whether he is genuinely defending the infant. A fight ensues, after which the Weaping crowd breaks up. Two families decide they 'dint want to stop at Weaping no mor' and join Riddley and Orfing on the road. As they leave, a young lad on the high walk by the gate sings out, 'Riddley Walkers ben to show / Riddley Walkers on the go / Dont go Riddley Walkers track / Drop Johns ryding on his back.'

So the story ends with 'weeping' and a question mark. Drop John is a ghostly figure who gives people 'a dropping fealing' in the belly when they see him. He will always follow Riddley and haunt him, so he announced much earlier. Although Riddley in a short space of time has engaged in many conversations and explored many new avenues of thought about life's meaning and purpose, he still doesn't know 'Why is Punch crookit? Why wil he all ways kil the babby if he can? Parbly I wont never know its jus on me to think on it'.

We ourselves are left to ponder the question, Is all this such a distant scenario? If we forget the setting (a couple of millenia after the 1 Big 1), there is so much to remind us of the strife in today's world, the jostling for power, and the thirst to produce ever bigger and more explosive weapons. Wholesale slaughter as we know continues apace in our world too, often prompted by factors not dissimilar from those in Hoban's book.

Is that hand of friendship today's much needed image of 'the Littl Shyning Man'?

Will it prevail over the explosive forces that divide man from man, nation from nation, and even religion from religion?

Tragically, as the 1st World War poet Wilfred Owen – reflecting on the biblical story of Abraham and Isaac, in which the latter's life was dramatically spared – observed in *The Parable of the Old Man and the*

Young (a poem later set to music by Benjamin Britten in his War Requiem after WW2),

> *The old man would not so, but slew his son,*
> *And half the seed of Europe, one by one.*

Hoban suggests that, in its human essentials, the world will not have changed in two and a half thousand years, come what may. It may not indeed be so very different from the late 13th century when this Psalter illustration was painted. There were no doubt many young Isaacs then whose lives were but little valued and the restraining hand of an angel was much sought after.

PIONEERS

A reed broom

A gift from a Chewa community at St Martin's Church, Mala on the shores of Lake Malawi in northern Mozambique

They found refuge here following the civil war that ravaged the country. Further north we saw some of the devastation including a burnt -out church and seminary.

In the late 19th century the most renowned missionary along this inaccessible coast was William Percival Johnson, who travelled on foot and by boat. His life style was extremely simple, and he had no dreams of building imposing churches. Instead he used a small mission ship for training pastoral recruits and for necessary medical treatment.

St Ambrose of Milan

THE CHURCH AS THE CORE OF HUMANITY

Aurelius Ambrosius was one of the outstanding, inspirational Christian leaders of the late 4th century church. Along with St Augustine of Hippo, St Gregory the Great and St Jerome, he was recognised as one of the great doctors (i.e. teachers) of the Church throughout the Middle Ages. It was Pope Boniface VIII who in 1298 made their already recognised feast days into major festivals. Ambrose has always been popular as a baptismal name, not least in the days of English recusants when his courage in confronting the imperial order was recalled.

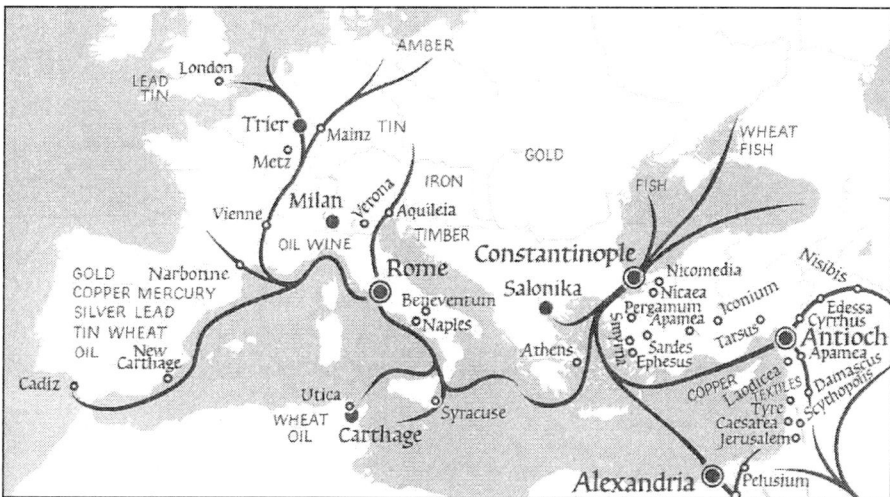

Principal towns and routes during Ambrose' time

Rome in his day had become increasingly remote from the centre of imperial affairs. No emperor since Constantine had lived there, and even the Western emperors based themselves in the north — in Trier (or Trèves, as the French call it), Arles and eventually Milan. Ambrosius, who had an elder brother Satyrus, was born around the year 340 in Trier, where his father seems to have been an acting Praetorian Prefect. There is a legend that as an infant, a swarm of bees settled on his face while he lay in his cradle, leaving behind a drop of honey. His father considered this a sign of his future eloquence and honeyed tongue: bees or beehives therefore often accompany his image. (During only the second mass at which I presided in Wye, a bee flew into the consecrated wine on the altar, which I took as a sign of his blessing on my ministry there!) When Ambrose was quite young, he lost his father who was executed as a traitor at a time of civil war. His mother moved to Rome and brought him up in a devout Christian household. Although Ambrose himself wasn't baptised until nearly two decades later, his elder sister Marcellina took the veil as a nun from Pope Liberius' hand in the year 357. The Pope was a frequent visitor to their home, and Ambrose was apparently fascinated by the way in which the womenfolk clustered around him, kissing his hand; he amused and infuriated his relatives by imitating the Pope's stately walk and offering his own hand to be kissed by the ladies.

As a young student he was exceedingly bright, and – unusually for the times – studied Greek as well as Latin and Roman law, and would have been familiar with a wide range of literature as well as philosophic ideas and probably some theology. So he was well equipped to enter imperial service himself, rising to become consular prefect (or Governor) of Liguria-Emilia. This took him in about the year 370 to Milan, which was then the second city after Rome. Now Milan had been the centre of the emperor Constantius' attempts to impose Arianism on the West, and when Ambrose reached Milan the Arian bishop, Auxentius, was still in office. Not many years later, in 374, Auxentius died, leaving an important vacancy to be filled. In those days this was not done behind the closed doors of the Vatican, but much more publicly as seems still to happen in the election of a new Coptic leader. The possibly apocryphal story is that when the congregation gathered for this purpose in Milan and remained undecided, a child somewhere on their periphery shouted out 'Ambrose for bishop'; and since Ambrose by now was a well-known figure, who as a catechumen had intervened to pacify different factions within the congregation, the cry was taken up and he was duly elected. Even if this tale is unsubstantiated, it bears some connection with Coptic procedures, where at the final stage a child comes forward blindfolded to select one of three names under consideration: the point is, that the decision must be understood as God's own choice, which may be conveyed better through an innocent child than through a possibly prejudiced ecclesiastical committee. (Children often fulfil such a religious purpose; compare the role of the infant Samuel in Israel's history with that of the Vestal Virgins in Rome or of the choirboys in Canterbury cathedral.)

What actually happened is more likely conveyed in Timothy Barnes' reconstruction. He suggests that there was a struggle between the Arian priests who had been ordained by Auxentius and the Catholic-minded laity:

> The deadlock was broken when the consularis of Aemilia and Liguria, whose theological sympathies cannot have been secret, offered himself as the candidate of the Nicene Christians of Milan by taking the unusual step of entering the basilica where the contested election was being conducted. Ambrose was elected unanimously because Auxentius' clergy were ready to compromise... For his part, the new bishop received those who had been ordained by Auxentius... It is a mark of Ambrose's skill as a politician that he avoided a doctrinal purge of his clergy and allowed homoean priests to continue to exercise their functions and enjoy their privileges. From December 374, however, no homoean could any longer expect to receive ordination as a priest in Milan.

There was one small detail that would surely today have disqualified Ambrose: he was still unbaptised. The ancient world, however, was more adept at taking legal hiccups in its stride; in eight days flat, Ambrose was not only baptised, but progressed rapidly through the minor clerical orders to be ordained priest in readiness for his consecration as bishop on 8th December 374. St Jerome's subsequent comment was scarcely complimentary: 'yesterday a catechumen, today a bishop; yesterday in the amphitheatre, today in the church; previously a fan of actors, now a consecrator of virgins.' Despite such a potentially damaging track record, a factor that must have weighed significantly in Ambrose's favour was his affluent background: since he was not married, there was the likelihood that some at least of his wealth would benefit the church in Milan, as indeed proved to be the case.

Having gained the see of Milan, he at once set himself to increase its influence further afield. He achieved this to such an extent that it was Ambrose, not Pope Damasus or his successor Siricius, who came to dominate the life of the Western Church in this last quarter of the 4th century. He managed to take on the metropolitan role over the north Italian bishoprics that had previously been exercised by Rome; indeed, he involved himself in episcopal appointments as far away as the Balkans, and attracted clergy and religious to Milan from Piacenza, Bologna, even North Africa. Following Rome's example, he presided over the creation of several great churches which would establish Milan as a truly Christian capital – perhaps even outshining Rome itself which was still in many ways dominated by paganism. The Basilica Nova at Milan, now buried under the present Duomo, had been built in the 350s, and was a gigantic church almost as big as St John Lateran; Ambrose added to it an octagonal freestanding baptistery. Elsewhere, using finances from his family estates, he dotted the perimeter of Milan with four new basilicas, S. Nazaro, S. Ambrogio, S. Simpliciano and S. Dionisio, although not all of them were completed in his lifetime; collectively they superimposed a cross upon the city.

Milan in the late 4th century, including Ambrose' episcopal complex

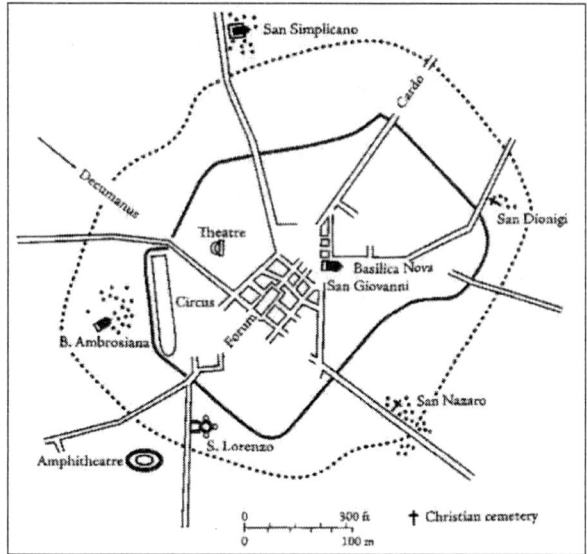

These were martyr's memorial churches, only lacking what Rome could claim so readily, namely, the actual remains of martyrs. This was an omission that Ambrose was naturally keen to remedy, so when exhumations in 386 uncovered what were arguably saintly skeletons he placed these relics (of 'Gervasius' and 'Protasius') with great ceremony beneath the altar in S. Ambrogio, where his brother Satyrus was buried and in whose crypt he was later buried himself. He described what happened in Milan in a letter to his sister, adding that 'during the translation a blind man was healed':

You must know that we have found some bodies of holy martyrs. For after I had dedicated the basilica, many, as it were, with one mouth began to address me, and said: Consecrate this as you did the Roman basilica.

116

And I answered: Certainly I will if I find any relics of martyrs... God favoured us, for even the clergy were afraid who were bidden to clear away the earth from the spot before the chancel screen of SS. Felix and Nabor... We found two men of marvellous stature, such as those of ancient days... On the following day we translated the relics to the basilica called Ambrosian.'

Some evidently expressed doubt about the accompanying miracle, but it was confirmed, both in his *Confessions* and in *The City of God*, by Augustine who was in Milan at the time.

It was not only in church matters that Ambrose gained wide respect for his energy and abilities. His previous experience stood him in good stead with the imperial court in Milan, and he was the first bishop asked to undertake an important diplomatic role on their behalf: in the winter of 383 he was sent to Trier to negotiate with the usurper Maximus, and followed this with another such visit a year later. The errands, however, proved fruitless.

More importantly, he proved his mettle as a determined defender of the Nicene faith, which was upheld in Rome but much disputed elsewhere throughout the 4th century. Yet he inherited a bishopric in which Arianism was deeply entrenched. So he set himself at the head of a movement to restore orthodoxy, mobilising the bishops of the West behind the Catholic cause. A symbolic gesture in the year 378 was his melting down of church plate to buy the freedom of prisoners of war held captive in the Balkans: although a notable act of mercy, it was also carefully calculated to distance himself from the Arians in Milan who were the original donors of the plate.

More outstanding clashes occurred in 385-6 after the imperial court had moved to Milan. Ambrose refused to surrender one of his churches for the use of Arian troops serving in the imperial army. He asserted that churches were 'temples', not to be allotted at the whim of an emperor as if they were neutral public spaces. The response was a new law (January 386) which gave the Arians free rights of assembly, and threatened that those who denied them would be treasonable and punishable with death. This was put to the test not long before Holy Week 386. Imperial messengers came to the basilica where Ambrose was gathered with his large congregation (some detractors claiming that he had bribed them with lavish distributions of gold coins); the people shouted down the emperor's request, and for several days following there was stalemate. Ambrose replaced traditional readings of the Psalms by antiphonal chanting, and then the singing of hymns which he had composed specially. He told the congregation that by reciting theological issues in memorable verses they too had become teachers of the faith. His hymn *Lux Beata Trinitas*, which became one of St Monica's favourites, was almost certainly sung, and the well-known *Aeterna Christi munera* may also have been in the repertoire.

O Trinity of blessèd light,
O Unity of princely might,
The fiery sun now goes his way;
Shed Thou within our hearts a ray.
To Thee our morning song of praise,
To Thee our evening prayer we raise;
O grant us with Thy saints on high
To praise Thee through eternity.
All laud to God the Father be,
All praise, eternal Son, to Thee,
All glory, as is ever meet,
To God the holy Paraclete.

The Church in these her princes boasts,
These victor chiefs of warriors hosts;
The soldiers of the heavenly hall,
The lights that rose on earth for all.
'Twas thus the yearning faith of saints,
The unconquered hope that never faints,
The love of Christ that knows not shame,
The prince of this world overcame.
In these the Father's glory shone;
In these the will of God the Son;
In these exults the Holy Ghost;
Through these rejoice the heavenly host.

The eternal gifts of Christ the King,
The Apostles' glorious deeds, we sing;
And while due hymns of praise we pay,
Our thankful hearts cast grief away.

Redeemer, hear us of Thy love,
That, with this glorious band above,
Hereafter, of Thine endless grace,
Thy servants also may have place.

On Palm Sunday he preached a defiant sermon in which he insisted that 'the emperor is within, and not above, the Church.' Various arrests were made and fines were imposed, with soldiers now present in greater numbers. Ambrose refused to appear in a hearing alongside an Arian bishop, nor would he leave the city. In the end it was the defection of some soldiers to Ambrose' cause that caused the court to back off. 'Imagine the happiness of all the congregation at this moment, the cheers of all the people, the thanksgiving,' he wrote. Ambrose thus not only made hymn-singing popular in the church, he also established a sense of the Christian masses as a united body and a force to be reckoned with. A few years later, he noted that 'the praises of a plebs… the rejoicing of a free people… is indeed a great bond of unity, by which the plebs gather together with one voice.'

There were other confrontations too, in which Ambrose marked out the boundaries. He had already outwitted Symmachus, the pagan Prefect of Rome, in persuading the young Emperor Valentinian II not to restore the annual grant of public funds to the Vestal Virgins in Rome. He denied the right of the imperial courts to judge in ecclesiastical cases. He (rather unreasonably) prevented church funds being used to rebuild a synagogue destroyed elsewhere in a religious riot. Finally he excommunicated the Emperor Theodosius for having ordered the punitive massacre of civilians at Thessalonica after the murder of an imperial official in the year 390 – forcing Theodosius to do public penance.

This readiness to hold firm to his convictions was probably why (as we noted) Ambrose was venerated so much by Catholics in the reign of Elizabeth I. It was not an uncommon name to be given then to their children: William, Lord Vine, the leading Catholic aristocrat who at one time sheltered Edmund Campion, so named one of his sons in 1570, while Ambrose Rookwood was an accomplice in the Gunpowder Plot. Again, one Fr Warford could write after the martyr Edward Stransham's death:

> The Martyr was wont to say that he would like to go to Italy (though in fact he never went) for many reasons; ranking, next after his desire to visit the tombs of the Apostles, **a wish to see the place and examine with his own eyes the rails, whence Theodosius was turned away by Blessed Ambrose**. [*This he could not have done, for every trace of the 'basilica nova intramurana' of Milan, where this took place, was obliterated nearly two centuries before, when the new Duomo was begun in 1386.*] In the writings of that holy Doctor he took great delight, and loved especially his greatness of mind, a greatness which was seen renewed in Stransham while withstanding with his life the Queen of England. Writing to him afterwards, I gave him a description of Milan and its Cathedral, with which he was so charmed, that, writing to me about it, he confessed that nothing had ever given him so much pleasure, and that he esteemed it a great favour. These, his last letters, are still in my possession in England.

Ambrose was certainly the real leader of the Western Church in his day; as his biographer Paulinus remarked of him, 'he had a concern for all the churches' – which was a Pauline text more often invoked by the popes. Yet his dominant position in Italy was built on a high doctrine of the papacy, not on any attempt to erode it. He frequently justified his activities as being carried out on behalf of the Pope. From Rome flowed, he said, 'the sacred faith of the Apostles... and all the rights of venerable communion'. He did indeed promote the cult of Peter and Paul in Milan, and Damasus encouraged him by sending him relics of these apostles. In S. Nazaro there is still preserved the silver casket in which they came.

If, unsurprisingly, his Arian enemies saw him as Pope Damasus' toady, he nevertheless maintained a proper regard for Milan's own traditions. When Monica, Augustine's mother, came to him concerned about variations in the churches' liturgical practices, he advised her to follow whatever was the local custom. Thus, in Milan she should follow Milanese ways, but when in Rome she should do as the Romans did. When Augustine himself sought the reason behind this, he was told that it was to prevent any scandal. For example, in North Africa Monica had evidently been accustomed to join in the martyrs' festivals that took place in burial grounds. These had a tendency to be rowdy occasions, with some drunken behaviour. So Ambrose prohibited any food or drink being offered, to avoid any resemblance to the conduct of pagan festivals. Instead, prayers were to be offered and any gifts were to go to the poor. There were variations too in the reception of candidates for baptism, whose feet Ambrose washed. And to this day the so-called Ambrosian rite of mass is still celebrated in Milan, as also is the Mozarabic rite in Toledo and Salamanca. It was an innovative Ambrose who helped to pave the way for more imaginative decorative schemes in church buildings – specifically the use of mosaics – by his careful theological analysis of the issues involved. The mosaic of Ambrose (seen above), which dates from about 50 years after his death, could be an actual likeness.

Augustine, the great theologian who succeeded him, paid much attention to his arguments. Indeed, it was the subtlety of Ambrose' mind and his novel ways of interpreting the scriptures that had led Augustine to seek baptism at Ambrose' hands. We recall that Augustine, who grew up in a Christian household in North Africa, had become a Manichee for a number of years and had carved out a career for himself in Rome as a leading intellectual, who, immersed like many others in Roman culture, rather despised Christianity as a backwoods religion lacking any proper philosophical and literary merit. The Bible in particular was not to be compared with the rich treasury of classical writings, indeed the Manicheans regarded at least its more ancient parts as a primitive muddle. But in Ambrose' sophisticated, allegorical treatment of the texts all this seemed very different – and extremely appealing: he interpreted Hebrew scriptures typologically, as prefiguring the life and person of Christ himself. He once explained this as follows:

You have read in the Apocalypse that the Lamb opened the sealed book which nobody hitherto had been able to open... By means of his Gospel, Jesus handed over the key of knowledge and gave it to us so that we may open.

Henry Chadwick commented:

At Milan, for the first time in his life, Augustine met a Christian intellectual who commanded his respect. Ambrose' sermons in the cathedral charmed him at first by their eloquence, but soon moved his mind by their argument, by their combination of Christian devotion with the language of Neoplatonic mysticism, and by their convincing interpretations of problematic passages in the Old Testament which answered the mocking objections of the Manichees.

Ambrose made no claims, however, to have resolved all doctrinal issues: 'My preference,' he wrote, 'is to encourage faith, not to define it.' Augustine wrote later of his own gradual change of heart and mind:

While I had an open mind for what he was saying deftly, what he was saying soundly reached me also, though only by degrees.

It was not just Sunday sermons that wrought this transformation; in his Lenten weeks of baptismal preparation he listened to Ambrose' instruction twice each day, for he gave the fullest possible attention to his *competentes*. They attended from Monday to Friday at the third and ninth hour, not only to hear Ambrose but to join in psalm-singing and prayer. They were urged to keep a strict diet and to abstain from sexual activity.

For their own biblical reading they were directed to ethical texts – Proverbs, Ecclesiasticus, and Wisdom. In the final week of preparation the candidates were initiated into the creed, which had to be learnt by heart and recited each day. Then at last came the baptismal rites at Easter, after which further instruction followed about the deeper meaning of the sacraments which they had received. Ambrose's text displayed in the baptistry summarises the heart of it:

> Here, whoever wishes to lay aside the shameful crimes of their lives, let them wash their hearts and take on a clean breast... What can be more divine than that, that the sin of the people falls away in a brief moment?

So Gary Wills observes:

> Much of medieval Christendom acquired its broad contours from what took place here. The Church would learn to act according to Ambrose' ruling patterns – his development of doctrinal rigour (especially on the Nicene Creed), the centrality of baptism, liturgical expansiveness, monastic discipline, the cult of saints, and episcopal control. And the Church would learn to think with the imaginative flights and intellectual daring of Augustine.

Before becoming a bishop it seems, however, that Ambrose had undertaken very little study of the Bible. Faced with the challenge of expounding it on a regular basis, he learnt much from the commentaries of the great Alexandrian teacher Origen as well as from Eusebius of Caesarea, Hilary of Poitiers, and the Jewish philosopher Philo. In his Lenten addresses he focused especially on four of the patriarchs:

> In Joseph there was a special incandescence of chastity...
> In Abraham you have learned the fierce adherence to faith,
> in Isaac the purity of a single intent,
> in Jacob a special resilience under harsh test.

New Testament passages offering fitting examples of conversion were the stories of the Samaritan woman at the well and the raising of Lazarus. In Peter Brown's words, Ambrose was able to take his hearers 'on a mystery tour of the Scriptures (or as he described it himself on 'excursions'). To expound the Bible was to peer into a deep, dark well of spiritual truths.'

Typical examples of his inspired exposition may be found in his discourses on the Psalms – as here, where he reflects on Psalm 1:

> Although the whole of sacred scripture breathes the spirit of God's grace, this is especially true of that delightful book, the book of the psalms ... History instructs, the law disciplines, prophecy foretells, correction shows us our faults and morality shows what should be done: but in the book of the psalms there is something more than all this and at the same time a sort of medicine for man's spiritual health. Whoever reads the psalms finds a special remedy to cure the wounds caused by his own passions. Whoever is at pains to read the psalms will find in them a sort of gymnasium for the use of all souls, a sort of stadium of virtue, where different sorts of exercises are set out before him, from which he can choose the best suited to train him to win his crown.

His regular elucidation of the Scriptures so revolutionised Augustine's mindset that – following his arrival in Milan when he had been received by Ambrose 'in a fatherly way' – after three years during which he had been suitably 'formed and instructed' by scripture, he and his son were baptised on Easter Eve 387.

There is a telling passage in Augustine's *Confessions* that, whenever he went to see the bishop, there was always a long queue of people waiting to talk over their problems; while in the brief moments when he was not so engaged, Ambrose was either restoring his body with the necessary food or nourishing his spirit with reading – and here Augustine marvels, because (contrary to contemporary custom) he read with his eyes only and his mouth shut, uttering no words. Silence, he once explained, citing Job's ultimate humility in the face of God's awesome greatness ('I have uttered what I did not understand, things too wonderful for me, which I did not know'), was much to be preferred to speech: Augustine was later to share his reticence[4]. In one of Ambrose' letters (to another bishop) he commended constant recourse to the scriptures as a vital preparation for preaching:

---

[4] Cyril of Jerusalem (mid 4th century) resorted to St Paul's advice to the Church in Corinth: 'Let the young women's group gather in such a way that, whether it is praying psalms or reading in silence, their lips move but the ears of others do not hear ... And let the married woman do likewise.' So he expected *women* to read silently.

He who reads much with understanding is filled. He who is filled, waters others, and therefore scripture says, 'If the clouds are full of rain, they empty themselves upon the earth.' Let your discourses then, be flowing, let them be clear and lucid, so that you may bring pleasure to the ears of the people by your discourse on morals, and with the charm of your word soothe the faithful, that they may readily follow your guidance. Let your addresses be full of understanding... their meaning should flash with intelligence.

In Ambrose' sermon *On Isaac*, he dwells on the soul's capacity 'to pass beyond intelligible things' and 'to pursue the divine', being 'strengthened and fed by it'. The transformation of the 'inner man' and his ascent towards God were common themes. Unlike many of his contemporaries, including the Manichaeans, he never conceived of God as some sort of 'superman' (to use today's jargon); rather, the likeness of a human being to God resided in the soul who would 'gaze on the glory of God and be remade in the same image.' By contrast, the body might be described as like 'mud'.

As well as quite a few extant biblical commentaries, ninety-one letters, quite a few hymns (as many as nineteen have been attributed to him), and various writings on faith and ethics, there are some (fragmentary) sermons. Most of Ambrose' compositions were dictated to his secretaries, although he was very careful not to impose too much upon them; thus he did not normally dictate at night when he would be 'troublesome and a burden to others.' In his older age he came to prefer writing in his own hand, so as to have time to ponder the words he was using.

Another of his works is entitled *On Naboth*, which was compiled from sermons he had recently delivered in the late 380s. Based on the Old Testament encounter between king Ahab and the prophet Naboth, it displays Ambrose' readiness, not merely to be a spiritual guide, but to grapple as necessary with issues of his day. These are addressed in a forthright manner – so he begins:

The story of Naboth is an ancient tale. But today it is an everyday occurrence.

Shouldering the prophetic mantle, he then lists some of the shocking abuses and injustices that would have been familiar to his audience – although scholars today reckon his examples were often literary clichés that didn't necessarily correspond to the contemporary scene. Never mind, they say, 'it is precisely the commonplace quality of the greed of the rich and the misery of the poor that Ambrose wished to conjure up'. Nor did Ambrose confine himself simply to preaching. He often lobbied the ruling classes on behalf of ill-treated individuals brought to his attention. On one sensational occasion, he even gate-crashed the emperor's private circus: he entered the arena by the gladiators' gateway (fortunately before the wild beasts were let loose) in order to petition the emperor in person. Peter Brown observes here:

> The On Naboth and similar sermons formed part of Ambrose' continued drive to build up a sense of a Christian community in Milan... This community had already stood the test of fire (in 385-86) in the incident of the basilicas. Now their sense of cohesion would be further sharpened by a challenge to the evil rich.

In one of his most important works *De Officiis* (On Duties), written in 388 (when he was getting on towards the age of 50) in deliberate imitation of Cicero's work bearing the same title, Ambrose summed up his personal vision of pastoral care. What mattered most to him was the co-responsibility Christians held for one another, whether rich or poor – their mutual solidarity:

> Good will is now enhanced by the communal nature of the church, by our partnership in faith, by our kinship as recipients of the grace of baptism, and by our sharing in the Mysteries... By these means the congregation of the holy church grows ever upwards into one body, joined and bound together in the unity of faith and love.

Nor was it only faith and love that rich and poor were called to share: a greater pooling of earthly wealth was also implied.

> God has ordained all things to be produced so that there should be food in common for all and that the earth should be the common possession of all. Nature has produced a common right for all, but greed has made it a right for the few.

Herein perhaps lies Ambrose's most important achievement:

[He] brought the poor into the Catholic community. He presented the care of the rich for the poor as a necessary consequence of the unity of all Christians. Last but not least, Ambrose presented the unity of the Catholic community of Milan as the living core of human society as a whole. A fractured human race could regain its long-lost solidarity by entering the Catholic Church.

Thus, here in late 4th century Milan, Christians were taught to understand themselves for the first time, not as a persecuted minority of true believers, but as the growing nucleus of God's true humanity.

It is also in *De Officiis* that Christians, at a time when the Church was becoming an increasingly important influence in public life, were first offered the rudiments of what later became known as Just War teaching. In his earlier days as a Roman governor Ambrose had been able to call upon the militia in order to maintain order, but as a bishop he was clear that fighting was not his preferred option: 'It is not our business to look to arms, but rather to the forces of peace.' While he commended an attitude of turning the other cheek he nevertheless recognised that we have no right to turn another person's cheek and may well be called upon to defend that person; not so doing might sometimes therefore be a failure of neighbourly love. By extension, the use of force to protect a nation may also on occasion be justified. Here, once again, Ambrose was able to draw upon ideas expressed two centuries earlier by Cicero, who argued that war is to be waged only in the pursuit of attaining peace; that it should spare non-combatants and be merciful to those who surrender; that it is only soldiers under oath of service who may legitimately fight; and that the humanity of one's enemy must be recognized, imposing restrictions therefore upon the conduct of war. Yet Ambrose, however conversant he was with Cicero's thinking, based his own arguments explicitly upon biblical sources – and once again paved the way for Augustine's more extended reflections upon the subject.

Ambrose died, alas, before he reached the age of 60, in 397. Fittingly it happened on the very eve of Easter. His body rested in the cathedral of Milan before being escorted on Easter Day by 'crowds beyond counting', headed by the newly baptised (some of whom claimed to have had a vision of him the previous night sitting on his customary seat in the cathedral), to his tomb in the Ambrosiana church. A generation later, Augustine of Hippo made sure his mentor would not be forgotten by commissioning Paulinus of Milan (who had served Ambrose as one of his many scribes and secretaries) to write a *Life of Ambrose*. It is a colourful account, and since Paulinus recorded that much of his work 'had been done for him' through Ambrose' careful editing of his own writings it needs to be balanced with other estimations of his personality and achievements; but it certainly indicates the high regard in which his contemporaries held him.

If I have given an impression of Ambrose as perhaps rather too assertive in his manner (and others would argue, very much a late Roman aristocrat in the way he attempted to enhance his authority – 'a carefully crafted public persona'), let me end by quoting again from *De Officiis*: the way to go about things, he wrote, is as far as possible *'sine perturbatione'* – without making a fuss:

> We must avoid giving the impression that we are acting more with an eye
> to self-glorification than to showing people mercy.

Despite their dramatic clashes, it is worth remembering that, when the Emperor Theodosius lay dying, it was Ambrose whom he asked to be at his side. He knew that while Ambrose (in his own words) 'deferred' to emperors, he did not 'truckle' to them, because he was in God's higher service. And when Ambrose delivered the funeral oration *De Obitu Theodosii*, he singled out above all Theodosius' readiness to forgive others:

> If it is a great thing to find anyone who is merciful or faithful, how much
> more so an emperor whom power impels toward vengeance, but whom,
> nevertheless, compassion recalls from taking vengeance?

Theodosius, he believed, had attained salvation through his humility; 'because he asked for forgiveness when sin stole upon him, his soul has returned to its rest.'

For all his failings, the same may be said too of St Ambrose.

St Ambrose (in the *Egino Codex of Verona,* late 790s)

A Doctor of the Church inspired by a youthful Christ

John Henry Newman

MANY CHANNELS OF GOD'S GRACE

What do most of us know of Newman? Two or three hymns: *'Praise to the Holiest in the height'* and *'Firmly I believe and truly'*, both of which come in his 1865 poem *The Dream of Gerontius*, set to music by Edward Elgar many years later; and of course that great favourite of the Victorians *'Lead, kindly light'* composed in 1833 when his ship was becalmed in the Mediterranean and he contemplated the 'encircling gloom' of the Church of England back home. Then there are two prayers of his we often use: one sometimes in our parish diaries, *'My God, you have created me to do you some definite service'* and the other frequently cited at funerals, *'O Lord, support us all day long of this troublous life'*. They serve to remind us that as well as being a theologian and a philosopher, Newman was also a pastor and a poet, whose focus seldom strayed from the mystery of God. His historical importance lies in his challenge to the prevailing rationalism of his times: he taught that it is what we know unclearly that matters most, that the Church expresses her beliefs implicitly as well as explicitly, that in any case all doctrines dissolve in God's own presence, and that the Christian life is a complex journey leading us into that presence. He used the term 'development' of his own journey and that of the universal Church, and so I shall use a chronological model to explore the way his ideas evolved and his influence grew.

John Henry Newman was born in 1801 into a prosperous London family of Anglican persuasion: 'I was brought up from a child to take great delight in reading the Bible... Of course I had perfect knowledge of my catechism' [Apol 96]. His father was a banker (as was Cardinal Manning's), yet lost much of his money in the widespread financial collapse that resulted from the ending of the Napoleonic Wars in 1815. Around this time John Henry himself suffered serious illness, but was supported by a schoolmaster who pointed him in a more Calvinistic direction which he claimed later as his first real conversion: '[I] received into my intellect impressions of dogma, which, through God's mercy, have never been effaced or obscured' [Apol 97]. By dogma he means what we would probably call 'eternal truth'. Even after his further

129

conversion to the Roman Catholic Church he never repudiated this early evangelicalism, but saw his faith in terms of 'development' – and I think the great Victorian public (of whatever Christian persuasion) who took his poetry to heart saw in it their own essential religious instincts. However, Newman also received certain other teenage impressions which he did repudiate in time: from Isaac Newton's commentaries on the prophetic books of Scripture he picked up the belief that the pope was Antichrist, a 'doctrine' which, he confessed, 'stained' his imagination for the next twenty-seven years [Apol 100].

In 1817 he entered Trinity College, Oxford where overwork brought him a much poorer degree than he merited. He redeemed himself almost immediately by gaining a prestigious fellowship to Oriel College, then the centre of a mini renaissance of Anglicanism. Here he imbibed lasting insights from several of his colleagues: (1) 'Scripture' as he later wrote 'begins a series of developments which it does not finish'. In other words he discovered the Church's tradition, in particular the early Fathers, extending beyond the Bible, drawing out its import; (2) If there have been developments in different times and places, the question of authority arises: on what grounds can one claim a particular development is valid? Wherein lies the authority of the Church of England – in its historic privileges, in its recourse to parliament? Hence, he came to weigh the significance of the apostolic succession; (3) Following on from this, at a time when the Tory and Anglican dominance of the Establishment was beginning to be challenged by Whigs and dissenters, opening up the vista of a parliament that might one day include not only non-Anglicans but agnostics and atheists as well, was it right that church affairs should be controlled by the State? Thus disestablishment, the right of the Church to self-government, was an issue to be taken seriously.

Newman was ordained a priest for the Church of England in 1824, and in 1828 became vicar of the University church of St Mary's, in the very centre of Oxford. Pastoral experience allied now with academic studies of the Fathers prompted in him an urgent sense of the Church's need to rediscover its true calling. As the acerbic Lytton Strachey wrote in his *Eminent Victorians*, 'For many generations the Church of England had slept the sleep of the... comfortable', seeing itself merely as 'a useful organisation for the maintenance of Religion, as by law established'. Today we might find it hard to recognise such a church: for example, in many places there was no permanent altar, just a table brought out a few times a year for use on what they called Sacrament Sunday. And where altars did remain by force of habit in the villages there are shocking accounts of farmers sitting round them drinking and playing cards. In Owen Chadwick's account, Newman understood this as a personal challenge: he 'came into the pulpit just when people felt the discontent but had not quite expressed it'. He glimpsed his own future in 'the necessity of there being men in the Church, like the R(oman) Catholic friars, free from all obstacles to their devoting themselves to its defence' [Letters ii, 150].

One much needed reform was the restoration of a true sacramental life: Newman saw its centrality in the early Church and learnt too from his friend and mentor John Keble how mere words and rationality are insufficient to feed the soul. The age of Enlightenment had by now given place to the Romantic Movement, which (although not always sympathetic to the Christian faith) emphasised above all the role of the imagination. So here is Newman's sermon on sacramental worship:

> At times we seem to catch a glimpse of a form which we shall hereafter see face to face. We approach, and in spite of the darkness, our hands, or our head, or our brow, or our lips become, as it were, sensible of the contact of something more than earthly. We know not where we are, but we have been bathing in water, and a voice tells us it is blood. Or we have a mark signed upon our foreheads, and it spake of Calvary. Or we recollect a hand laid upon our heads, and surely it had the print of nails in it, and resembled His who with a touch gave sight to the blind and raised the dead. Or we have been eating and drinking; and it was not a dream surely, that One fed us from His wounded side, and renewed our nature by the heavenly meat He gave. Thus in many ways He, who is Judge to us, prepares us to be judged, – He, who is to glorify us, prepares us to be glorified, that He may not takes us unawares; but that when the voice of the Archangel sounds, and we are called to meet the Bridegroom, we may be ready.

His audience in Oxford largely consisted of undergraduates, drawn there in the first instance by the scent of rebellion but held by Newman's own radiant spirituality. Matthew Arnold remembered his preaching, 'In the most entrancing of voices, breaking the silence with words and thoughts which were a religious music, sweet, subtle, mournful.' In a short time 'Newmania' as they called it became the university's new creed, and set the Church of England on altogether a new course – bearing in mind that roughly half of all Oxbridge students in those days would enter the ordained ministry. In a world of growing prosperity brought about by the Industrial Revolution it became above all Newman's voice that spoke of deeper truths and higher callings. Without such a challenge (to give but one example) it is unlikely that so much Anglican missionary work would have been attempted abroad, for it was often young men inspired by his teachings who renounced ambition for a life of hardship, including sometimes an early death.

His special field of interest – the Arian crisis of the fourth century – not only recalled a neglected spirituality, but also alerted Newman to past theological tensions. His hero was the bishop of Alexandria, St Athanasius, who – despite years of exile – championed the cause of Nicene orthodoxy, which in the end prevailed over the 'watered-down' version preferred by bishops too close to the imperial establishment. Newman saw many parallels in contemporary Church life; and when in 1833 he toured the Eastern Mediterranean to familiarise himself with places he had merely read about, Athanasius' voyages came vividly to mind and moved him to pray [Letters iii, 155]:

When shall our northern Church her champion see
Raised by high heaven's decree
To shield the ancient faith at his own harm?

Then in Naples he read in the newspapers of events back home: the Whig government's Bill to suppress ten bishoprics of the (Anglican) Church of Ireland – a major affront in his eyes and in those of his clerical friends, Keble, Froude, Pusey, all of whom rejected the Erastian view that the State had any right to do this. It was then Keble who launched the so-called 'Oxford Movement' with a sermon on 14th July 1833 entitled National Apostasy, but it was Newman's genius for publicity that issued their further protests in the form of Tracts selling for a penny each. In the end there were ninety such *Tracts for the Times* written over the next eight years (hence the movement's alternative description as Tractarianism) – wide-ranging polemical statements arguing for a Catholic Revival within the Church of England, with, it should be noted, both Popery and Dissent among the targets.

Newman wrote twenty-four of these Tracts himself, his main idea being to see the Church of England as a *via media*, a moderate reformed Catholicism, taking his inspiration from the patristic tradition. Yet continuing studies unsettled his confidence [Apol 182]:

My stronghold was Antiquity; now here, in the middle of the fifth century, I found, as it seemed to me, the Christendom of the sixteenth and the nineteenth centuries reflected.

He had come to realise that alongside the extremists, there were also moderate heretics, and in his research on Athanasius he reached a like conclusion: that the *via media*, the moderate party (which was where he located the Church of England), these were the moderate heretics rather than the orthodox. Then there were the words to which Nicolas Wiseman, in time the first Archbishop of Westminster, had directed him: 'a mere sentence, the words of St Augustine, struck me with a power which I had never felt from any words before... *Securus judicat orbis terrarum* ('If everyone agrees, the verdict must be right')! By those words of the ancient Father, the theory of the via media was absolutely pulverised' [Apol 185]. He now appreciated that merely positioning oneself centrally in a debate isn't the way to win the argument. One needs a 'deliberate judgment in which the whole Church at length rests and acquiesces' as 'a final sentence against such portions of it as protest and secede': or, put differently, it is a process of dynamic interaction that leads to the truth.

Newman's advocacy for the Church of England was henceforth revised. In the famous *Tract 90*, published in 1841, he offered an interpretation of her Thirty-Nine Articles in a sense which would harmonise them, to the greatest degree possible, with the (primitive rather than Roman) Catholic faith. He argued that they were published before the decrees of the reforming Council of Trent, hence their critique of Roman Catholicism only referred to its corrupt late medieval form. 'Apostolical' Anglicans, he said, had no duties to the framers of the articles, whose uncatholic positions were well known, whereas they did have an obligation, both to the Catholic Church and to their own, to 'take our reformed confessions in the most Catholic sense they will admit' [Via Media II,344]. Such was his renown that this tract could not be ignored. Inevitably, therefore, *Tract 90* precipitated a violent controversy, drew down the formal censure of the Vice-Chancellor of the University, its Heads of Houses and Proctors, and was condemned in the pastoral charges of a number of individual bishops; his own bishop, Bagot of Oxford, sought to impose silence upon its author. It was a defining moment for many in the Oxford Movement, for whom this was a tract too far.

For anyone shifting their allegiance from one church to another the question may be asked, Were they pushed, or did they jump? Almost always the answer is a mixture of both. The unpopular Newman now began to shed his official roles as a minister of the established Church. From 1842 on, he lived in a semi-monastic establishment in the village of Littlemore, outside Oxford: a life mainly of study and prayer with a few friends – but with some continuing pastoral engagement (in catechizing at the local school he had found occasion to lecture 'against uncombed hair and dirty faces and hands; but I find I am not deep in the philosophy of school-girl tidiness'). 'Meanwhile', wrote Strachey,

The English Roman Catholics were growing impatient; was the great conversion never coming, for which they had prayed so fervently and so long? Dr Wiseman, at the head of them, was watching and waiting with special eagerness. His hand was held out under the ripening fruit; the delicious morsel seemed to be trembling on its stalk; and yet it did not fall. At last, unable to bear the suspense any longer, he dispatched to Littlemore Father Smith, an old pupil of Newman's, who had lately joined the Roman communion, with instructions that he should do his best, under cover of a simple visit of friendship, to discover how the land lay. Father Smith was received somewhat coldly, and the conversation ran entirely on topics which had nothing to do with religion. When the company separated before dinner, he was beginning to think that his errand had been useless; but on their reassembling he suddenly noticed that Newman had changed his trousers, and that the colour of the pair which he was now wearing was grey. At the earliest moment, the emissary rushed back post-haste to Dr Wiseman. 'All is well,' he exclaimed; 'Newman no longer considers that he is in Anglican orders.' 'Praise be to God!' answered Dr Wiseman. 'But how do you know ?' Father Smith described what he had seen. 'Oh, is that all? My dear father, how can you be so foolish?' But Father Smith was not to be shaken. 'I know the man,' he said, 'and I know what it means. Newman will come and he will come soon.' And Father Smith was right.

In 1845 Newman was received into the Church of Rome by the Italian Passionist priest Dominic

Barberi. Perhaps a key issue for him was the role of the papacy in distinguishing true developments from false (while here he lauded Pope Leo's vital contribution in the early 5th century it is also worth noting the very positive impression he had formed of the papal liturgy on his visit to Rome in 1833). Revelation, he argued, is not given if there is no authority in the church to decide what it is. Without it there can only be 'a comprehension of opinions'. So he now published his *Essay on the Development of Christian Doctrine* which had been in the making for some time, but foreshadowed, for example, by the last of his University Sermons in Oxford. Reviewers at the time dismissed his arguments, failing to see that he was addressing a really crucial predicament. If he failed to do this entirely satisfactorily, the lasting value of the Essay is to have implanted the idea of development within the conscious mind of the Church – and of course it is an idea that embraces not only doctrine, but also liturgy and church architecture (for which reason Newman was not enamoured of Pugin's ongoing Gothic Revival). David Brown singles out the historical importance of 'his refusal to treat theology as a complete or closed system... The way of heresy was found in arrested development, burying the gospel treasure in the ground rather than risking it in the mental currencies of the world'. The way forward was by daring to combine what seemed to be opposites, resulting in some 'fresh evolution' from the original idea, 'which can indeed be said to be never entirely exhausted'.

If Christianity be a universal religion, suited not simply to one locality or period, but to all times and places, it cannot but vary in its relationships and dealings with the world around it, that is, it will develop. Principles require a very various application according as persons and circumstances vary, and must be thrown into new shapes according to the form of society which they are to serve. [Dev 58]

In Newman's most memorable words [Dev 36,40]:

A great idea is elicited and expanded by trial, and battles into perfection and supremacy... [when] old principles reappear under new forms. It changes with them in order to remain the same. In a higher world it is otherwise, but here below to live is to change, and to be perfect is to have changed often.

Once ordained priest in Rome, Newman followed the advice of his new superior, Nicholas Wiseman, vicar-apostolic of the Midland District, and threw in his lot with the Oratorians. These were communities of secular priests with a rule of life, but without traditional religious vows, offering opportunities for scholarship as well as for pastoral work. So came about the foundation of Birmingham Oratory. And indeed Catholic fortunes generally seemed to be reviving. Yet with the restoration of the hierarchy in 1850 there was violent public opposition. In response Newman gave a lecture course on *The Present Position of Catholics in England*, aiming to challenge the wide misrepresentation of Catholic belief, in particular the views of an ex-Dominican friar Giovanni Achilli about the workings of the Inquisition. Achilli was pretty disreputable and had already been defrocked for immorality, which Wiseman had recorded in *The Dublin Review*. The article had passed without comment, so Newman, having first taken legal advice, simply reasserted what was already in print – but then found himself charged with defamation. Had Wiseman responded initially to Newman's request for supporting documentary evidence, the case would almost certainly never have reached court. As it was, the case hung over Newman for two years, while large sums were collected across the Catholic world to defray the costs of the trial – Newman being acclaimed as the Church's champion. Personally, however, he suffered the possible outcome of a prison sentence and during the hearing spent 'day and night almost' before the Blessed Sacrament with remarkable serenity. He impressed even the judge who handed down a nominal fine and said afterwards: 'I was overpowered – the immense crowd, the anxious and critical audience, his slender figure, and strange mysterious cloudy face... What a sweet musical, almost unearthly voice it was, so unlike any other we had heard'.

Meanwhile, from 1851 onwards, a new sphere of opportunity had arisen: Newman was now the Rector of the (short-lived) Catholic University of Ireland in Dublin. This allowed him to develop his vision of what university education should be, in a Catholic perspective. His *'Discourses on the Scope and Nature of University Education'*, is still in print (and still much commended) as the first half of his influential *The Idea of a University*, which takes as its main theme, the unity of all human understanding:

All branches of knowledge are connected together, because the subject-matter of knowledge is intimately united in itself, as being the acts and the work of the Creator. [Idea 94]

In this respect he was far ahead of those who determinedly resisted scientific enquiry or the advancement of knowledge: so, for example, he was able to appreciate Charles Darwin's discoveries much more than some of his contemporaries. He was strongly in favour of an educated laity, and in a contemporary letter he expressed his regret that his own bishop, W.B.Ullathorne, had 'a horror of laymen'.

On his return to England in 1858, Newman (reluctantly) became editor of *The Rambler*, a lay-controlled, rather left-wing periodical , which in the end foundered financially. He wrote an early article for it, *'On Consulting the Faithful in Matters of Doctrine'* (1859), but found himself reported to Rome by the Bishop of Newport, and was very much under a shadow there for several years following. Once again there was misunderstanding of what he was trying to say, and the alarm was misplaced: the point he made about the Arian crisis was historically sound:

There were untrustworthy councils, unfaithful bishops, there was weakness, fear of consequences, misguidance, delusion, hallucination, endless, hopeless, extending itself into nearly every corner of the Catholic Church.

The situation was saved by the laity. As St Hilary of Poitiers commented at the time:

The ears of the common people are holier than the hearts of the priests. [Consult 77,85]

So Newman insisted on a properly comprehensive view of apostolic tradition:

I think I am right in saying that the tradition of the apostles... manifests itself variously at various times: sometimes by the mouth of the episcopacy, sometimes by the doctors, sometimes by the people, sometimes by liturgies, rites, ceremonies, and customs, by events, disputes, movements, and all those other phenomena which are comprised under the name of history. It follows that none of these channels of tradition may be treated with disrespect; granting at the same time fully, that the gift of discerning, discriminating, defining, promulgating, and enforcing any portion of that tradition resides solely in the ecclesia docens. [Consult 63]

Newman not only respected the faith of lay people, but was pastorally sensitive towards them and 'tender of the popular religious sense'. In words that ought to be heeded today, he urged:

What the genius of the Church cannot bear is, changes in thought being hurried, abrupt, violent – out of tenderness to souls, for unlearned and narrow-minded men get unsettled and miserable. The great thing is to move all together and then the change, as geological changes, must be very slow.

But having stated his view that it is 'not the wise and powerful, but the obscure, the unlearned, and the weak' who constitute 'the real strength' of the Church, Newman found himself as unpopular with the more respectable classes of Victorian society as with Ultramontanes in his Church, and had to keep his head down.

The tide turned in 1864, after the Broad Church Anglican Charles Kingsley had publicly attributed to him words that indicated a cavalier attitude to truthfulness among Catholic priests. In three months of intensive writing Newman compiled his *Apologia Pro Vita Sua*, a religious autobiography which won him the sympathy of Catholics and non-Catholics alike. Strachey observed: 'Kingsley could no more understand the nature of Newman's intelligence than a subaltern in a line regiment can understand the Brahmin of Benares', adding that it was 'his very desire to explain what he had in his mind exactly and completely, with all the refinements of which his subtle brain was capable, that persons such as Kingsley were puzzled into thinking him dishonest'. Yet Newman's frankness about his own doubts and struggles won him many admirers, with his nuanced appreciation of his Anglican heritage and a not-uncritical stance towards Catholicism revealing a man free of bigotry who was passionate about spiritual truth:

Catholic Christendom is no simple exhibition of religious absolutism, but presents a continuous picture of authority and private judgment alternately advancing and retreating as the ebb and flow of the tide. [Apol 286]

And as Chadwick noted, 'For the first time in English history, a Roman Catholic priest rejoiced publicly in many of the truths taught by Protestants'. He urged Catholics to 'assist and sustain' the National Church 'if it be in our power, in the interests of dogmatic truth'. Robert Runcie once observed:

In his room in the Oratory at Birmingham he kept a whole series of mementoes to remind him of his years at Trinity, at Oriel and as vicar of St Mary's... Just as in his Anglican days he had made use of the prayers of the Roman breviary, so at the end of his life as a cardinal the Preces Privatae of Launcelot Andrews were still on his prayer desk.

In 1870 Newman published his long-distilled work of apologetics, *An Essay in Aid of a Grammar of Assent* – or, in simpler language, a study of the messy process whereby human beings (and not just learned academics) come to faith, and discover something of God's purposes for them – with 'certitude', not mere irrationality. Above all he wanted to establish that the act of faith was in the broadest sense 'reasonable'. This in his view was the crucial problem of his times. Key to his thinking is the insight that personal experience counts for more than external ideas. 'While I can prove Christianity divine to my own satisfaction, I shall not be able to force it upon anyone else' [GA 408]. Indeed, 'The medicines necessary for our souls are very different from each other. Thus God leads us by strange ways'. He was convinced that heart and mind have to grow together into God's truth. But he used a rather obscure phrase to express this: he spoke of 'antecedent probabilities', which to later Roman Catholic auditors seemed to exude an aura of doubt, although his own meaning is spelled out in an Anglican sermon of 1839, *Love the Safeguard of Faith against Superstition*. What I think he meant was that if any of us is to be persuaded by the evidences of faith, we have to be open and ready and responsive; it is 'the state of our heart' which counts. The gift of faith calls for 'antecedent expectancy' – a preparedness in each one of us to appreciate spiritual signs and moments. So 'the antecedent probability of a revelation' is 'estimated variously according to the desire of it existing in each breast'. Newman understood that the actual means of grace may be very ordinary indeed:

There is nothing miraculous or extraordinary in [God's] dealings with us. He works through our natural faculties and circumstances of life... A man is going on as usual; he comes home one day, and finds a letter, or a message, or a person, whereby a sudden trial comes on him, which, if met religiously, will be the means of advancing him to a higher state of religious excellence, which at present he as little comprehends as the unspeakable words heard by St Paul in paradise. [PS viii, 24]

He even allowed that, just as we may be brought into the Church at the hand of an unbeliever, so God may on occasion speak to us through the rites and customs of non-Christian people.

Thus Newman, who distrusted mere intellect, helped to overturn the prevailing reliance upon purely rational instruction. Earlier on in The Rambler he had written this:

People are variously constituted; what influences one does not influence another... I am touched by my five senses, by what my eyes behold and my ears hear. I am touched by what I read about, not by what I myself create... I gain more from the life of our Lord in the Gospels than from a treatise de Deo. I gain more from three verses of St John than from the three points of a meditation. I like a Spanish crucifix of painted wood more than one from Italy, which is made of gold. I am more touched by the Seven Dolours [of the Blessed Virgin] than by the Immaculate Conception... I do not say that my way is better than another's; but it is my way, and an allowable way.

Today it is commonly accepted that initiation into the Catholic Church is a process which varies according to personal need, and is (for example) as much about belonging to a community of faith as about believing certain dogmas. Conversion is not just the changing of opinions, but a change of heart – 'and this is evidently not done in a moment – it is a slow work' [PS viii, 15].

The heart is commonly reached, not through the reason, but through the imagination, by means of direct impressions, by the testimony of facts and events, by history, by description. Persons influence us, voices melt us, looks subdue us, deeds inflame us. [Tamworth 6]

So there are many contributory stimuli: devotional artefacts and visual aids play their part; so does scripture; personal testimony counts; as does active participation in the life of the Church and the formation of new habits – hence prayer should seek God's help in changing one's likes and dislikes, one's tastes and views [PS iv, 17]. Newman understood that

God's grace, awakening the individual's conscience, may work through a host of channels – first, perhaps as an inner religious emotion, but then as a serious quest for God's truth, and ultimately as a longing to encounter him. Supremely he insisted that it is in the collective experience of the whole Church that fullness of truth is to be found:

And I hold in veneration / For the love of Him alone
Holy Church as His creation / And her teachings as His own.

When, in the latter 1860s, a new ecumenical Council (Vatican 1) was announced by Pius IX especially to consider the definition of papal infallibility, it carried serious potential implications for one of Newman's persuasion. He was opposed to the definition; yet he regarded it as inopportune rather than unfounded. After all, Catholic theologians had long held 'that what the Pope said *ex cathedra*, was true, when the Bishops had received it:

What has [now] been passed, is to the effect that what he determines ex cathedra is true independently of the reception by the Bishops – but nothing has been passed as to what is meant by 'ex cathedra' – and this falls back to the Bishops and the Church to determine quite as much as before. Really therefore nothing has been passed of consequence. Again, the decree is limited to 'faith and morals' – whereas what the Ultra party wished to pass was political principles. [Letters xxv, 224]

In 1875, an attack on the dogma by the British prime minister, William Gladstone, enabled Newman to state his own view of the matter (in his *Letter to the Duke of Norfolk*), with the nuances which such extreme Ultramontanes as his fellow-convert, Cardinal Manning of Westminster had left out. He disarmed critics by listing numerous instances of past papal bad behaviour, but managed to upset the Curia in Rome by referring also to the 'malaria' at the foot of St Peter's. Manning however defended him, recognising how positively he had changed public perceptions.

In his old age Newman's wisdom came to be accorded public recognition. In 1877 he was elected an honorary fellow of Trinity College. In 1879, the new pope, Leo XIII, made him cardinal deacon of S. Giorgio in Velabro.

My cardinal (exclaimed the pope to a Catholic peer, Lord Selborne)! It was not easy, it was not easy. They said he was too liberal, but I had determined to honour the Church in honouring Newman. I always had a cult for him I am proud that I was able to honour such a man.

This was not the stamp of approval upon his every utterance (there being no doctrine of creeping infallibility), but it did endorse Newman's principal concerns: the recognition of truth in whatever quarter it lay – in other church traditions as in the secular sphere – hence too the rights of critical enquiry, the appreciation of historical development within Christian thinking, and the role of lay people alongside bishops and theologians in discerning and upholding the faith entrusted to God's Church. To suggest that Newman was 'liberal' was to misunderstand his lifelong quest for God's truth: when, in acceding to the honour bestowed upon him, he testified how 'for thirty, forty, fifty years I have resisted to the best of my powers the spirit of Liberalism in religion', he meant above all the tendency to regard truth as relative, that 'one creed is as good as another' – which no doubt is today's politically correct opinion.

Nor was Leo's recognition an idiosyncratic lapse of judgment. Bishop Christopher Butler once suggested that Newman possessed 'a sort of prophetic charisma' about the direction Rome would eventually take, and – *mirabile dictu* – during the Second Vatican Council a seminar was indeed organised to consider his view of the laity's role. In the Council's *Decree concerning non-Christian religions* too there are striking resemblances to the strategy he had urged in his first major work, *The Arians of the Fourth Century*; that after St Paul's manner the apologist or missionary should 'seek some points in the existing superstitions as the basis of his own instructions, instead of indiscriminately condemning and discarding the whole assemblage of heathen opinions and practices' [Arians 84]. Regarding papal infallibility, *Lumen Gentium* states that it 'extends as far as the deposit of divine revelation', in words almost identical with Newman's: 'the Pope is not infallible beyond the deposit of faith originally given'. So Paul VI may not have erred in calling it Newman's Council. Here was his very prediction coming true:

If you look into history, you find Popes continually completing the acts of their predecessors, and Councils too – sometimes only half the truth is brought out at one time – I doubt not a coming Pope or a coming Council will so explain and guard what has now been passed by the late Council [Vatican 1], so as to clear up all that troubles us now. [Letters xxv, 322]

All recent Popes have lauded Newman for his 'courageous research' and his 'toilsome' but 'most meaningful' and 'most conclusive' thought. Yet papal endorsement of a visionary teacher is one thing, whereas the promotion of eventual canonisation is another. Newman's own words are again apposite:

We advance to the truth by experience of error; we succeed through failures. We know not how to do right except by having done wrong... Such is the process by which we succeed; we walk to heaven backward. [PS v, 107-8]

The vivid imagery of 'walking backward' suggests one who frequently looked in a different direction, stumbling in the process and possibly bumping into other people. Newman was very much aware of his failings and imperfections; his advice to others 'let us not be content with ourselves... let us look out for a better country, that is, a heavenly [PS viii, 242]' was ever directed towards himself. In other words, he endeavoured to practise what he so eloquently preached. He continued striving after God, 'one step' at a time, without necessarily seeing 'the distant scene'. When, in *The Dream of Gerontius* (1865) his imagination roams further, describing a spirit who flies after death towards the feet of the Crucified but who is then 'seized, and scorched, and shrivelled', 'consumed, yet quickened, by the glance of God', we surely sense the author's own feeling of deep unworthiness. In a letter to a convert (Miss Munro) he stressed that there was nothing saintly about himself:

I may have a high view of many things, but it is the consequence of education and of a peculiar cast of intellect – but this is very different from being what I admire... It is enough for me to black the saints' shoes – if St Philip uses blacking, in heaven.

There are some other letters, out of the vast collection that still remains, in which certain obvious failings can be glimpsed: at times he could be prickly, stubborn, and too quick to take offence. He was, we discover, never reconciled to his brothers Frank (who had leanings towards Unitarianism) and Charles (an unbeliever, with a fondness for drink). He made enemies of both his fellow converts F.W. Faber and Henry Manning.

Nevertheless, it remains true that he inspired holiness in others, and that may well be our better guide to his sanctity.

> True religion is a hidden life in the heart; and though it cannot exist without deeds, yet these are for the most part secret deeds, secret charities, secret prayers, secret self-denials, secret struggles, secret victories... Though we have seldom means of knowing at the time who are God's own Saints, yet after all is over we have; and then on looking back on what is past, perhaps after they are dead and gone, if we knew them, we may ask ourselves what power they had over us, whether they attracted us, influenced us, humbled us, whether they made our hearts burn within us. [PS ii, 241]

For Newman, sanctity lay not in any extraordinary or heroic service, but in continuing to perform the ordinary duties of the day well – often what the world might reckon as 'petty actions' such as succouring the distressed, bearing with the froward, and enduring ingratitude [PS vi, 324]. True to his own teaching, he declined to spend his final years living in favoured apartments in Rome. He preferred a shabbier and quieter existence in Birmingham, closer to the people for whom he cared most and conformed in spirit to the One who 'would now be called with contempt a vagrant' [PS vi, 45]. He also, it should not be forgotten, preferred 'English habits of belief and devotion to foreign' [Diff ii, 21]. Indeed, there is a fulsome expression of gratitude in the *Apologia* to Pius IX for giving the English a Church of their own, by which he meant much more than a restored hierarchy, namely, 'our own habits of mind, our own manner of reasoning, our own tastes, and our own virtues, finding a place and thereby a sanctification, in the Catholic Church' [Apol 299]. His own role in this is not mentioned here, but was certainly appreciated in his obituary in *The Tablet*:

> He has clothed Catholic philosophy and Catholic doctrine with a familiar garb, and set them both to the large music of our English speech.

He died on 11th August 1890. Owen Chadwick noted:

Vanity Fair, 1877

144

On the pall at his funeral he had his cardinal's motto, cor ad cor loquitur (heart speaks to heart). And on the memorial tablet, by his request, were the perfectly fitting words, ex umbris et imaginibus in veritatem; that is, coming out of the shadows and the reflections into the truth.

Newman's writings

Apol Apologia Pro Vita Sua (1864)

Arians The Arians of the Fourth Century (1833)

Consult On Consulting the Faithful in Matters of Doctrine (1859)

Dev Essay on the Development of Christian Doctrine (1845)

Diff Difficulties felt by Anglicans in Catholic Teaching (1850)

GA Essay in Aid of a Grammar of Assent (1870)

Idea The Idea of a University (1851)

Letters The Letters and Diaries of John Henry Newman

PS Parochial and Plain Sermons

Tamworth Tamworth Reading Room [Letters to The Times] (1841)

Via Media The Via Media of the Anglican Church (1833-1841)

Missionaries beyond the bounds

SPREADING THE CHRISTIAN FAITH IN AFRICA

Early expansion

Three particular Africans are mentioned in the New Testament. In each of the Synoptic Gospels, **Simon of Cyrene** is listed as the man compelled by the Romans to carry the cross of Jesus as he was taken out to be crucified:

And as they came out, they found a man of Cyrene, Simon by name: him they compelled to bear his cross.

His home town Cyrene was located in Libya. It was then a Greek colony, but had a Jewish community where 100,000 Judean Jews had been forced to settle during the reign of Ptolemy Soter (323–285 BC). No doubt Simon was in Jerusalem as a Jew intent upon observing the festival of Passover; the Cyrenian Jews actually had their own synagogue there where many went for the annual feasts. Since Simon's sons Rufus and Alexander are specifically mentioned by name in Mark 15.21, it is considered likely that they were well-known to the early Christian community in Rome, for whom Mark's Gospel may originally have been compiled – sometime after Peter's martyrdom in the 60s AD? There was certainly a Rufus in Rome when Paul addressed his letter to the Christians there; he is described as 'eminent in the Lord'. Tradition claims that Simon's sons became missionaries, perhaps linking them (or alternatively Simon himself) with the 'men of Cyrene' who preached the Gospel to the Greeks in Antioch [Acts 11:20].

Another African resident, about whom rather more information is supplied in the book of Acts, is the one-time Alexandrian Jew **Apollos**. He may certainly be described as a missionary:

Now a Jew named Apol'los, a native of Alexandria, came to Ephesus. He was an eloquent man, well versed in the scriptures. He had been instructed in the way of the Lord; and being fervent in spirit, he spoke and taught accurately the things concerning Jesus, though he knew only the baptism of John. He began to speak boldly in the synagogue; but when Priscilla and Aq'uila heard him, they took him and expounded to him the way of God more accurately. And when he wished to cross to Acha'ia, the brethren encouraged him, and wrote to the disciples to receive him. When he arrived, he greatly helped those who through grace had believed, for he powerfully confuted the Jews in public, showing by the scriptures that the Christ was Jesus. [Acts 18.24-28]

The third African to whom reference is made [Acts 8.26-40] is the Jew evangelised by Philip on 'the road that goes down from Jerusalem to Gaza'. His name is not given, but he is described as '**an Ethiopian, a eunuch**, a minister of the Candace, queen of the Ethiopians, in charge of all her treasure.' He had 'come to Jerusalem to worship', and was on his return journey. After his baptism, he saw Philip no more, but 'went on his way rejoicing.' Today he would be called a 'Cushite', from the land of Cush (to the south of Egypt) which might well be reckoned as Lower Nubia, where the Candace (sometimes spelt with a K) was a recognised figure. Given that Jeremiah once posed the question, 'Can the Ethiopian change his skin or the leopard his spots?' [Jer 13.23], it seems likely that Cushites were of a darker skin than Israelites: this was perhaps one of the reasons why Miriam and Aaron once had criticised Moses for marrying a Cushite woman. We may surmise that, apart from those who were ethnic Jews, one of the first to be converted to the Christian faith was a black African. In later legend he is joined by one of the *magi*: 'Balthasar', as he came to be known in the Middle Ages, was increasingly depicted as an African.

The Adoration of the Magi (El Greco 1568)

It is perhaps not entirely a coincidence that Cyrene, Alexandria and 'Ethiopia' (meaning the lands to the south of Egypt) were precisely those parts of Africa where the Church took root early on. Coptic Christians herald St Mark as their apostle. Whatever the truth of this, there was certainly a powerful appeal of the gospel to those in Egypt who suffered under harsh Roman rule at that time. From the late 2nd century it was here in Egypt and also in North Africa (which once served as the bread basket of Rome) that the Church saw outstanding teachers of the faith emerge, such as Clement of Alexandria, Tertullian, Cyprian and Augustine. Again, it was in Egypt during the late 3rd century that St Antony laid the foundations of Christian monasticism in his desert retreats, followed by the more communal arrangements of St Pachomius.

Broadly speaking though, the teachings and practices of the early African Fathers were linked much more closely with the Mediterranean world, and with their Graeco-Roman inheritance, than with the so-called primal religion and culture more commonly associated with their own continent. Yet there were such developments in the kingdom of Ethiopia (rather than Cush, where the 'eunuch' mentioned above disappears from view) a little later. According to the late 4th century historian Rufinus, the Ethiopian Church dates its origin to an incident at a Red Sea port when two Syrian brothers on a voyage with their uncle were captured as slaves and taken to the court in Axum. Here they won considerable favour, and in time were able to meet with fellow Christian traders in the country, and indeed to effect a number of local conversions. One of the brothers, Frumentius, visited Alexandria and appealed to Athanasius for missionary support. The latter records that he ordained Frumentius himself to be the first *abuna* (bishop) for the kingdom, although the actual year (320s? 346?) remains uncertain. He was challenged to tailor some church practices to suit the Amharic culture; reports reached the Roman Emperor that he was overstepping the mark, but demands for him to be examined for doctrinal errors were resisted by his own king Ezana. Indeed, the ruling Aksumite elite insisted on appropriating key pre-Christian cultural motifs, not least in architectural expression and in the liturgical use of existing *stelae*.

4th cent Axumite coin

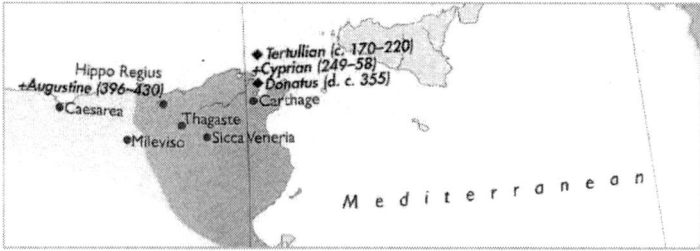

Early African theologians -
around Carthage (*above*) and Alexandria (*below*)

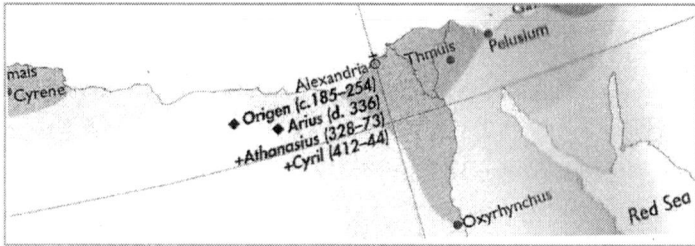

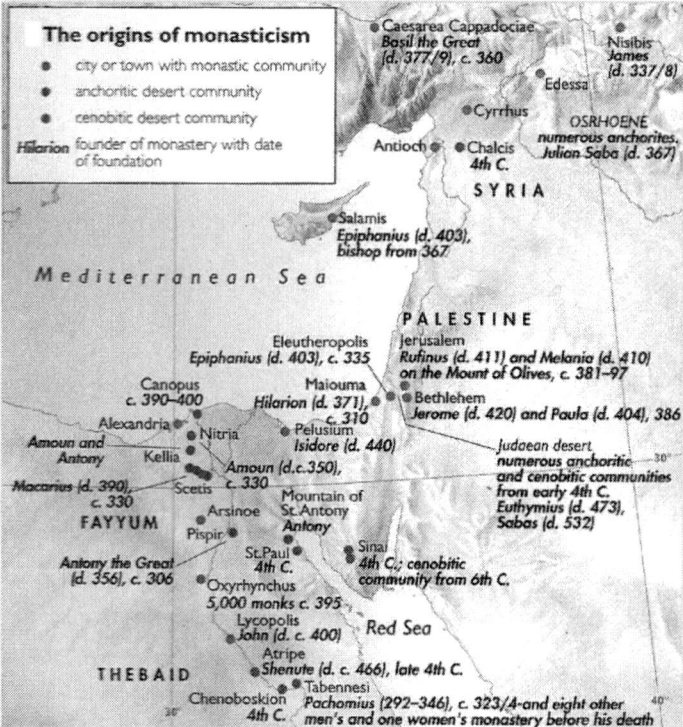

The origins of monasticism

● city or town with monastic community

● anchoritic desert community

● cenobitic desert community

Hilarion founder of monastery with date of foundation

It seems that the greatest development in this direction was made a couple of centuries later by the renowned St Yared, who introduced the use of drums, dancing and the *sistrum* or rattle, as well as encouraging healing ceremonies which invoked a host of saints and angels.

African Christianity under threat

Much later, when Islam spread westwards from the 7th century onwards, Christianity largely disappeared from Africa. Egypt fell to Muslim armies in 639, as did Carthage in 697, although some places retained their Christian identity until perhaps the 11th century or even later. It survived much longer in Egypt as the minority Coptic Church, probably because of its usefulness in providing professional, literary and commercial skills to the Muslim rulers. In the Nile Valley to the south, in Nubia and in Ethiopia it also escaped. Excavations in the former region have uncovered a number of medieval churches and monasteries, although these show a gradual weakening of Coptic and Byzantine influence: the archaeologist David Edwards has noted that in many places 'pagan forms of burial survive until very late, indicating an extremely patchy uptake of Christianity, or unusual syncretistic practices at work'. After the early 16th century, however, little remained of Nubian Christianity except 'some archaic folk customs among the now Muslim peasantry', such as the use of crosses to ward off sickness.

However, because of its relative isolation (and perhaps also because of its legendary hospitality to Muslim refugees when Muhammad was still in Mecca), the Ethiopian Orthodox Church has continued intact from the 4th century until the present day. Its greatest threat occurred in the 16th century when European support was sought against violent Muslim incursions. The four hundred Portuguese musketeers who were sent certainly helped the Christian kingdom to survive; yet they also paved the way for a Jesuit missionary presence, which proved to be a mixed blessing. Initially, the Jesuits were sympathetic to local customs; but when the Portuguese Alphonsus Mendez became *abuna*, his attempts to reform the Ethiopian Church to bring it into line with Roman Catholic theology and practice caused the country to erupt. The Jesuits were eventually expelled in 1632. Questions about reconciling indigenous culture and existing religious practice with those of the universal Church were thus left unresolved.

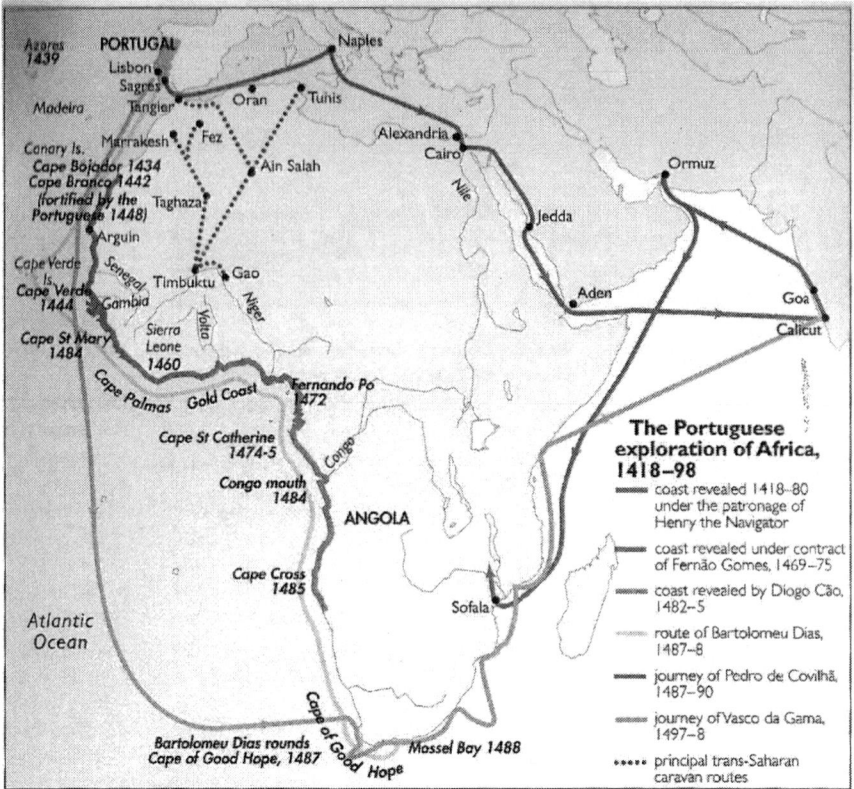

The Portuguese exploration of Africa, 1418–98

- coast revealed 1418–80 under the patronage of Henry the Navigator
- coast revealed under contract of Fernão Gomes, 1469–75
- coast revealed by Diogo Cão, 1482–5
- route of Bartolomeu Dias, 1487–8
- journey of Pedro de Covilhã, 1487–90
- journey of Vasco da Gama, 1497–8
- principal trans-Saharan caravan routes

Map labels: Azores 1439; PORTUGAL; Lisbon; Sagres; Madeira; Tangier; Oran; Naples; Tunis; Marrakesh; Fez; Ain Salah; Alexandria; Cairo; Ormuz; Canary Is.; Cape Bojador 1434; Cape Branco 1442 (fortified by the Portuguese 1448); Taghaza; Jedda; Arguin; Cape Verde Is.; Cape Verde 1444; Gambia; Senegal; Timbuktu; Gao; Niger; Aden; Goa; Calicut; Cape St Mary 1484; Sierra Leone 1460; Volta; Cape Palmas; Gold Coast; Fernando Pó 1472; Cape St Catherine 1474-5; Congo mouth 1484; Congo; ANGOLA; Sofala; Atlantic Ocean; Cape Cross 1485; Bartolomeu Dias rounds Cape of Good Hope, 1487; Cape of Good Hope; Mossel Bay 1488; Nile

A new phase of exposure to Christianity had in fact already begun in the 15th century with the establishment of various Portuguese trading posts. They had a foothold in Morocco by 1415, the Gold Coast in 1481, and Portuguese East Africa (Mozambique) and Zanzibar in 1498. On the east coast they were drawn up the Zambezi River by news of Mwenemutapa, a ruler reputed to have fabulous wealth in gold. In their efforts to locate him, the Portuguese established two settlements in 1531 far up the Zambezi – at Sena and even further inland at Tete, some 260 miles from the sea. Yet although the Jesuit Gonzalo de Silveira reached Mwenemutapa's court at Kalanga (in present day Zimbabwe) in 1560, he was soon exposed and put to death. Further initiatives were made by Dominican priests as well, and in the 1620s the reigning Mutapa was actually baptised along with his queen. But in general the Christian 'community' extended little beyond the Portuguese traders and their dependents. This is borne out by excavations at the one-time church of Dambarare (west of Harare), where buried remains of young white males were found within the building, with African females and some of mixed race outside. Contacts with the local population were evidently sporadic, and even such tentative missionary activity petered out by the 18th century, following a period of considerable unrest in the 1690s.

Of particular interest though is the evangelisation undertaken by secular priests from Portugal further south in the kingdom of Kongo (modern Angola) in the last decade or so of that century: a formal see was established in 1596. Initially the secular priests were sympathetic to indigenous traditions, and gained the support of visiting priests and their superiors in Rome. The subsequent Jesuit incursion in the mid 16th century failed as in Ethiopia, since by this time the local rulers were in control of church developments. However, in 1706 a local prophetess, Kimpa Vita, known also as Donna Beatrice, was put to death following demands by Capuchin missionaries. They were understandably critical of her claim to have received a vision from St Antony (of Padua) in which she was warned that the colonial churches were in error and that Jesus himself was a black Kongolese. As attitudes hardened, 'what had been considered orthodox before', writes Aylward Shorter, were now seen as 'no more than interesting and unedifying survivals'. Although the Catholic presence regained more customary forms, Donna Beatrice's popular following never died away, and is regarded by many as the forerunner of the modern African Instituted Churches.

Expeditions to the more remote African interior elsewhere were for centuries quite rare, other than the trading caravans which crossed North Africa to reach destinations such as Timbuktu. What sometimes drew the Portuguese further inland was their search for trading opportunities, for mineral wealth and, no doubt, more slaves captured in the ever-recurrent inter-tribal warfare. The 17th century saw a mini-scramble for these African spoils as British, Danish, Dutch and French coastal forts were also established. Chaplaincies for the most part looked after the spiritual welfare of European soldiers and traders, and only to a limited degree (for example, up the Zambezi) engaged in local outreach. There is little evidence of any attempts at engaging creatively with the prevailing culture, beyond the ordination of a few Africans as priests or ministers. An obvious failing was the apparent lack of willingness among the clergy to learn the local language. Nor were there any statements of official policy corresponding to those that accompanied the more considerable work in Asia, such as the landmark instruction of 1659 from the Sacred Congregation de Propagande Fide which urged the Vicars Apostolic of Tonkin and Cochinchina:

Do not in any way attempt, and do not on any pretext persuade these people to change their rites, habits and customs, unless they are openly opposed to religion and good morals... It is not your country but your faith you must bring.

New missionary initiatives in Africa

Nevertheless, later in the following century there were significant developments in Africa. For one thing, the tide was turning against the slave trade (eventually outlawed in Britain in 1807, but persisting in many places until the present day); for another, a variety of European missionary agencies were formed with a view to evangelising the native populations, initially in regions bordering the coast such as (in modern terms) Ghana, Sierra Leone, Congo and the Cape, but progressively further inland. Whereas the Portuguese presence had been exclusively Catholic, these new missions were often from different Protestant churches (Moravian, Calvinist, Baptist, Presbyterian, Anglican...) and worked on other continents as well. One of their fundamental failings was therefore to export divisions between European-based denominations much further afield (incidentally lending themselves open to exploitation by canny local rulers, such as the Kabaka of Buganda who agreed to receive Bible lessons from whoever would provide him with gunpowder). Even the Church of England shares some responsibility for the disunity thus sown: SPG (the Society for the Propagation of the Gospel, founded by the Revd Thomas Bray in 1701) and CMS (Church Mission Society, originally *The Society for Missions to Africa and the East*, founded by active evangelical Christians in 1799) were principal representatives of different Anglican parties, resulting in overseas missions with the theological ethos of their parent body. (In modern terms, this might be seen as a global variation on the 'post-code lottery' that affects some public services in Britain today. In terms of the Anglican Communion, it is a significant factor in its current de facto schism.)

The Christian 'scramble for Africa' was firmly under way by the mid 19th century. It is of course too vast and complex a subject to be dealt with adequately here, hence my focus will be on just two important contributors to the mission enterprise. As it happens they were both born within a year of each other, just over two hundred years ago: **David Livingstone**, considered usually as a Scottish Presbyterian, renowned as an explorer; and **John Colenso**, from the Church of England, a controversial bishop of Natal. Both of them had the interests of the

African at the heart of what they did, and inevitably incurred much criticism from authorities back in Britain. For example, as we shall see, Livingstone had so many varied encounters with the slave trade (which on the east coast of Africa had been little affected by the eradication of trans-Atlantic trafficking) that he realised how essential it was for this evil to be rooted out, and therefore that legitimate commerce to replace it must accompany any realistic programme of evangelisation. This was not an entirely new idea, having already been suggested by anti-slave campaigners such as Fowell Buxton (William Wilberforce's successor), but the discovery of possible trade routes into interior regions of Africa now seemed to make its implementation feasible. However, it turned the apparently straightforward task of mission into an altogether more complex matter in which Livingstone's enthusiasm in the end outstripped his judgment. Colenso, a man schooled in the rigorous logic of the Cambridge mathematics tripos, found aspects of the prevailing biblical hermeneutic not only personally inadequate but unconvincing for his Zulu congregations. He also found the disrespectful and sometimes underhand way in which they were treated quite abhorrent, and stood up for their cause against colonial officials. Consequently, he had to fight battles on the home front too. He was not, however, always as diplomatic in maintaining his own cause as he might have been.

Opening up the interior

In the year 1800 there were very few Christians in the whole of Africa, certainly compared with the millions who were Muslims, particularly in the north. The situation was much changed a hundred years later, thanks to the very considerable missionary efforts, mainly in the second half of the 19th century: in 1900 it is estimated that there were by then 8.7 million Christians as against 34.5 million Muslims. Today's churches have now well surpassed the Muslim total (estimates suggest that in the year 2000 there were over 500 million Christians compared with perhaps 350 million Muslims), although head counts do not necessarily tell us much about the quality of Christian commitment. In many churches – not least the African Initiated Churches – syncretistic ideas are frequently found, just as in Britain personal beliefs may often depart significantly from what is upheld as orthodox teaching.

It is important to remember that the seeds of faith take time to root themselves, and even then grow unevenly. Certainly this was **David Livingstone**'s own experience. A brief survey of his upbringing and early life may be helpful in setting the scene for his future calling. He was born in 1813 in Blantyre (later appropriated as the name of the main commercial town in Malawi) and was initially taught to read and write by his father Neil, a commercial traveller. At the age of ten he started work in a local cotton mill, which provided two hours of schooling for youngsters like himself at the close of the working day. In addition, he bought himself a Latin grammar which he was able to study in spare moments. His real inspiration, though, came when he was turned twenty: his father, who belonged to the local Congregational church, brought home a pamphlet written by a missionary in China, which encouraged young men to become medical missionaries there. Almost at once David started saving enough money to pay the entry fee to Anderson's College, Glasgow, a few miles from his home. He began studying medicine there in 1836. After two years he offered his services to the London Missionary Society (LMS), which was not aligned strongly with any denomination. They arranged for him to undergo training at their Essex college, and then paid for a final year of medical studies in London.

After passing his exams in Glasgow and thus gaining his medical degree, his plan to serve in China was frustrated by the outbreak of war there. Instead LMS sent him to South Africa where he arrived at Simon's Bay in March 1841 just before his 28th birthday. His destination, which he reached by ox wagon the following July, was Robert Moffat's mission station several hundred miles inland at Kuruman. He had met Moffat in London prior to his voyage.

Here Livingstone experienced his first shock. Moffat, a fellow Scot from a similar background (although with Methodist sympathies), had been living in Kuruman for nearly twenty years, and yet had only forty converts to his credit. He approved of Moffat's linguistic efforts, such as his continuing work of translating the Bible into Setswana, but otherwise found little to inspire him:

There is a lamentable deadness prevailing in the whole of this field – there are no conversions, the only work proceeding with anything like briskness is translation of the Bible into the language of the people.

The one thing Livingstone felt he could do was to apply himself to getting a better grasp of the language (which he had already started to learn on the boat). After falling out with an English companion and taking local Tswanas with him instead, he travelled further north on different occasions to immerse himself in the local scene and to scout out possible sites for future mission stations. The fact that Moffat himself had made such excursions and had sent written reports to the Royal Geographical Society may also have suggested their usefulness in arousing interest and support back in Britain. Several years later, in 1847, he wrote to the 'foreign secretary' of LMS that a missionary's role was not to stay labouring in a single place (like Moffat), but – having planted a new congregation – to let them have their own African pastor and to continue outreach elsewhere:

> An onward movement ought to be made, whether men will hear or they will forebear.

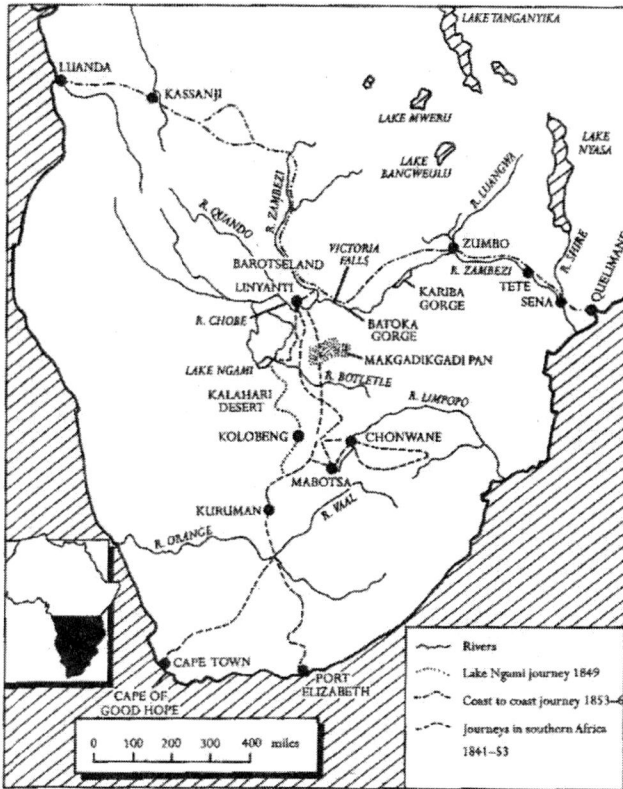

Livingstone's journeys 1841-1856

On an early expedition to Mabotsa, Livingstone was attacked by a lion and suffered severe damage to his left arm. It was Moffat's eldest daughter Mary who then nursed him in Kuruman for several months. They were eventually married, and settled first at Chonwane but (after a water shortage there) moved to Kolobeng where they stayed for four years. Here Livingstone made his one and only conversion, of Sechele the local chief, who was baptised in 1848. However, although Sechele had promised to retain only one of his wives, he subsequently backtracked, much to Livingstone's disappointment.

His lack of missionary success began to suggest other plans to him: as he discovered more about the prevalence of slave-trading, the urgent need to supplant it with a stable commerce in agricultural output as well as in mining came to be seen as a necessary foundation for the growth of a Christian society. Such legitimate commerce could only flourish, however, if there were viable trade routes – and in the 1850s his missionary enthusiasm, which never waned, turned his attention to exploring how effectively the interior wealth of Africa could be bartered with the outside world in exchange for the blessings of Christianity.

This implied the need for 'travel and research' as a necessary prelude to the advance of the Gospel, but of course it was not an idea that commended itself easily to the London Missionary Society, who were paying Livingstone a salary of £100 per annum to fulfil more conventional expectations. In the plan he submitted to them, he suggested that cash crops such as cotton (recalling his own youthful employment) might be pioneered in a suitable location, if such could be found. An opportunity to explore further afield arose in 1849 when he joined a shooting party who were visiting from India in search of large game. He became more aware as a result that the booming European market for ivory was a significant factor in the slave trade, relying as it did upon cheap transportation of the tusks. The trip's high point for him was the discovery of Lake Ngami to the far north of Kolokeng: he wrote a report of their journey to LMS, as a result of which it was passed to the Royal Geographical Society who awarded him their gold medal.

Lake Ngami had been the furthest limit of exploration on that trip: without a boat, the party could travel no further. So far all Livingstone's African journeys had been by means of ox wagons or on foot, but at this point his interest turned to river navigation. He therefore went north a couple more times to explore the upper reaches and tributaries of the Zambezi. His family accompanied him, with unfortunate consequences such as malaria and the birth in a remote spot of yet another child. It became clear to him that he was placing too many demands upon Mary and the children, who were sent back in 1852 to Scotland to live with his parents – not to be met again until four years later. He also appreciated the need for better protection against malaria, and after experimenting with quinine developed his own prophylactic pill. With some financial support from one of the earlier shooting party and on two years' paid leave from LMS he was now able to explore more freely, and managed to travel north-westwards from Linyanti, reaching the coast at Luanda in May 1854. The British commissioner there took care of him for over three months while he recovered from fever and then made preparations to return to Linyanti in the hope of following the Zambezi on foot all the way eastwards to the coast. A year later he reached the falls that he named after Queen Victoria: 'scenes so lovely,' he wrote, 'must have been gazed upon by angels in their flight.' He left the river for some time now while searching the territory northwards for possible sites of a mission station, high enough to be largely free of malaria. He did the same lower down the Zambezi's course on subsequent occasions too, but this was to prove a costly mistake: he eventually reached Quelimane not far from the river's estuary in May 1856 unaware of having bypassed several unnavigable rapids.

His aim was now to return to England, where he would make his discoveries known and gain support for a boat to return upstream to the very heart of Africa, thereby demonstrating the viability of the plans that he had nurtured for a number of years. Although he was in receipt of a letter from the London Missionary Society rejecting the idea of a new mission station so far inland, he was encouraged both that a naval ship was awaiting him at Quelimane with supplies and that the Royal Geographical Society was pleased with his earlier crossing to Luanda – as yet they were ignorant of his successful transcontinental crossing. On arrival in London the following December he was presented by the RGS with their Victoria Medal, and the next month commenced writing up his journeys. *Missionary Travels and Researches in South Africa* was completed in the middle of 1857, and was a huge publishing success that November. Just before its publication he finally parted company from LMS (although not from their missionaries in southern Africa) as he now had the assurance of government support for his future projects. Both he and the government were no doubt encouraged by the huge popular success of his lecture tour around the country. This included his famous speech in the Senate House in Cambridge on 4th December which ended with his much-quoted final plea:

I beg to direct your attention to Africa. I know that in a few years I shall be cut off in that country, which is now open; do not let it be shut again! I go back to Africa to try to make an open path for commerce and Christianity; do you carry out the work which I have begun. I leave it with you.

In fact, Livingstone's new appointment was announced in the House of Commons on 11th December 1857. For a six year period, starting on 22nd February 1858, he was to be a 'roving consul' in the region of the Zambezi River. This at once caused a diplomatic storm with the Portuguese; the outcome was to limit his authority largely to Quelimane and to the interior area beyond their control known as Barotseland, where he now aspired to settle. He had pondered the nature of his mission, and in his Travels had approved St Boniface's policy in 8th century Germany: as he understood it, his mission there had been effective through the various monastic communities that he planted. They cared for the poor, they ran schools, and they introduced new farming practices – all of which resonated with Livingstone's own ideas. At last he was ready to put them to the test in Barotseland: armed with a £5000 vote in Parliament for his expedition, he set about recruiting colleagues. Apart from his wife Mary, he included a naval officer, a doctor who was also a botanist, a photographer, a geologist, an artist, an engineer. As he explained in a letter to one of them:

It may be hoped that by encouraging the natives to occupy themselves in the development of the resources of their country a considerable advance will be made towards the extinction of the slave trade, as the natives will not be long in discovering that the former will eventually become a more certain source of profit than the latter.

In his own dealings with these 'natives' he had always been sensitive and forbearing, and he enjoined his new colleagues to act likewise. Those in positions of authority should, he wrote, always be treated with great respect. In fact, Livingstone's Achilles heel proved to be his frequent failure to apply the same standards to his relationships with European colleagues (three of whom he eventually sacked).

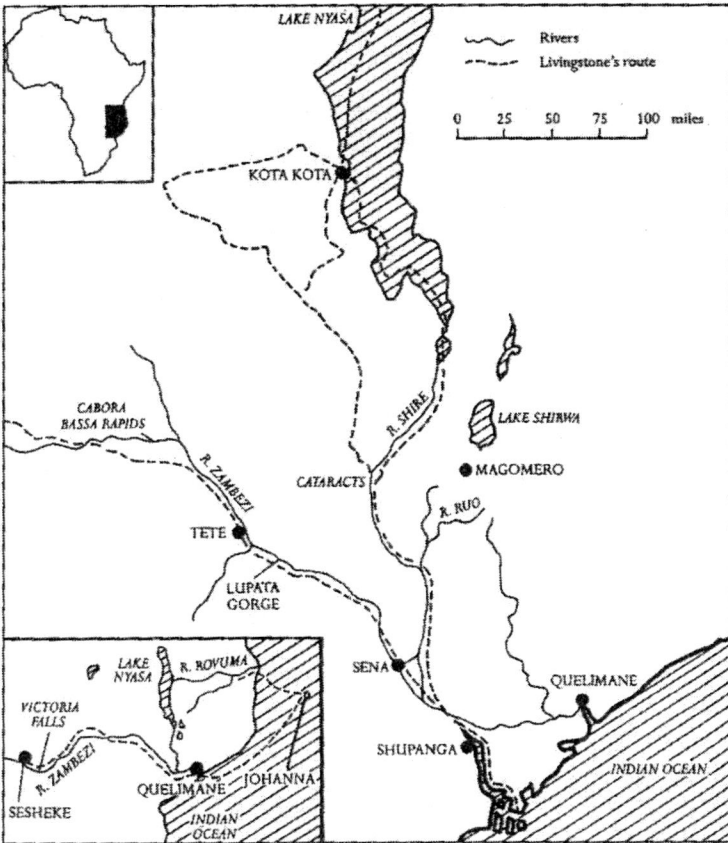

Livingstone's Zambezi and Shire expeditions of 1858-63

After navigating the Zambezi for about forty miles, it was found impossible to take the larger vessel in which they had sailed from Birkenhead any further; so Livingstone's steam launch, the *Ma Robert* (named after Mary, known to Africans as 'mother of her firstborn Robert') was reassembled and, along with smaller boats, loaded with expedition's equipment and stores. Although with some difficulty the party then reached Tete on 8th September 1858, two months later they encountered the Cabora Bassa (or Kabrabasa) rapids which Livingstone had bypassed on his historic trek eastwards. It immediately became clear that any hopes of settling in Barotseland had to be abandoned.

The impassible Cabora Bassa rapids
(Thomas Baines, completed 1859)

The Victoria Falls
(Thomas Baines, 1862)

Dr John Kirk, who was also with Livingstone on the Zambezi, commented:

Mr Baines has given actual views, and has so scrupulously adhered to nature, that anyone familiar with the vegetation may name the very plants represented in his paintings.

The *Ma Robert* on the Zambezi
(painted by Thomas Baines shortly after her launch in May 1858)

The party therefore turned back, and undaunted looked to an alternative possibility about which Livingstone had heard two years earlier. Lower down its course the Zambezi was fed by a broad river, the Shire, which apparently had its source in a large inland lake. Perhaps this would be more navigable, at least as far as a healthy location where the project could be re-sited? A smaller group set out to reconnoitre the prospects. After two hundred miles travelling up the Shire they reached once again an impasse of cataracts (some miles below the present city of Blantyre), so resolved to prepare for an expedition continuing from this point on foot. They returned to the cataracts before the end of August 1859, and three weeks later had 'discovered' Lake Nyasa (in fact, the Portuguese had been here earlier): 'Nyasa', it may be observed, is an African word meaning 'lake'.

It transpired that this whole region was rife with parties of slaves being transported to Zanzibar via various coastal ports such as Kilwa.

Such scenes rekindled Livingstone's determination to root out the trade, which he could now see required strong measures.

Livingstone was offered three small black girls for a shilling each

He appealed to Henry Venn, the CMS Secretary, for a new Church of England mission, and ploughed ahead by ordering two more steamers, one for the Zambezi itself, and the other which – after reassembling – could operate on Lake Nyasa. While he waited for them to be delivered, he headed over to Barotseland to return some of his native helpers to their homes as well as to meet LMS missionaries relocating northwards to Linyanti on the Upper Zambezi; they alas suffered serious losses from malaria just before he reached them. When his party were back in Tete again, letters awaited him with the news that missionaries were already travelling from the Cape to set up a new station in the region of the Shire. He hastened to meet them at the Kongone mouth of the Zambezi during the first week of February 1861.

Universities Mission to Central Africa (UMCA)

This development was one of the fruits of Livingstone's time in Britain, not least of his 1857 speeches both in Cambridge and in Oxford which generated much enthusiasm and energy to 'carry on the work' he had outlined. The universities of Durham and Dublin responded to invitations from Oxford and Cambridge to join them, and so the Central African Mission was born. Those who arrived early in 1861 on two different battle-cruisers numbered seven in all: Charles Frederick Mackenzie, previously archdeacon to Bishop Colenso of Natal, but recently ordained

164

'Bishop of the Mission to tribes dwelling in the neighbourhood of Lake Nyasa and the River Shire' by Bishop Gray of Cape Town; Deacon Henry Rowley; Rev Lovell Proctor; Rev H.C. Scudamore; Horace Waller (a lay missionary); plus S.A. Gamble (a carpenter) and Alfred Adams (agricultural worker). A further few were expected within a couple of months or so. The vanguard was welcomed by Livingstone himself, his brother Charles and John Kirk, the expedition's doctor. Even though the newcomers professed a different churchmanship, Livingstone regarded the advance of the Christian faith as far more important than what for him were minor theological disagreements.

Yet almost at once an argument developed over a proposed change of plans. Livingstone was ever wary of Portuguese interference and had noted new forts at the Kongone; so he now aimed to reach the Upper Shire plateau by a different route, if it proved possible. His idea was to use the Rovuma river which rises to the east of Lake Nyasa and flows thence towards the Indian Ocean. Despite the advice of the senior officer on the naval vessels that it was barely navigable, Livingstone insisted on exploring that option first. Mackenzie reluctantly gave way, not wishing to fall out with a more experienced traveller than himself. As predicted, however, it was a fruitless trip up the coast – they steamed up the Rovuma for a mere twenty-five miles before having to turn back. Nor did the reversion to the Shire river go according to plan: their boat, the *Pioneer*, had to leave many supplies behind in an old hulk; its stock of coal was by now inadequate to complete the journey, and much time was spent cutting a daily ration of wood for fuel; the water level was lower than on Livingstone's previous trip and the sandbanks were therefore much more of an obstacle. So, instead of reaching their intended mooring at Chibisa's before the end of March, as Mackenzie had been advised, it actually took until 8th July 1861.

Here further decisions had to be made: Chibisa himself was absent, but a delegation of Mang'anja had arrived seeking his help against the Yao, claiming that the latter had been armed by the Portuguese and were steadily enslaving their people. How much support Mackenzie should lend them was the first question; the second, in the face of such obvious security threats, was where they should settle themselves. Livingstone was never one for engaging in local disputes, but felt that guns were needed for self-protection; and further, that a reasonably defensible site must be found for the mission. Mackenzie had not previously had to take such precautions; as a man of God his instinct was against bearing arms, and certainly against using any, but the strong views of others in the party

165

brought him to acquiesce. Leaving Rowley, Gamble and Adams behind at Chibisa's to build huts for future storage purposes, the main party continued their journey on 15th July. They carried supplies to last at least six weeks, and reached what Mackenzie considered a fine location 3000 feet higher up the next day. Shortly afterwards they encountered a caravan of eighty-four slaves being driven along and lost little time in cutting them free of their bonds and yokes. While Livingstone regarded this as a necessary duty, others were aroused and readied themselves for more such engagements, using any necessary force.

A few days' further march brought them to Magomero, which Livingstone had to persuade Mackenzie was an ideal place to settle because a steep-sided river looped round it on three sides. The local chief Chigunda welcomed them, seeing their presence as an extra defence against Yao attackers. Other local chiefs had differing views, but Livingstone was as ever tactful in dealing with them. After only a few days he left the missionaries to establish themselves, and returned to the boat awaiting him at Chibisa's.

Magomero, as sketched in October 1861
The larger hut in the background was the 'Bishop's Palace',
completed in September.

Much trouble now lay ahead for the missionaries. They held an important discussion after their Sunday service on 11th August as to their relationship with the Mang'anja people vis-à-vis the Yao. The unanimous conclusion was that they now owed them a duty of support, provided that

166

the Mang'anja swore an oath not to take any slaves themselves. Having confirmed this with local chiefs the next day, Mackenzie then went to the nearest Yao leaders to talk peace with them. He and his three colleagues went unarmed, with Mang'anja forces poised not far away if trouble should arise. Their overture being rejected, a brief battle ensued, which proved costly to Mackenzie himself. The Yao were defeated, but Mackenzie had retrieved his gun – and had fired it 'to the best of my skill': he added in his defence that his action was undertaken after 'some deliberation ... I do not doubt now that it was right' – an opinion certainly not shared by many Victorian churchgoers back in Britain when they heard the news. There were subsequent engagements with the Yao, who were forced to abandon their slave-trading in the neighbourhood. Yet Mackenzie soon discovered that it was now the Mang'anja who were doing the same. Livingstone's parting advice proved much sounder than the 'deliberations' of those newly on the scene.

Work to establish the mission (which soon included a considerable number of freed slaves) continued apace. A surrounding stockade was erected fairly quickly, with huts then built for accommodation, plus two storehouses, a kitchen, a goat house, a hen house and chicken coop; a start was made on St Paul's church (which was never finished, eventually the same dedication being transferred to the cathedral in Blantyre); a simple school, together with a boys' dormitory, provided for three age-ranges plus daily classes for adults – about two dozen young Africans freed from slavery attended, one of whom (Chimwala) was considered as a potential future Christian leader. The missionaries themselves were also serious students, making determined efforts to learn the local language. However, they experienced great disappointment on discovering that in some respects they had been misled by Livingstone: his 'abundant' game was nowhere to be seen except much lower down in the Shire valley, nor was there any sign of cotton at this altitude (in later years coffee and tobacco plantations were to be found here). Mackenzie soon realised too that, in terms of agriculture, the Africans 'know far more about it than I do.'

Meanwhile, Livingstone had been exploring further north around Lake Nyasa, before sending the message on 12th November that he was back at Chibisa's about to return to the Zambezi mouth to welcome their next batch of missionaries. He admitted that the *Pioneer* drew too much water for much of the Shire River, hence he would bring the lady newcomers and the extra stores only as far as the confluence of the Shire with its tributary, the river Ruo – an estimated 130 miles trek from Magomero. Mackenzie immediately set off with Meller to catch Livingstone before he

167

sailed south, but to no avail: the plan remained, with 1st January agreed for the rendezvous. The one positive outcome of Mackenzie's forced march to Chibisa's (60+ miles in little more than a day) was his delight in finding Rev Henry Burrup newly arrived ahead of the other male recruits (Dickinson and Clark), having used his initiative to travel up from the coast. Fr Burrup (as he was known) was therefore back with them in Magomero on 19th November, his colleagues some ten days later.

The expedition to bring back the ladies (Mackenzie's sister Anne together with the recently wed Mrs Burrup) together with replenishment of their stores was led by Procter and Scudamore, who left on 2nd December. Given the strong disagreements over the advisability of bringing any women at all to a remote mission station, it can scarcely be termed a 'welcome' party: Mackenzie had, however, won the day by arguing that the men alone could scarcely minister effectively to the African women, and that both the example and instruction of Christian ladies would be badly needed. In the event it was not the ladies, but the various ensuing attempts to reach the mouth of the Ruo that met with disaster upon disaster. Sparing the details, the first expedition faced armed hostility and not all the party eventually staggered back to base. A second group led by Mackenzie himself set out on 23rd December, once again getting caught up in fighting and returning to Magomero. The third attempt was limited to Mackenzie and Burrup together with their African bearers, and this time took the safer route down to Chibisa's, reaching it after five days of pouring rain, continuing thence by canoe down to the Ruo. In the course of this two day journey, one of the canoes which carried their medical supplies capsized and for much of the trip in any case they were plagued by mosquitoes. They waited for Livingstone (whose *Pioneer* had made very slow progress heading downstream through the sandbanks) at an island village from 11th January for the rest of the month. Both Burrup and Mackenzie were now seriously ill with diarrhoea and fever, and on 31st January 1862 the latter died: Burrup buried him over on the mainland. He himself with the three bearers struggled against the current to paddle back to Chibisa's, but before reaching it had to get out and walk. Burrup was now so weak that he was finally carried on a crude stretcher up to Magomero. He was there for eight days before he too died on 22nd February 1862 and was then buried nearby.

Both these deaths occurred before the ladies reached Chibisa's on 4th March under the naval protection of one Commander Wilson, accompanied by Livingstone's colleague Dr Kirk. Here Kirk learnt of the problems of the past three months, including the news of Mackenzie's death, but not yet of Burrup's: hence the party, after making (what proved to be unnecessary) efforts to gain help for Magomero, in due course turned back to rejoin Livingstone on the Zambezi. The ladies then set sail back to the Cape. Meanwhile Livingstone remained on the river at Shupanga with his wife Mary, who had journeyed east with Miss Mackenzie and Mrs Burrup, determined to be no longer separated from her husband. Alas, she died of a fever on 27th April.

Although the UMCA mission struggled on a little longer, even moving back on 25th April to occupy a site close to Chibisa's, it remained there only for 15 months. A new bishop, William George Tozer, reached the Kongone on 8th May 1863 with a band of six more workers from England. He rapidly concluded that even Chibisa's was too far from the essential supply lines, and the mission then experimented with another of Livingstone's recommendations – Mount Morambula, just north of the Shire's junction with the Zambezi: 'Had it been English,' he claimed, 'we should have had a sanatorium, and possibly a college, on the mountain.' Unfortunately, though, – apart from being barren and marshy on top, and very often cold and covered in cloud – it was in Portuguese territory, which brought objections from some of Tozer's followers. Yet what concerned the new bishop above all was the fact that, apart from freeing quite a number of slaves and then looking after their welfare, very little had yet been attempted to teach the Christian religion to the Africans. He believed a new start was necessary elsewhere; even Mount Morambula might only be a temporary trial, given the very recent news of Livingstone's own recall by the Foreign Office – who by now regarded any Zambezi project as doomed to failure. Without Livingstone there would be far fewer naval vessels calling at the Kongone, hence the isolation would increase. So it was that, after starting to resettle on the mountain in August 1863, everything was dismantled by the following January 1864.

Livingstone, of course, had previously envisaged the possibility of reaching the interior by a more northern route (the Rovuma River). Although a second attempt (in September 1862) had confirmed its impracticability, the idea of skirting round Portuguese territory commended itself to Tozer, and with Captain Gardner's backing the mission transferred itself to Zanzibar, which was a busy hub for shipping, from April 1864. Ten years later, under Bishop Steere, it began to re-establish itself inland just east of 'Nyasaland' – today's Malawi. Indeed, in 1880 Likoma Island became the headquarters of the mission, with an impressive cathedral begun just over twenty years later.

Livingstone in 1864

Livingstone himself disappeared in 1866 searching for the source of the Nile, although five years later the American journalist Henry Morton Stanley found him and trumpeted his achievements in the media. After he died at Ilala (in Zambia) in 1873, there was a renewed surge of enthusiasm for missions in Africa – so that now a church flourishes even in Magomero, which would certainly rejoice the hearts of those who first sowed the faith there.

The cross remains to mark Fr Burrup's grave
Chiradzulu mountain can be seen in the background to the SW

In 2002-3 as parish priest of Zomba, I had charge of Magomero. The chapel seen here was built in 1980, but was now too small. Sitting on my left was Fr Brighton Malasa, a former student, who was looking after some of our two dozen outstations. He subsequently became Bishop of Upper Shire.

170

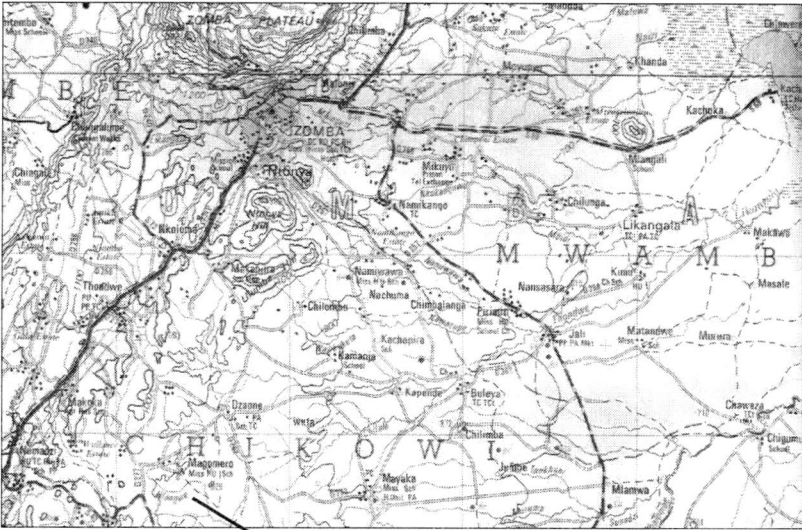

A recent map: Magomero lies about 6 miles south of Zomba

Unfinished business

Livingstone's passion was always to open up the interior of Africa to the Christian faith. It is obvious that he met with many unexpected difficulties and that his plans were not always well researched or well conceived. His greatest weakness was perhaps his failure to listen to criticisms or alternative suggestions from his English colleagues – whereas one of his real strengths was his ability to relate well to the Africans whom he encountered.

He was certainly right to identify slavery as a major problem that needed to be addressed, but it was so bound up with rivalry between local tribes, the competing European powers, and the economic interests of Arabs and others not even on the continent, that his simplistic solution focusing principally on trading alternatives ('commerce') was never likely to work. In fact, other missions arriving later in the region of Nyasaland found eventual acceptance for very different reasons (indeed, missiologists today would recognise many possible forms of apostolic engagement):

- Robert Laws, a Scottish Presbyterian who arrived in 1878, met with initial suspicion and hostility until in 1886 his prayers for rain were answered dramatically.
- The Catholic Montfort Fathers reached a village just south of Lake Nyasa in 1901, and unwittingly placed a medallion of Mary on an imposing baobab tree: this was well-received, being seen as an offering to the spirits of the land.
- Further south the White Fathers held a novena of prayer in 1913, a year of severe drought, which seemed to open the heavens. The local cult was thereby dealt a near death blow.
- Success was certainly more common wherever the missionaries learnt the local language and respected as much as possible of the local customs.
- The benefits of Western healthcare and the advantages of schooling also proved crucial factors, even if liable to store up problems for the future.

Although Livingstone was quite appalled on his later explorations further north to discover how ubiquitous slave-trading had become, it was actually his former colleague Dr John Kirk (with whom his relationship was particularly unstable) who only a short time after Livingstone's death brought an end to the principal slave market in Zanzibar. Unlike those who had failed before him, he was thoroughly versed in the intricate web of local interests and knew better than anyone how to deal diplomatically and effectively with the parties concerned. Above all, he managed to persuade them that they would prosper financially much better without reliance on an increasingly precarious slave trade. This did not end the trade elsewhere, but Kirk could reasonably claim that by the end of the 1870s little was left of it along his stretch of Africa's east coast.

In the campaign to eradicate the trade, credit must also be given to many other Christian initiatives elsewhere on the continent for playing their part. St Daniel Comboni was a younger Italian contemporary of Livingstone whose witness stands out. In the early 1860s he developed his ideas about missionary work, which were published as his *Plan for the rebirth of Africa*: 'Save Africa through Africa' was his particular slogan. He founded the Verona Fathers in 1867 in pursuit of this aim, together with an order of missionary sisters in 1872. He was appointed *Pro Vicar Apostolic* in the same year with responsibility for Sudan, Nubia and the region south of the great lakes. This brought him into direct touch with the slave trade that was still much in evidence in Sudan, and in the later 1870s he devoted much energy to mitigating its effects. He died all too soon in 1881.

Mention must be made too of the French bishop (Cardinal from 1882) Charles Lavigerie who was slightly older than Comboni, but who came to focus on similar problems. He became Archbishop of Algiers in 1868 just at the time of a great famine; his care for those who were orphaned soon preoccupied him, but his work was considered by the colonial authorities to threaten the *modus vivendi* with the majority Muslim population. Lavigerie made it clear, however, that he had come to serve the whole population of Algeria. In the same year he founded the Missionaries of Africa (known as the White Fathers) to extend his mission even further afield. They were joined the following year by the founding of the White Sisters. By 1874 there were missionaries in Tunis, Tripoli, East Africa and the Congo. In the 1880s they began to send him disturbing reports about the vicious trading in slaves, especially in the Sahel, including what is now known as South Sudan. This was brought to the attention of Pope Leo XIII, who charged Lavigerie with responsibility for raising awareness of it throughout Europe. Thus, the mantle of Livingstone fell upon him, and he campaigned vigorously and effectively against the slave trade in the years 1888-1889. He was able to narrate horrific details of the slave markets he had seen himself, the firing of entire villages in the search for slaves, and the deprivations that many of them suffered as a consequence. One particular response came in 1894 from an aristocratic Austrian lady, Mary Theresa Ledochowska, who then founded the Sisters of St Peter Claver to serve the African missions.

Despite their best efforts, and those of many others, slavery remains very much alive in the modern world – and continues indeed in the same East African regions – even though it is known under different terms such as 'human trafficking', 'hijacking refugees', or 'sexual exploitation'. A story worth remembering, however, is that of Josephine Bakhita, who at the age of six was taken from her village in Darfur, Sudan and was then enslaved in different households for the next eight years: yet, on being freed through the agency of an Italian diplomat, she became a Christian, was professed as a Verona sister, and in the year 2000 was canonised.

A mixed heritage

Daniel Comboni's slogan of the 1860s, 'Save Africa through Africans', was scarcely common currency at the time. In Livingstone's words of 1857, Africa needed 'those two pioneers of civilisation – Christianity and commerce', and although he himself focused on the latter two Cs, the catch phrase which dominated much future thinking was rather the three Cs. So Thomas Pakenham in his book *The Scramble for Africa* remarks of the Berlin Conference held in 1885:

> Berlin marked a turning point in the history of Africa and Europe. For the first time, great men like Bismark had linked their names at an international conference to Livingstone's lofty ideals: to introduce the '3Cs' – commerce, Christianity, civilisation – into the dark places of Africa.

Indeed, in 1873 the Vatican Congregation of Indulgences, supported by Pope Pius IX, took an equally bleak view of Africa, identifying black people as the cursed offspring of Ham, destined to be 'a slave of slaves' [Gen 9.25]:

> Let us pray for the most miserable Ethiopian peoples in Central africa, who form a tenth of humanity, so that God may take away from their hearts the curse of Ham and give them the blessings of Jesus Christ, our God and Lord.

In more extravagant language, the influential 19th century philosopher Georg Hegel had earlier described the Negro as exhibiting 'the natural man in his completely wild and untamed state', a view which seemed to harmonise with the evolutionary ideas popularised by Darwin in his writings from the late 1850s onwards. At least the Vatican prayer offered some hope of salvation from this primitive state.

Undoubtedly, the still flourishing slave trade, and the cruelty and inhumanity associated with it, gave Africans generally a very bad reputation elsewhere. The popular view in Europe was therefore their urgent need for 'civilisation'. There was, of course, undoubtedly far too much ignorance of the 'other' Africa to allow for a balanced appreciation at this time: there was as yet little awareness of her own ancient civilisations, or her artistic treasures, or the widespread 'primal' awareness of spiritual realities. Even so, one must question whether Europe was entirely up to the task she had set herself – how 'civilised' were the nations who now sought to convert others to their own beliefs and practices? For example, given that the enslaving of others was very much bound up with the rivalries between tribes, had Europe herself renounced her own national rivalries? – obviously not, when one considers the uncivilised savagery that broke out in the devastating wars of the 20th century.

Again, if one returns to the growth of commerce, so dear to Livingstone, did the European traders, settlers, and troops who smoothed its path invariably witness to the highest ideals of the Christian faith, or was this seen by them merely as the concern of pious do-gooders? Here we turn to look at the colonial activities in South Africa, where Mackenzie had his first experience of African life under his bishop, the controversial **John William Colenso** (who like him had been a student of mathematics at Cambridge). As time progressed, he found himself again and again defending the cause of the native African, whom he came to respect far more than some of his white compatriots.

Colenso became Bishop of Natal in 1853, only six years after Gray had been consecrated the first bishop (of Cape Town) for this expanding colony, which dated back officially to the treaty of Paris held in 1815. For twenty years before Gray took over, pastoral responsibility had rested with the Bishop of Calcutta. Several missionaries sent by SPG and SPCK had already served in the Cape since the early 1820s, and there Rev Fearon Fallows (yet another mathematician, who devoted his time to astronomy) reported in 1823 on their distinct lack of progress. He noted that the state of religion, 'if there be any', was low, with the exception of the Muslim faith which was rather more flourishing. Nonconformist missionaries were also present, but Fallows assessed their efforts as largely fruitless. The religious prospects in Natal thirty years later were evidently not much better, and the political situation looked unstable, with racial tensions and economic difficulties.

Before leaving for South Africa, Colenso spent several weeks improving his medical knowledge at the recently opened missionary college of St Augustine in Canterbury, before his consecration on 30th November. He sailed from Plymouth on 15th December and reached Durban (founded in 1835) on 30th January 1854. He found there an unfinished St Paul's church, with a colonial chaplain who ministered to the white settlers who numbered about 1200. His aim was to visit Natal (a British colony since 1845) as thoroughly as possible before returning to

England in mid 1854 to raise both funds and missionary helpers. Although there were some chaplains who ministered to the Europeans (or served the military encampments), and some Catholic, Wesleyan or Calvinist missionaries, there were few existing Anglican missions. One previous missionary of note was Rev F. Owen of the CMS who arrived in August 1837, but left a few months later – his life miraculously spared by the 'inhuman tyrant' Dingane (Shaka's successor) at the time of the massacre of Piet Retief and his Boer companions. During the period of Zulu ascendancy, which began under Shaka around 1812, much of Natal was depopulated, with other tribes fleeing to escape his savagery.

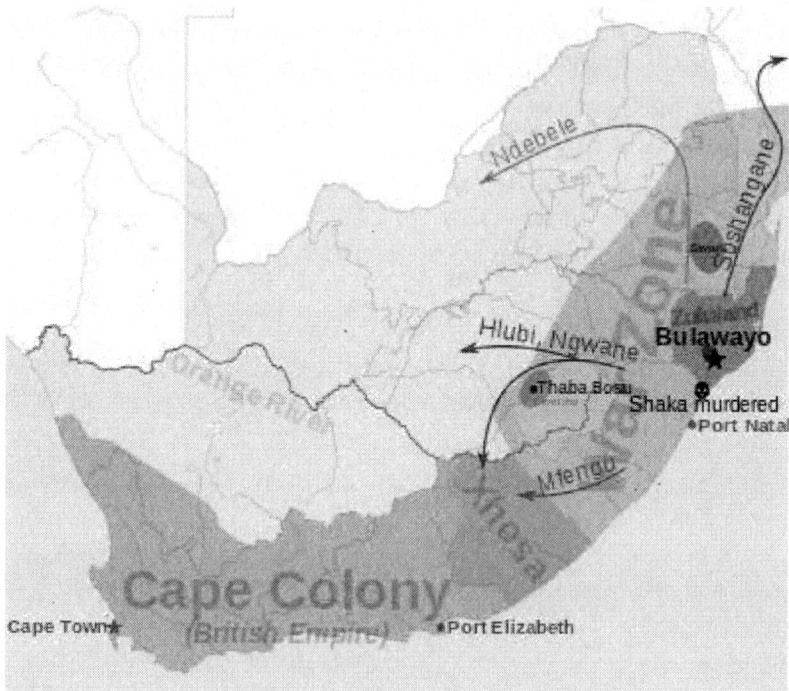

The Basotho, initially at Thaba Bosiu, were also part of this migration

Colenso lost no time in getting to know this troubled history and as much as possible about the present inhabitants of Natal (about 6000 Europeans and 100,000 or more 'Kafirs' as he termed the black population). It was several years since Bishop Gray had been here, so Colenso spent a full ten weeks travelling as widely as possible. He was particularly concerned that both he and his future missionaries should be able to speak Zulu:

176

The only Zulu grammar as yet published, is that of Mr. Schroeder, written in the Danish language – the work of an excellent missionary and able philologist, but not suited for beginners, or for English students generally. There are Kafir Grammars, by Messrs. Boyce and Appleyard; but the dialectic variations of the language spoken by the British Kafirs, for whose use these were written, from that spoken by the Natal Kafirs, or Zulus, are considerable, though their principles are identical.

He wrote a full report of his findings for publication back in England, and incorporated a version of Shroeder's *Grammar* into a similar work of his own, again for publication. (Over the next seven years he provided translations of over half the Bible, including the whole New Testament, as well as a Zulu dictionary and several school books.) A key point to be noted is his realisation that, although all the Natal Africans may be termed Zulus, yet they were mostly distinct groupings who had actually hidden from Shaka, or had fled the region before later returning. Colenso was a pastor who aimed to understand his potential flock, and to look after their welfare in a way which had not so far been much attempted.

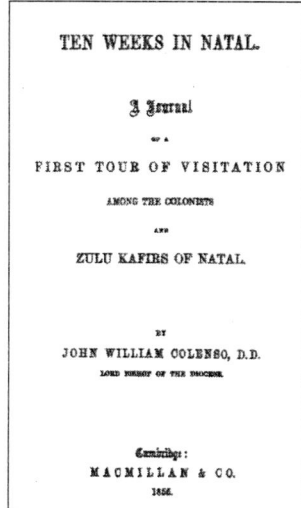

TEN WEEKS IN NATAL.

A Journal

OF A

FIRST TOUR OF VISITATION

AMONG THE COLONISTS

AND

ZULU KAFIRS OF NATAL.

BY

JOHN WILLIAM COLENSO, D.D.

LORD BISHOP OF THE DIOCESE.

Cambridge:

MACMILLAN & CO.

1855.

There were some, however, who shared his concerns – and his early preconceptions – as the following conversation with a certain Captain Struben of Ladysmith reveals:

Capt. Struben spoke [of the Kafirs] with a warm and affectionate interest, and with such a hopeful desire for their real welfare, as quite refreshed and cheered me. He said, however, much of the mistakes made by missionaries in beginning at the wrong end, and expecting to get through Christianity to industry, instead of through industrial pursuits to the reception of Christianity. On this point, indeed, all, with whom I have conversed upon the subject, are agreed... But we must not expect too much of these poor heathens, or that their minds, overgrown with error, (like their native hills around them, with the wild luxuriance and matted grass of ages,) shall be capable of receiving at once and cherishing that advanced Christianity, to which we in England have been brought through centuries of cultivation.

Nevertheless, Colenso gradually modified his views. He learnt from another source of the high regard in which Moshoeshoe (king of the Basotho) was held, and of his much 'advanced' faith and culture (in time he became a Roman Catholic, a move which other Basotho then also made). He was introduced to various local Kafirs whose judgment was widely appreciated. They gave him considerable help in understanding the religious beliefs and terminology of their fellow tribesmen, as well as in appreciating better how to conduct his mission: 'a missionary,' they told him, 'must be like an experienced hunter. He must not show himself, and frighten the game away: but he must get around them, and so catch them.' Soon after these conversations he was also much encouraged in meeting some young Kafirs, who struck him as 'fine children, with well-formed, intelligent foreheads – those from the coast of a lighter colour, those from the interior of a deeper black.' Likewise on another occasion he questioned a group of Kafir children and found that 'their answers were quick and accurate enough, to show that they are not at all wanting, as a race, in intelligence'.

As for potential aggressive behaviour, he remarks later:

> It is certainly somewhat strange that the only act of violence, which came under my own personal notice, while I remained in the colony, was committed not by the fierce, untutored, heathen savage, but by educated Christian Englishmen.

Where the above Capt Struben went on to complain of the readiness of Kafir workers to leave their place of work and to return to their native kraal, Colenso commented on this natural tendency in more sympathetic terms:

> I must confess, I see no reason whatever to charge this practice upon them, as a sign of their want of feeling; but rather I find in it a sign of hope,—a token that they have human feelings like ours, and are therefore accessible to the tidings of great joy, for themselves and for those they love, which shall reveal to them their Great Friend and Father in Heaven. They are ready always to come back after the holidays, and greet their old masters with a brightened eye, wherever they meet them. Sensible persons, however, and those of old experience in the colony, know how to manage, and have no difficulty of this kind with their Kafirs.

His own aim, he says, was to show 'from the very first that I did not consider true religion to consist in a system of restrictions and negations, but in a real spirit of devotion to God's service and love to our fellow-men.' He noted the advice of one Mr Allison who 'warned me not to bring out any missionaries, who were not of the right stamp—elevated, self-denying, self-sacrificing men; and especially to look to their wives, for these often ruined a mission by their tempers and animosities.' Necessarily he began to think of his future mission strategy:

The great defect of the missionary system, adopted in South Africa by the various bodies of Christians [is this]: they do not sufficiently concentrate their forces, but seek to cover a large extent of territory, by planting a number of separate stations, each of which is meant to influence its own little circle of heathens. But... I am convinced that much of their strength is wasted; and I cannot but believe, that greater results may be expected, and with a far less expenditure of means, from establishing, in the first instance, one strong central institution... under the immediate eye of the bishop himself.

He envisaged therefore centralised schooling and training facilities, well-staffed and able to provide any necessary accommodation, close to an urban centre rather than in a remote rural settlement. (This model may not always be appropriate, but it seemed to me in the days of my Somerset ministry near Taunton – a county and market town – that the Catholic provision of a central church together with a large modern one where there was new development made more sense than the Anglican deanery divided into forty parishes covering the same area. The total number of churchgoers was roughly equal; but with, for example, young people found in just twos or threes – if at all – in the Anglican churches very little youth work took place there, unlike the two Catholic churches. The cost of maintaining buildings and the use of clergy time was also very different.)

There was also the fundamental question about the appropriate response to facets of existing Kafir rituals, practices and beliefs. Already Colenso had been urged to stamp out polygamy, but he felt strongly that men who converted should not cause a rift between parents and their children, which would inevitably have followed if they renounced all but one wife. The cast-off wives would, he observed, probably be forced into adultery. The issue was not a new one for the Church – St Augustine had argued that in Old Testament times polygamy 'was allowed in order to have a more numerous posterity'. Even though mainstream churches had consistently opposed it, there was still a pastoral difference between a convert who came with several wives and a married Christian seeking to marry a further wife. A few years earlier, David Livingstone had taken a tough stance, but soon discovered a serious consequence:

All the friends of the divorced wives became the opponents of our religion.

The well-regarded Moshoeshoe observed in similar vein that, without the insistence on monogamy, 'we should soon be Christians.' As it was, Colenso expressed himself forcibly (and controversially for the year 1854) that 'the usual practice of enforcing the separation of wives from their husbands upon their conversion to Christianity is quite unwarrantable and opposed to the plain teaching of our Lord.' It was not that he disagreed at all in viewing polygamy itself wrong, but that the break-up of existing families was surely unChristian – an example of attempting to put new wine into old bottles, as he graphically expressed it. He approved, however, the recent decision of American missionaries elsewhere that polygamists received into the Church should not be allowed to take up any offices therein (compare the instruction in 1 Timothy 3.2 that 'a bishop must be above reproach, the husband of one wife').

Some colonists who learnt of his 'lax' stance became less supportive of his ministry as a result. Yet he felt so strongly that in 1862 he addressed a long (one hundred page) letter on the subject to the Archbishop of Canterbury, making clear also that 'the practice of polygamy is at variance with the whole spirit of Christianity, just as much as that of slavery is, and must eventually be rooted out.' The topic was subsequently debated at the 1888 Lambeth Conference, and Colenso's position of 'gradualism' was rejected – only to find itself approved a hundred years later at the 1988 Lambeth gathering. Today's African Catholic bishops and priests continue to discuss pastoral ways forward, and are seldom too rigid or legalistic.

Another question arose about the observance of native feasts. He comments in his diary:

The feast of first-fruits, as now observed, is a purely heathen ceremony, but has undoubtedly a right meaning at the bottom; and, instead of setting our face against all these practices, our wisdom will surely be, in accordance with the sage advice of Gregory the Great, to adopt such as are really grounded on truth, and restore them to their right use, or rather raise them in the end still higher, by making them Christian celebrations.

Colenso was therefore well aware of Christian tradition, as he was of biblical teaching, and took heed of earlier precedents which again justified his sensitivities towards the Kafirs in his care. In this instance he thought it might be possible to introduce the Lord's Prayer into the proceedings, perhaps with some preliminary explanation of its meaning to the chief and his counsellors. This he was soon able to attempt through an interpreter, and he carefully noted the progress of their dialogue:

It was very interesting to observe with what fixed attention they listened to [the explanation], and what rational remarks they made upon it.

He was much heartened by their appreciative summary:

We've missed the truth by very little, after all: for we pray to unseen spirits, and you to one unseen Being.

Arising from this conversation was an important matter of terminology that he pondered frequently: what Kafir word should be used for this 'one unseen Being' that might best convey its Christian meaning? Towards the end of his ten week tour he received a letter from an American missionary whom he had met at Umtwalumi, which reassured him about the human sympathies of the Kafirs, and – whatever they called him – their faith in 'God'. When his wife was very ill, Mr Wilder had received frequent visits from local 'heathens' who were very supportive:

Heathen though they were, they would talk to me of God's mercy, of His sovereignty and power, of my duty to trust Him, because he would do all things well.

One of the final visits he made before sailing back to England for recruiting purposes was to the Catholic bishop in Maritzburg. He had already met many of the 'separated brethren' on his rounds:

I found him a very gentlemanly Frenchman, with a benignant expression of countenance, and an appearance of sincerity and earnestness about him, which I was rejoiced to witness. He told me that there were not yet any Missionaries of his Church among the natives; but he was about, without delay, to set some at work. One of my last duties, before I left Durban, was to write a short farewell note of brotherly love to him, as I had not been able to call and take my leave of him in Maritzburg. I believe that I can thus live in charity and union with my brethren in Christ, who are striving to walk religiously before God, and to bring forth fruit to their common Master, although I may not, and certainly do not, agree with them on all points.

The serious work began on his return, again recorded by him in much detail: *First Steps* (published in 1860) continues some of the story, especially his contacts with local chiefs, and indeed the Zulu king Mpande, to discuss possible openings for missionary work. In the background we are made aware of the continuing dispute about the Zulu succession, which resulted in much conflict. This never wholly died down, and in later years too the Anglo-Zulu war broke out. So, as well as finding ways and means to bring the Gospel to the African people, Colenso increasingly found himself caught up in issues of 'justice and peace'.

It was, as we have seen, always a priority for him to express Christian teaching in terms that resonated with the Kafirs. His work of Bible translation continued, and he spent much time attempting to master the Zulu language as well as in discussing how best to express the meaning of the text. In particular, he rejected previous renderings of the term for God, such as *uYehova* or *uDio*, as loan words. He insisted (against considerable opposition) on using existing Zulu terminology, believing that their own religious beliefs provided a basis on which to build; so the word 'God' was expressed as *uNkulunkula* or *uMvelinqangi*.

It was, however, not only a translation of the Bible on which he laboured; he was much concerned with the proper interpretation of its contents. Throughout the 1860s and 1870s he made many published contributions to biblical criticism. Thus, having noted F.D. Maurice's controversial attempts to bring the love of God much more in focus ('I am obliged to believe in an abyss of love which is deeper than the abyss of death'), he took up the issue in his own *Commentary on St Paul's Epistle to the Romans* (1861), arguing against the hellfire preaching which was much prevalent in the colony at this time. His apparent 'universalist' theology seemed to Bishop Gray to discount the gravity of human sin, and he found Colenso guilty of heresy. Colenso took his case to the Juridical Committee of the Privy Council in London, who found that Gray had acted *ultra vires* – and so set in motion (1) a schism in Natal following Gray's appointment of a rival candidate for the see in 1867 and (2) a chain of events which in the end resulted in the Colonial Clergy Act of 1874 under which Gray became an Archbishop, with henceforth his and other Anglican provinces becoming legally independent of Canterbury. If Colenso was increasingly unpopular among his fellow countrymen within Natal, he nevertheless retained support from the Kafir population, who in the end saw him as *Sobantu*, their father and protector.

He was also influenced by the publication in England of the equally controversial *Essays and Reviews* (1860), which was an attempt to reconcile Christian ideas with recent critical (and scientific) thinking. The essay *On the interpretation of scripture* was contributed by Benjamin Jowett, who argued that the Bible ought to be treated as scholars treated classical texts. One may observe that this is a somewhat ambiguous idea: so much depends on how far the *context* of a text's composition, usage, and validation (as conveying divine truth) is taken into account. It might therefore lead to fluctuating assessments of a text's significance, but given that 'meaning' can be 'ever old and ever new' under the guidance of the Holy Spirit this is not an unknown problem. Whereas the early Fathers realised that 'literal', 'moral' and 'spiritual' interpretations might all have some relevance, some later commentators, alas, took far too literal a stance – paying, in particular, little attention to the varied genres of scriptural texts: and in so far as Colenso challenged their readings, including some relating to the Pentateuch, he was well justified, even if much criticised. Yet his motive in doing so was to present scripture in accessible ways to his potential Kafir converts. At no point did he want to insult their intelligence by glossing over difficulties in the text; 'How is it possible,' he asked, 'to teach the Zulu to cast off their superstitious belief in witchcraft, if they are required to believe that all the stories of sorcery and demonology which they find in the Bible... are infallibly true?... The time is come, through the revelations of modern science, when, thanks to God, the traditional belief in the divine infallibility of Scripture can, with a clear conscience, be abandoned – can, in fact, be no longer maintained.'

There is an extant series of sermons he preached in 1865 (to the congregations in Durban and Maritzburg) which clarify where he stood in the face of distortions that readily circulated. The following is extracted from a November sermon entitled *Love abounding in knowledge and judgment*:

> When I say that the Bible contains God's Word, I do not mean, as some have supposed, that we may pick and choose among the contents of the Bible – that we can separate those books or portions of the Bible, which are God's Word, from those books or portions, which are not... I say that

183

this Word is 'the spirit and the life,' which breathes in the written words, not the 'mere flesh' or letter of the words themselves. 'The flesh profiteth nothing: the words that I speak unto you, they are spirit, they are life.'...

But, if God has given us so freely the knowledge of Himself in the Holy Scriptures, which His Providence has 'caused to be written for our learning', He has also given us in this our day most wonderful illumination by the light of the different Sciences, which all come to us from Him, who is 'the Father of Lights, the Giver of every good and perfect gift'...

[Hence] we may not read [the Bible] with unreasoning acquiescence in every line and letter of the book, or rather that series of books, written by different men in different ages, bound up in one, which we call the Bible, but may read it with an intelligent faith, with the understanding as well as the heart. Thus we need not be disquieted though the progress of Modern Criticism should take from us much in the Scriptures, which perhaps without sufficient reason we had hitherto regarded as infallibly certain and true...

We must consider for what end the Bible is given to us, namely, to bring our spirits near to God; and we must seek, therefore, the proofs of the inspiration of its writers, not in matters of Science or History, but in those words of Eternal Life, which come to us with a power that is not of this world, and find us out in our inner being, with messages from God to the soul.

In fact, to demonstrate where literalism fell short, he provided an hilarious analysis of the implied daily maintenance on board Noah's Ark. Allowing for two 'unclean' and fourteen 'clean' animals of every known kind, with sufficient larder space for their food, he demonstrated that each human on board with Noah would have to tend 8500 animals daily: without any breaks for rest, this would have to be achieved at the rate of one every ten seconds!

Such writings were undoubtedly ahead of their time, and only served to further isolate Colenso. In the 1870s the causes of friction moved from biblical criticism to more immediate issues of colonial misrule. The discovery of diamonds at Kimberley attracted many African

LANGALIBALELE AND THE

AMAHLUBI TRIBE

COMPILED UPON THE OFFICIAL RECORD OF THE TRIALS OF
THE CHIEF, HIS SONS AND INDUNA AND OTHER MEMBERS
OF THE AMAHLUBI TRIBE

BY THE

BISHOP OF NATAL

Printed by
SPOTTISWOODE & CO., NEW-STREET SQUARE, LONDON
1874

workers, who were sometimes rewarded with firearms instead of money. Hlubi tribesmen were better placed than many to be engaged in this work, and the Natal government learnt that some young men had brought their guns home. In 1873 the magistrate in Estcourt demanded that these be properly registered. As Langalibalele, the Hlubi chief, did not know who held guns, he refused to enforce the order. Eight particular men were then named, but only five appeared before the magistrate. Langalibalele himself was sent for, but refused on grounds of ill health. His arrest was then ordered, at which point Langalibalele and his people made plans to flee to Basutoland. Here he was eventually handed over to the pursuing forces and put on trial, as a result of which he was banished to Robben Island far away while others in his tribe had cattle seized and forced labour inflicted. Colenso was not slow in taking up their cause, challenging the travesty of the court proceedings and campaigning for intervention from the Colonial Secretary in London. As a result the Governor of Natal was recalled and the sentences reduced – but Colenso was much vilified locally.

Matters got worse as the decade progressed. In 1875 the Colonial Secretary, following the successful federation in Canada, had hopes of achieving something similar in South Africa (particularly as it would make cheap black labour available for the plantations and mines). However, this was rejected by the Boers in the Orange Free State and in the Transvaal. Two years later Sir Bartle Frere was sent out as High Commissioner to bring it about. Transvaal itself was forcibly annexed, but the neighbouring Zulu kingdom was more problematic. Up to this point the British had supported the Zulus in their border disputes with the Boers but now unsurprisingly took a different view. Yet in July 1878 a commission found almost entirely in favour of the Zulu contention. Frere characterized their judgment as 'one-sided and unfair to the Boers', and demanded compensation be paid by the Zulus to the Boers. Soon afterwards there were three border incidents which Frere seized upon: despite warnings from London ('it is the desire of Her Majesty's Government not to furnish means for a campaign of invasion and conquest'), he presented King Cetshwayo with an ultimatum that the Zulu army be disbanded and the Zulus accept a British resident. No reply was made, so on 11th January 1879 British forces invaded Cetshwayo's territory, and the Anglo-Zulu War began, lasting a full six months.

Throughout the campaign Colenso criticised Frere's action and provided a detailed analysis of official colonial reports to expose his policy in print This contrasted sharply with the response of most other missionaries, who – having met with little success among the Zulus over a number of years – wrote copiously to the press and indeed to their respective governments in favour of war. The long-experienced military officer Anthony Durnford who had served on the boundary commission was appalled by their attitude and was one of the few who supported Colenso's views. He wrote home:

> These missionaries are at the bottom of all evil. They want war so that they might take the Zulu country, and thus give them homes in a good and pleasant land. They have not been turned out. They came of their own accord. The Zulus do not want them and I for one cannot see why we should cram these men down their throats.

After initial setbacks the decisive battle of Kwanodwengu in July 1879 brought the war to an end – 'a bloody but barren victory' in Colenso's words. Eight weeks later Cetshwayo himself was captured and sent into exile in the Cape – but Colenso continued to argue for his restoration (achieved when, again with much backing from Colenso, he was allowed to travel to England three years later to meet Queen Victoria) and for Zulu rights until his own death in Maritzburg in 1883. It had become more than apparent to him that there was no clear cut divide between supposedly enlightened Europeans and the benighted heathen of Africa: virtue and vice were evidently much more evenly distributed.

* * * * * * *

Livingstone and **Colenso** were in their different ways both pioneers of the faith, and therefore inevitably both sometimes made errors of judgment, perhaps offending, hurting or misleading others in the process. But, as a Catholic bishop once vividly put it, 'the word *church* is much more a *verb* than a *noun*'; so we continue to salute both men for expanding the horizons of our ongoing Christian mission, and for their courage and resilience in so doing. They were products of an adventurous Victorian age, which begs the question: How many would be ready to face similar challenges today?

EXPLORATIONS

A weathered rock

from the shore of Lake Galilee
It evokes the Holy Land's hilly terrain,
the cave of Golgotha, and 'Cephas' the rock.

'The very stone which the builders rejected has become the head of the corner.'

No doubt this stone was misshapen as they judged it, unsuitable for their preconceived design.

Change in the Church

GUIDED BY GOD'S SPIRIT

A developing church

Before our grandson Samuel reached school-age, we sometimes mentioned to him how different life was in the past: no computers, no cars, no lorries, no aeroplanes, no electricity even. It was difficult for him to imagine such a world. So too it is hard for us to conceive a Church that had no dedicated places of worship, no liturgical books, no yearly cycle of feasts and fasts, no agreed structures of ministry, and no Bible as we know it today. Yet the first Christian community of all had something even more precious – their own personal knowledge of Jesus, which they rapidly shared through testimony and preaching. In time these oral reminiscences came to be backed up by one or more written accounts, and much came to be learnt from the interpretation of the Hebrew scriptures. Much of what we take for granted in the Church then took years (if not centuries) to develop, although it is not uncommon to find some Christians who would regard a particular expression of the faith that dates back, perhaps for less than a hundred years, as *essential* to the Church's identity. Sometimes the current hymnbook is so exalted, or the vestments that are worn, or the use of bells, or the position of the altar. When people occasionally quiz me as to why I seldom wear a clerical shirt, the simple answer is that St Peter never wore one either.

I want to focus in some detail on how just a few of the features with which we are familiar in the Church gradually took shape in those early centuries. The crucial question is always, Have we as a Christian people remained true to the apostolic faith? The supplementary question is, Are some developments, which were appropriate in an age gone by, now in need of further adjustment to take account of the changing world in which we live? These are matters for later consideration, but first we take a look at how some facets of church life evolved at the start.

We begin with the Church's gatherings for worship. Meetings of Christian believers mentioned in the New Testament seem to envisage fairly intimate occasions. The Church was of course born in a house (probably in the 'upper room') on the day of Pentecost [Acts 2.1-4], as in Duccio's painting below.

Duccio's Pentecost (1308-11)
now in Museo Dell' Opera Del Duomo, Siena

Luke refers repeatedly in Acts to believers using their homes both for teaching and for worship; Paul explicitly mentions 'house churches'. Evidence of larger assemblies is limited to initial opportunities within synagogues or otherwise out of doors. The main exception seems to be in Ephesus where Paul uses 'the hall of Tyrannus' [Acts 19.9] for two whole years for teaching purposes. A later reference, maybe around 185, comes in the apocryphal Martyrdom of Paul which indicates that he rented a barn (perhaps a 'granary' or a 'warehouse') outside Rome 'where he and the brethren taught the word of truth'. The most famous account from the same period occurs at the trial of Justin Martyr:

Rusticus the prefect said, 'Where do you assemble?' Justin said, 'Where each one chooses and can: for do you fancy that we all meet in the very same place? Not so; because the God of the Christians is not

190

circumscribed by place; but being invisible, fills heaven and earth, and everywhere is worshipped and glorified by the faithful.' Rusticus the prefect said, 'Tell me where you assemble, or into what place do you collect your followers.' Justin said, 'I live above one Martinus, at the Timiotinian Bath; and during the whole time (and I am now living in Rome for the second time) I am unaware of any other meeting than his.'

By this date we know that such private gatherings required official permission, so Rusticus was probably fishing for information about any *unauthorised* meetings. His contemporary Celsus wrote an anti-Christian polemic and mentions that in his day Christians gathered in domestic venues or in shops. In larger urban centres or cities we have to imagine a network of these, rather than a single venue. The first hint of premises set apart specifically for worship is found in the apologist Minucius Felix: he uses the term *sacraria* which begins to suggest a few cultic furnishings in the building – although at this stage no sacred images. The archaeological record identifies Dura-Europos in Syria as the site of the earliest known 'house church' building; it has biblical frescoes probably from around the year 230, including one depicting Adam and Eve, with another of Christ the Shepherd.

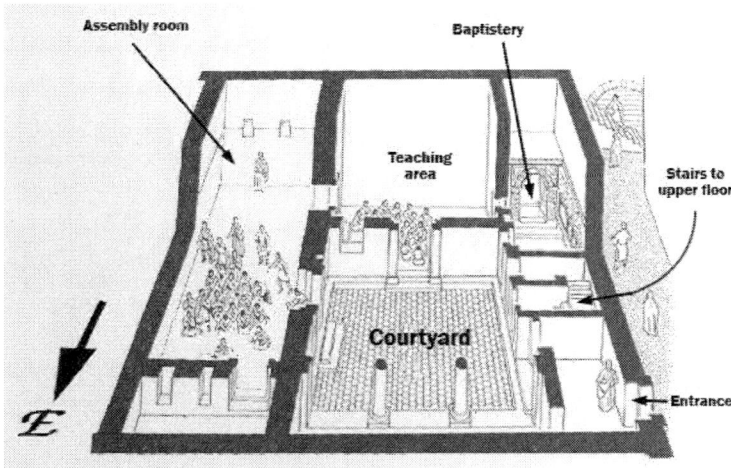

Christian community house at Dura-Europos

In most respects this 'house church' is no different in its layout from an ordinary domestic dwelling; but the baptistery (seen on the left) is the one exception. The depth of its bath suggests that baptisms (as allowed in the much earlier *Didache* whenever water supplies were limited) may have been by sprinkling, rather than by immersion. The capacity of the worship (or assembly) room has been estimated as no more than seventy people. By way of comparison, there is a surviving pre-Constantinian inventory which names precisely forty-nine Christians who were arrested in a private house near Carthage in 304. Even though this was probably the typical number that could be accommodated, it does remind us that in these early centuries church gatherings were places where Christians knew each other well.

It is striking that in the gospel accounts of Jesus' feeding miracle, the crowd is not just a mass of anonymous people, but is organised into remarkably similar small groups, each perhaps roughly the size of a house church gathering. Mark tells us that Jesus 'commanded them all to sit down by companies upon the green grass. So they sat down in groups, by hundreds and fifties.' Some commentators liken this to the organisation of an army, but I suspect that this may reflect their own experience of being over-regimented by the Church. Mark's Greek text actually says συμπόσια συμπόσια [*symposia symposia* Mk 6.39], which suggests sitting down as for a banquet rather than in military formation. When we turn to Luke, we find he omits the reference to hundreds, and says that the people were simply in groups of 'about fifty' [Lk 9.14]. Thus, in these two presentations at least, the miracle may be understood as an anticipation, not simply of the Christian Eucharist, but more particularly of the way the Church gathered typically in small assemblies. 'One sees foreshadowed' wrote St Ambrose in his *Commentary on St Luke*, 'a better and greater Church whose numbers are without limit.' And Mark's hint of a banquet may remind us too that initially the Eucharist was incorporated within an agape meal – as we shall shortly discover.

If the assembly was in a *domus*, a private house, it might have a dining room which opened on to a portico, and this would offer both space and a degree of privacy. But the word 'apartment' is in fact the word used in Acts 20.8, and this was probably in a block of flats where the 'outsiders or

192

unbelievers' of 1 Corinthians 14.24 might more easily have observed the proceedings. Such squalid *insulae*, which sometimes rose to five or six stories, would undoubtedly have been where the poorer brethren lived in Rome. Tacitus tells us that a 'tremendous crowd' of Christians were executed there by Nero in the year 64, and it seems likely that most of these lacked the legal protection of Roman citizenship and were therefore of lower social status. So in Rome at any rate we need think more of slum dwellings where immigrants lived. Think of the people greeted by Paul in his letter to the Romans: two-thirds of them had Greek names ('Asyncritus, Phlegon, Hermes...'). If they were in immigrant slums, you can understand why there was a need for barns to be rented for worship. But it might be different elsewhere. In Jerusalem, for example, there was room for some seating ('a sound came from heaven... and filled all the house where they were sitting'). James, however, warns about the discriminatory use of seating ('if... you pay attention to the one who wears the fine clothing and say, "Have a seat here, please," while you say to the poor man, "Stand there" or "Sit at my feet," have you not made distinctions among yourselves?). We recall that Paul too was concerned about discriminatory behaviour, in the church at Corinth.

Each one goes ahead with his own meal... Do you not have houses to eat and drink in? Or do you despise the church of God and humiliate those who have nothing?... So then, my brethren, when you come together to eat, wait for one another – if any one is hungry, let him eat at home. [1 Cor 11.21–22; 33–34]

The Eucharist is described here as a 'meal', while the letter of Jude later uses the term 'love feasts' – in his experience too often blemished with 'bold carousing' [v12]. We begin to realise that, whereas our sacred elements of bread and wine are consumed as fragments in the hand or on the tongue and as a sip of wine, in the early centuries the Church usually incorporated its liturgy within a more substantial *agape*. When some 50 or 60 years later Pliny the Younger, as Roman governor in Bithynia, reported to the emperor Trajan what had been told him about local Christian practices he describes two separate gatherings held each Sunday: (1) a regular meeting before dawn to sing responsively a hymn to Christ 'as to a god', and to bind themselves by an oath to serious moral behaviour and (2) an assembly later on the same day to partake of ordinary and innocent food. This latter assembly is clearly the Eucharist, which was generally held in the evening to accommodate those who of necessity worked during the day. 'Ordinary' food does not preclude the idea that, even if the portions of bread and wine were 'adequate', they might at the same time be regarded as a sacramental gift.

A whole century later Tertullian certainly makes it clear that hunger was properly abated in the *agapes* known to him:

> The participants, before reclining, taste first of prayer to God. As much is eaten as satisfies the cravings of hunger; as much is drunk as befits the chaste. They say it is enough, as those who remember that even during the night they have to worship God; they talk as those who know that the Lord is one of their auditors. After manual ablution, and the bringing in of lights, each is asked to stand forth and sing, as he can, a hymn to God, either one from the holy Scriptures or one of his own composing – a proof of the measure of our drinking. As the feast commenced with prayer, so with prayer it is closed.

So too Clement of Alexandria during the same late 2nd/early 3rd century period says this:

> Dishonouring the good and saving work of the Word, the consecrated agape, with pots and pouring of sauce; and by drink and delicacies and smoke desecrating that name, they are deceived in their idea, having expected that the promise of God might be bought with suppers... Let our diet be light and digestible, and suitable for keeping awake.

Once again, notice the language he uses: *consecrated agape*, in which the diet was *light and digestible*, consumed at *supper* time.

A natural question follows: what, if anything other than bread and wine, was consumed at an *agape* or Eucharist (Ignatius of Antioch uses the terms interchangeably)? There is little evidence of any other items at all. The *Apostolic Tradition* indicates that around this time the candidates at a baptismal Eucharist received milk and honey, mixed together 'for the fulfilment of the promise to the fathers, which spoke of a land flowing with milk and honey.' Occasional offerings of oil, cheese or olives are mentioned, and were presumably shared among those present, after thanks were given for them 'in the same general manner' as at the offering of the bread and wine, 'though not with the same words'. For modern Westerners, a meal has a variety of ingredients and often more than one course. We forget that life in other parts of the world, as universally in the past, is perforce much more basic. In many cultures there is a staple diet such as rice or maize, sometimes flavoured with herbs or vegetables, sometimes not – so we should not be surprised if little other than bread was once eaten at the Church's *agape*. Irenaeus of Lyons (c. 130-202) tells us that in his day, 'the mixed chalice (wine taken with water) and the baked loaf (no mention here of individual wafers)' were the essential elements to 'receive the word of God'.

Growing numbers of Christians inevitably made the common *agape* increasingly more difficult to stage. The difficulties were practical, rather than theological. Cyprian of Carthage makes this very point in a letter of 253 to a fellow bishop Caecilius:

> When we dine, we cannot call the people together to our banquet so that we may celebrate the truth of the sacrament with all the brotherhood present.

The sacrament, he indicates, was a *dinner* or a *banquet* at which the whole congregation was expected to be present. It seems therefore that from the early or mid 3rd century *agapes* as such became less common, leaving the Eucharist much more like the liturgical celebration we know today. The process would certainly have been accelerated in the following century when Constantine sanctioned a public recognition of Christianity and the erection of basilicas where the emphasis was often on impressive ritual more than on the needful fellowship among believers.

By this time too, public worship had developed both liturgical structures and a corpus of recognised texts. If one looks back to the apostolic era, there would then have been more variability, with a significant input that was somewhat impromptu. Since the original twelve disciples were all Jews, the pattern of worship familiar to them would have been that of the synagogue – its chants, its readings and its prayers. They adopted it as Christians, but injected into it the teachings which Jesus had imparted, together with recollections of his life and death and resurrection. All this was preliminary to their eucharistic celebration, when week by week they faithfully observed what he had asked them to do 'in remembrance' of him. The law and the prophets would still have been read in their turn, but letters from Christian leaders elsewhere might also have been read; and little by little the 'memoirs' of the apostles – the Gospels as we call them now – would have been written down and copies passed around.

Here, though, is Paul's much earlier instruction to the Corinthians:

When you come together, each one has a hymn, a lesson, a revelation, a tongue, or an interpretation. Let all things be done for edification.

Although he doubts that all are prophets or teachers [1 Cor 12.29], Paul indicates that prophecy (and commentary on the scriptures) was in principle welcome from any believer present, although it was more edifying to limit the number contributing to just two or three *male* members (if any outsiders were present, they would in those days probably have been scandalised if women had been too vocal). The relatively informal character of Christian worship is borne out in the letter to the Colossians [3.16]

Teach and admonish one another in all wisdom, and sing psalms and hymns and spiritual songs.

In synagogues it was the elders or the 'rulers' who were responsible for discipline, and for the provision of teaching: the elders and overseers in the house churches, however they were chosen or appointed, no doubt had a similar role. According to Matthew [10.41] there were sometimes visiting prophets, who in principle were to be welcomed; yet expounding scripture was too important to be left entirely to chance, and needed careful supervision. There are many references in the New Testament to distorted teachings making inroads into the Church, and this led inevitably to much more careful supervision. Fairly soon this meant proper structures of authorised ministry. We read Paul's farewell warnings in Acts:

Take heed to yourselves and to all the flock, in which the Holy Spirit has made you overseers, to care for the church of God... I know that after my departure fierce wolves will come in among you, not sparing the flock; and from among your own selves will arise men speaking perverse things, to draw away the disciples after them. Therefore be alert. [Acts 20.27-31]

Clement of Rome, writing to the church in Corinth at the end of the 1st century, makes it clear that there was to be nothing casual about the rites of the Church:

There ought to be strict order and method in our performance of such acts as the Master has prescribed for certain times and seasons. Now, it was his command that the offering of gifts and the conduct of public services should not be haphazard or irregular, but should take place at fixed times and hours. Moreover, in the exercise of his supreme will he has himself declared in what place and by what persons he desires this to be done, if it is all to be devoutly performed in accordance with his wishes and acceptably to his will... The High Priest, for example, has his own proper services assigned to him, the priesthood has its own station, there are particular ministries laid down for the Levites, and the layman is bound by regulations affecting the laity.

We need to appreciate that by now there was intense scrutiny of God's word in the Old Testament, and Clement is here giving a Christian interpretation to the prescriptions that regulated the offering of temple sacrifices. Thus, different orders of ministry emerged in the Church, in parallel with the various Jewish offices: the one who exercised local oversight (for which the Greek term was *episcope*) supplanted the High Priest; the body of elders were the presbyters or priests who assisted him; the new Levites were the deacons (from the Greek word *diakonos*, one who serves). Ignatius of Antioch writes a few years later to the church in Smyrna (we know it as Izmir) that the bishop's approval is essential in all things, for example:

The sole Eucharist you should consider valid is the one that is celebrated by the bishop himself, or by some person authorised by him.

By the middle of the 2nd century, Justin Martyr records the (now accepted) common structure of Sunday worship:

And on the day called Sunday, all who live in cities or in the country gather together to one place, and the memoirs of the apostles or the writings of the prophets are read, as long as time permits; then, when the reader has ceased, the president verbally instructs, and exhorts to the imitation of these good things. Then we all rise together and pray, and, as we before said, when our prayer is ended, bread and wine and water are brought, and the president in like manner offers prayers and thanksgivings, according to his ability, and the people assent, saying Amen; and there is a distribution to each, and a participation of that over which thanks have been given, and to those who are absent a portion is sent by the deacons. And they who are well to do, and willing, give what each thinks fit; and what is collected is deposited with the president, who succours the orphans and widows and those who, through sickness or any other cause, are in want, and those who are in bonds and the strangers sojourning among us, and in a word takes care of all who are in need.

Some aspects of the prayer that followed the president's 'instruction' may perhaps be glimpsed in Tertullian's later description:

We meet together as an assembly and congregation, that, offering up prayer to God as with united force, we may wrestle with Him in our supplications... We pray for the emperors, for their ministers and for all in authority, for the welfare of the world, for the prevalence of peace, for the delay of the final consummation.

Note, however, that when Justin mentions what we would term the 'Eucharistic prayer' he indicates that there was as yet no fixed form of words: the president prays 'according to his ability'. This is also implied in his previous description of a Eucharist that included baptism:

There is then brought to the president of the brethren bread and a cup of wine mixed with water; and he, taking them, gives praise and glory to the Father of the universe, through the name of the Son and of the Holy Ghost, and offers thanks at considerable length for our being counted worthy to receive these things at his hands. And when he has concluded the prayers and thanksgivings, all the people present express their assent by saying Amen.

Although he refers elsewhere to 'the institution narrative' (as we call it) this is an explanatory note: its mandatory liturgical use appears to have been a later development.

Although the Eucharistic (thanksgiving) prayer was offered according to president's 'ability', its pattern and its themes were not necessarily his own. These were what Hippolytus, an early 3rd century Roman presbyter, recorded in the *Apostolic Tradition*. He was concerned that innovations were being made in his day, and so set down what he understood to be the more ancient structure of the prayer:

Driven by love towards all the saints, we have arrived at the essence of the tradition which is proper for the Churches. This is so that those who are well informed may keep the tradition which has lasted until now, according to the explanation we give of it, and so that others by taking note of it may be strengthened (against the fall or error which has recently occurred because of ignorance and ignorant people).

There follows his model prayer for a bishop to use when concelebrating with his presbyters. Hippolytus expressly states, however, that he has the right to use his own form of words – so long as they convey orthodox teaching. Hippolytus' documented prayer then proved very influential in the century that followed, but there was never uniformity across the far-flung Christian world. The later Latin, Greek, Coptic, or Armenian texts that appeared in liturgical books became normative in their own regions, but were not altogether in uniformity with each other. Some ancient liturgies such as the Ambrosian Rite of Milan and the Mozarabic Rite of central Spain are still in use today within the Catholic Church.

Variations are also found in the selection (the canon) of those Christian scriptures that gradually came into wide circulation. The letters of Paul were brought together, the Gospels emerged one by one alongside other writings such as *The Shepherd of Hermas*, but it took time for copies to be made; hence their usage was initially quite restricted. The process of canonisation was never determined by papal authority or by a general church council, but by the common agreement that their teaching conformed to the oral tradition handed down through the apostles and their successors. In the end, certain norms were established, chiefly the proven antiquity of the text and/or its apostolic authorship and/or its usage in one of the main centres of Christianity such as Alexandria or Rome. Even then such criteria were not sufficient to establish orthodoxy: the issue that mattered above all was whether the text was faithful to the teaching of the Lord himself? Although the New Testament as we know it was more or less in place by the mid 4th century, our Western version has never been quite the same as some other collections such as the Syrian, Nestorian or Coptic New Testaments. The book of Revelation is not a canonical text for the Syrians, while the letter of Jude has also had an erratic career. The Copts include the *1st and 2nd letters of Clement*, and the early writings known as *Barnabas* and *The Shepherd of Hermas* continued to be read publicly in the West long after the end of the 4th century.

Some further changes

We have observed that, as the Church developed in these early centuries, it remained important for its unity to be maintained across a wide geographical area. Doctrinal uniformity was regarded as essential, but church order and liturgical practices displayed a degree of flexibility. In most places the Church remained open to further changes, whose details cannot all be considered here. Hence we must pass over matters such as the construction and furnishing of church buildings, the use of hymns and chants, the part that music and singing came to play, the repertoire of postures and devotional gestures, the rise of monastic orders, the place of women and children, and the role of celibacy. Likewise the history of particular rites of baptism (and that of confirmation which in time became detached from it), of marriage, of ordination, and of confession, would require several lengthy treatises.

More briefly though, it is possible to summarise a few other developments:

- The use of images and relics remained highly contentious for a long time. The rapid rise of Islam which rejected the display of images (in line with the second biblical commandment) prompted the iconoclast controversy within the Eastern Church in the 8th and 9th centuries. In the end it was the 'incarnate' nature of Christ that proved decisive in legitimising icons. As for relics: they began to be venerated from the time of St Polycarp's death in the 2nd century and eventually proved so popular that in late Saxon times they were the main continental import into Britain (along with many fakes). Although theologians such as St Augustine challenged much misplaced piety, in the end the magisterium bowed to popular demand, conceding that such cults might be instrumental in arousing or even strengthening Christian faith. There were subsequently few in later centuries who were prepared to criticise them, with noteworthy exceptions such as Guibert, the late 11th century abbot of Nogent in France, and – 400 years after him – Jean Gerson, chancellor of the university of Paris, until of course the Reformation attempted to sweep them entirely away. In recent years more attention has been given to authenticating relics (for example, with the help of carbon dating and DNA testing), and to focusing devotion upon the merits of the saints rather than upon the physical aura of their sanctity.

- Whereas in the sub-apostolic era those who had died as Christian martyrs were recognised as having already attained a place in heaven, when persecution became less common it was the witness of outstanding faith in other ways that brought local recognition of sainthood. However, there was growing unease about this 'unregulated saints market' (to use Robert Barro's phrase). Hence, not only was episcopal approval regarded as important, but little by little the Pope became involved as well. The first known papal canonisation occurred in 993, but a further two hundred years elapsed before it was decided in 1234 that formal papal approval was required. Over the centuries since then the procedures have been adjusted a number of times. Thus, in 1917 the requirement of a 50 year gap between beatification and canonisation was introduced. Prior to 1983 two recorded miracles were necessary for beatification, but this was then reduced to one. Recently Pope Francis has dispensed with the need for miraculous evidence in the case of his predecessors. There has also been a trend to name many more saints than in the past, which has provoked speculation about some of the likely factors – such as the challenges from rising Protestantism, secularism and indeed feminism (in response to which there is now an increasing proportion of female saints). However, there is a concern about the huge costs of promoting the cause of any candidate.
- Personal devotions eventually came to include the Rosary, which took shape over quite a lengthy period from the 12th century onwards. While many spiritual practices arose from time to time within the Church, few have gained such a widespread and abiding following as the simple recitation of the Rosary. Similarly, it is now the norm for catholic churches to portray the Stations of the Cross, whose origin lies in the early pilgrimages to Jerusalem. For those unable to make such a long and arduous visit, they provided the physical means to walk the same spiritual steps. From the later medieval period it was the Franciscans who promoted them; in 1686 they were allowed to erect stations within their churches (as well as previously outside). In 1731, Pope Clement XII extended the same right to all churches so long as a Franciscan gave direction. At the same time the number of stations was fixed at fourteen. In 1857, the involvement of Franciscans was waived as regards England, a permission that soon became universal. More recently, it has become quite common to recall the Lord's resurrection in a 15th station.

- The response to moral issues took a significant turn in the 4th century when Constantine allowed religious toleration. With many now adopting the Christian faith, serious attention was given to questions of public as well as private morality – thus, there was a shift from the mainly pacifist views of the first three centuries to a formulation of 'just war' teachings. The biggest challenge faced when the Church subsequently expanded into continents like Africa has been, and often continues to be, the practice of polygamy. Indeed, missionaries were prone to conceal those parts of Genesis where patriarchal habits were liable to be 'misunderstood'. In Western societies the frequent breakdown of family life has likewise called for pastoral measures that were perhaps previously little needed. The advances in medical science have also stimulated much reflection on issues such as genetic modification, in vitro fertilisation, contraception, and terminal care.

- The crucial doctrinal dispute of the early Church concerned the person of Christ. This was partially resolved in 325 by the agreement known as the Nicene Creed, which was revised in 381. Despite the further attempt at clarity in the Chalcedonian Definition of 451, differences still remained, as inevitably they did too concerning Marian teachings. The Council of Ephesus declared her to be theotokos ('God bearer') in 431. The feast of her conception was introduced in the Eastern Church in the 8th century before being adopted by the Western Church two centuries later, long before the dogma of her immaculate conception was pronounced in 1854. At the popular level though there were always misconceptions about the BVM. In Muhammad's time some Christians regarded her as the third person of the Trinity, while by the 12th century the cult of the Virgin had become localised in so many different shrines that some pilgrims accepted a plurality of Virgins – as caricatured in the conversation once overheard in a later age by Thomas More: 'Of all Our Ladies I love best our Lady of Walsingham,' said one; 'and I,' saith the other, 'our Lady of Ipswich.'

- Although the Pope's role in the exercise of church authority was never in doubt, the extent of this unifying oversight was not always agreed. One of those who insisted on his own episcopal rights was St Cyprian, bishop of Carthage in the mid 3rd century. The subsequent dominance of the bishops of Rome did not accord well with some secular rulers in the Middle Ages, nor with many of the Reformers. Again, while Orthodox churches respect the Pope's position, they see him as primus inter pares; and although the 1st Vatican Council pronounced his infallibility (under certain conditions), the 2nd Vatican Council was also mindful of his collaboration with the synod of bishops. Pope Francis is readier than some of his predecessors to enhance this sense of collaboration.

In all such topics, there is a fascinating history which shows Christians learning to accommodate different needs and altered circumstances – and yet in the process attracting both criticism and misunderstandings. Kenan Osborne has commented:

> History indicates again and again that pastoral need at the local or regional level led to changes and developments... *with papal or conciliar approbation occurring only later.* Nor can one say that changes and developments took place only because of a well-formulated theological position. The theological academy generally provided a theological base only after the rituals had changed... When the praxis in the Church changes, as it is doing today, the theological rationale for the new praxis also changes.

We must not therefore imagine that at some point in the past this ongoing process has ever achieved finality: the Holy Spirit was promised to guide the Church into all truth, and his activity has never ceased since the day of Pentecost. We should also note that even when new norms have emerged, pastoral realities sometimes call for variations in their implementation. The situation in England in the late 16th century provides one such example: of necessity there was then no hierarchy, no real structure to the Church – and no regular sacramental practice. The role of women, who could move around undetected more easily than men, actually became more prominent.

Similar observations might apply today in many parts of the world: for example, in some large African parishes with perhaps two dozen outstations, it is impossible for there to be a Sunday mass celebrated in all of them. Some Christian communities may therefore have Sunday devotions led by a lay catechist, whereas their Eucharistic assembly may perforce take place mid-week when a priest is available. Such a model has already been adopted in some European parishes where resources are now more limited. As secularisation takes greater hold, other changes to familiar practices may well happen.

An inclusive church

A landmark in the Church's evolution was the so-called Council of Jerusalem, held around the year 50 to resolve a vital issue concerning newly converted pagans: should they be circumcised, as were Jews, and indeed should they observe the entire Mosaic law? Paul, who believed firmly that it was faith in Christ that mattered and that it was Christian love that truly fulfilled the law, argued against a legalistic approach and won over 'the apostles and elders' headed by James, brother of the Lord. All they insisted upon was that such Gentiles should abstain from idols, from consuming animal blood, and from unchastity – although of course they envisaged that all Christians would live devout and moral lives. So it was established that in the Church there does not have to be complete uniformity in all things, or – as we might express it today – there can be 'unity in diversity'.

This principle also undergirded Paul's own missionary approach. As he told the Christians in Corinth: 'To the weak I became weak, that I might win the weak. I have become all things to all men, that I might by all means save some' [1 Cor 9.22]. We might describe this as a policy of inclusivity, which implies that not only may people of any age or ethnicity be received into the Church, but so too many of their customs and cultures may be seen as gifted by God and ripe for Christian baptism. Within the unity of the Church, variations of practice may well be appropriate today. Flexibility is inherent in the implementation of the Gospel, because it enables its universal appeal to be realised in many different contexts. (If one compares Christian mission with Britain's foreign policy over the years, we do not do too badly. Parts of Africa, for example, had their own form of democracy long before we imposed *our version* on them: indeed, their object was often more laudable than ours – their traditions sought consensus rather than mere majority rule, which can leave minorities unrepresented and probably disaffected.) The Church for her part may not always allow sufficient diversity, but there are good precedents to inspire us both in scripture and in the historical record.

One vital teaching should be noted before looking at any particular examples. Paul wrote this, in his letter to the Romans:

Do not be conformed to this world, but be transformed by the renewal of your mind. [Rom 12.2 cf. 1 Pet 1.14]

So in the work of evangelisation, we need to clarify: what is fundamental to the Christian faith? We proclaim the life, death and resurrection of Jesus in many different ways, especially in the Eucharist, but do we have a *hierarchy* of values or of aspirations that draw us closer to him? Again, Paul can help us here: 'I will show you a more excellent way', he tells the Corinthians. This is evidenced in Jesus' own approach, as in his explicit response when criticised for allowing his disciples to eat grains of corn on a Saturday: 'The Sabbath was made for man, and not man for the Sabbath' [Mk 2.27]. He indicated thereby that human needs may well take precedence over man-made (or even Church-made) regulations: thus, compassion and mercy predominate when Jesus dines with publicans and sinners; he offers 'the water of life' to the woman at the well despite her previous record of five husbands; he gives his body and blood at the Last Supper to the one who is about to betray him as well as to those who desert him. Paul's summary therefore goes to the heart of the Gospel when he describes love as the gift we should desire above all else; it is the validation of the Church's witness because it is the living reality of Christ himself.

In the centuries that followed the apostolic era, the Church was sometimes persecuted and remained fairly hidden from public gaze, although its works of mercy drew many outsiders to it. In the 4th century all this changed. The scale of engagement with the pagan world, and the many opportunities for proclaiming the Gospel, provoked considerable thought about what should be affirmed in this wider arena and what might need to be purged. Earlier theologians such as Justin Martyr and Clement of Alexandria could be quite generous in their evaluation. Justin famously coined the idea of Christians before Christ:

Those who lived reasonably are Christians, even though they have been thought atheists; as, among the Greeks, Socrates and Heraclitus, and men like them; and among the barbarians, Abraham, and Ananias, and Azarias, and Misael, and Elias, and many others whose actions and names we now decline to recount, because we know it would be tedious.

Clement too found inspired truth in Homer, whom he called 'an unwilling prophet', just as Augustine subsequently referred to Virgil as 'a prophet unaware'.

In the later 4th century Basil of Caesarea suggested that Christian discrimination is like the activity of bees, which make honey from the freshest flowers but fly past others with less to offer. Yet concessions may sometimes be necessary, he thought, considering that conversion is generally a gradual process. Jerome was prepared to make allowances for profane fashions in personal appearance – but he said one should beware of thorns even in a garden of fragrant roses. Again, the challenge of cultural transformation was likened by Gregory Nazianzen to Moses sweetening the bitter waters of Marah by throwing wood into them, while Gregory of Nyssa advised that any marriage with the pagan world must ensure that the offspring remains 'untainted' – a valid if unspecific cautionary note.

The process of discernment was necessarily lengthy and ongoing. It took many pastoral encounters and intellectual debates to discover what was really central to the Church's life and witness, as contrasted with what was culturally assumed or indeed merely peripheral. Here, it was above all Augustine who led the way; he was less prone than some of his contemporaries to make hasty judgments, despite thereby attracting the accusation of defending Christian mediocrity. For example, on the question of what constituted heresy he observed:

> It is, in fact, extremely difficult to formulate a definition, and when we
> try to enumerate all of them, we have to be on our guard, not to pass over
> some which are really heresies or to include some which are not.

So idiosyncrasies and an excess of devotional zeal may be theologically dubious without demanding outright condemnation; ordinary believers, too, may practise traditional customs without realising that they conflict with Christian teaching. Augustine did believe, however, that a real difference existed between what was demonically inspired and what was mere human convention, and between what was essential and what could actually be judged as superfluous.

Yet his making of careful distinctions seems to mark the end of an era. In the 5th century the burden was shifting imperceptibly from discovering the truth to disseminating it, from discerning 'the working of the Holy Spirit in the world' to insisting on 'the Holy Spirit of discipline within the church'. Correspondingly, bishops became more coercive. The Church was settling down to be an institution with sharper boundaries than it had known before. The historian Robert Markus wrote:

> The bishops were constantly alert to traces of the unregenerate past, and
> they were ready to diagnose its presence in daily practices that seemed
> innocuous to most people... (Thus) the festivals of the pagan calendar,

observed by Christians problematically in the mid-fourth century, were growing suspect and by the end of the fifth century were in large measure eliminated from the Christian calendar. Examples of the boundaries of Christianity being more rigidly drawn could be multiplied.

If in many places pagan celebrations were by now in decline, this could not be said of the situation in England in the 5th and 6th centuries, following the withdrawal of Roman troops. Hostile invasions in this period had driven Christianity to the margins, and a rescue mission was eventually launched by Pope Gregory. Augustine (not the bishop already mentioned, but a monk from Rome) reached Kent in 597. Envoys returned to Gregory with the news of their favourable reception, but also requesting his further advice. The letter back with Mellitus included the advice to retain the pagan temples, and – having destroyed the idols within them – to consecrate them with holy water and set up altars (if possible, enclosing saintly relics), so that now the people would be able to worship the one true God in a customary setting. In similar vein he hoped Augustine would find suitable celebrations to replace the pagan festivals (and nearly three centuries earlier this is how the mid-winter feast we know as Christmas had made its way into the Christian calendar). Gregory concluded that it was impossible to win entrenched minds from their error overnight. As he so graphically expressed it, a climber does not reach the top of a mountain by a single stride, but gradually, step by step. The Venerable Bede subsequently wrote here of the need for 'preliminary training'; others might refer to the exercise of pastoral discretion in the care and oversight of the newly Christianised.

Gregory's wisdom informed church policy ever thereafter. There were certainly times when zealots wanted to mould others in their own extreme ways, but for men like Augustine of Hippo and Gregory the aim was for a catholicity which allowed for various expressions and degrees of the faith, in other words, for an inclusive Church.

Harold Drake, a church historian, has written:

Christianity faced two challenges to succeed: the first, to develop sufficient appeal to the majority culture to attract a critical mass of members; the second, to do so without letting that culture completely absorb its identity and the alternative message it offered.

There is an obvious tension between these two objectives, which is already seen in the Gospels. For example, Luke first recalls how discipleship demands renunciation, 'No one who puts his hand to the plough and looks back is fit for the kingdom of God' [Lk 9.62]. But shortly afterwards Jesus explains how generous regard for others will then sometimes imply the acceptance of unfamiliar customs – 'eat what is set before you', he says, indicating that refusal of such hospitality – a failure to engage with a different culture – might lead to the rejection of their mission altogether.

A particular issue in this missionary engagement concerns the use or otherwise of the vernacular language. The first Christians were Palestinian Jews, who spoke Aramaic in their homes but used Hebrew in their scriptures and their formal worship. Christian worship was rooted, as we have noted, in house churches where Aramaic was undoubtedly spoken (given the retention of Aramaic words and phrases within the New Testament – *maranatha*, for example, clearly being taken from its liturgical usage). However, the Christian faith spread rapidly elsewhere, and the Eucharist came to be celebrated in many languages, including Syriac, Coptic, and Armenian. In most of the Mediterranean world, the *koine* – or 'common' language – was Greek, which became the language of liturgy in that region and remained so until the early 3rd century. There are many words still in use that have Greek roots: for example, *Eucharist, liturgy, baptism, evangelise, bishop, martyr, and catechumen* as well as the familiar petition retained in its Greek form *Kyrie eleison*. But in the 3rd and 4th centuries Latin began to replace Greek as the common language, perhaps influenced by its long-standing usage in North Africa. By the 6th century, the Roman Canon (known today as Eucharistic Prayer 1) emerged completely in Latin and was prescribed for use exactly as written. It had of course developed from previous liturgies, partly in Greek and partly in Latin, which in turn had superseded the earlier often less formal liturgies.

For native speakers of Latin this presented no difficulty, but for people living beyond the former boundaries of the Roman Empire this could well prove an obstacle to conversion – to what would inevitably seem a 'foreign' religion, even if arguably 'truer' than their existing beliefs. The difficulty is well highlighted in Cyril and Methodius' 9th century mission to the Slavs. They were brothers from Thessalonica, who were sent north in response to a request from the Khazars for Christian teachers. They soon learned the Khazar language and achieved many conversions. Then there came a request from the Moravians for a preacher of the Gospel – a German mission having previously failed through ignorance of the Slavonic tongue. Cyril and Methodius, who already knew the language, were their obvious replacements. Cyril did even more than was anticipated: he invented an alphabet and, with the help of Methodius, translated the Gospels and the necessary liturgical books into Slavonic. Their success in the 860s, was however, challenged by the Germans and resulted in a summons to Rome. But Pope Adrian II was convinced of their orthodoxy, and so commended their missionary activity, sanctioned the Slavonic Liturgy, and ordained Cyril and Methodius as bishops.

Cyril died in Rome soon afterwards, while Methodius returned to Moravia. It was not long before opposition mounted again; this resulted in his imprisonment for three years. The Pope – who was now John VIII – intervened and, after making further inquiry, again agreed the use of Slavonic in the liturgy, while decreeing that the Gospel should be read first in Latin and then in Slavonic. Methodius managed to complete his Slavonic translation of the Bible in his monastery in Constantinople, and eventually died in 885.

Extract from a late 10ᵗʰ century Glagolitic Gospel Book

The illustration here shows the beginning of St Mark's Gospel, with Mark himself receiving angelic inspiration. It is written in Old Church Slavonic using the Glagolitic script usually attributed to Cyril and Methodius.

Manuscripts of other vernacular translations (e.g. into Gothic, Syriac, Arabic, or Armenian) as early as the 6th century are also extant, and the 'Celtic' art of the Lindisfarne Gospels (c. 700) is of course much renowned. Bilingual Psalters, with parallel columns in Greek and Arabic, dating from the 8th century have been found at St Catherine's Monastery on Mount Sinai.

This might be heralded as a 'landmark victory', but it proved to be an exception for centuries yet to come. Even though Latin evolved into various modern languages, it retained its exclusive position in the Roman Rite until the 2nd Vatican Council. Although monk-scholars such as St Bede added partial translations to the Latin text of biblical manuscripts, it was not until John Wyclif (in the 14th century) and William Tyndale (in the early 16th century) that complete English translations of the Bible came into more widespread circulation. These met with strong disapproval from the Church, since their authors were men of reforming zeal. Further, it was considered dangerous for those who lacked hermeneutical training to have ready access to the Scriptures: given the widespread misreading of texts among both clergy and laity even today, this hesitation is not without some foundation.

The English Reformation resulted, as we know, in an entirely vernacular Anglican liturgy, a move which the Catholic Church allowed some 400 years later (while retaining the Roman Missal in Latin as the normative rite) and thus respected the original instinct of Christianity that people should worship in a language they understand:

How is it that we hear, each of us in his own native language? [Acts 2.8]

Yet despite the apparent freedom to use a 'native' translation, the ensuing result may still not correspond too well with local forms of expression, leaving some people (including English-speaking Catholics?[5]) still feeling 'excluded' by the underlying Latin style. James Okoye has articulated similar reservations as an African:

---

[5] The new English translation of the Roman Missal, which came into use in 2011, does better justice than its predecessor to scriptural references in the text, but leaves some prayers – literally rendered from the Latin – opaque to many of the faithful and not always easy to deliver verbally, given their propensity to include a multitude of subordinate clauses. Of more traditional importance is the need to engage with people's hearts and minds, as indeed Christ did himself.

Africa is an oral culture which uses words for communicating feeling and beauty; repetition sustains and strengthens feelings. The Roman liturgy privileges doctrine; Africa privileges experience.

Indeed, Catholic bishops in West Africa asserted in 1989 that Africa's cultural affinities are much more with the *Jewish roots* of Christianity than with its subsequent Greco-Roman developments.

Nor is it only in Africa that such comments can arise. When Timothy Radcliffe visited Asia, he experienced a style of worship in which the repetitive element was also prominent:

Many religions are marked by this tradition of the repetition of sacred words... I heard a Buddhist service, and it seemed to consist in the endless repetition of holy words... The constant reiteration of words can work a slow but deep transformation of our hearts.

An early Christian example of this usage is the threefold *Kyrie eleison* – as also the Ter-sanctus ('Holy, holy, holy') – still retained in the Mass. Both of these are derived from 'the Jewish roots of Christianity' in the Bible, in which repetition is an idiomatic means of intensifying what is being expressed.

W.A.Graham in *Beyond the Written Word* reminds us that in many cultures religious rites have purposes going beyond the communication of specific content. He refers to the 'sensual' dimension:

(I) suggest that seeing, hearing, and touching in particular are essential elements in religious life as we observe it. They deserve greater attention than our bias in favour of the mental and emotional aspects typically allows.

To illustrate his point, he points to modes such as chant, repetitious singing, artistic or dramatic representation, the pageantry of solemn procession, even the devout touching of holy objects. John Barton in his *Hulsean Lectures* (1990) comments too on the way the Gospel is proclaimed at Mass:

In Catholic and Orthodox liturgy, the reading of the Gospel is attended with special ceremonies that emphasize the holiness of the 'message' it communicates... [so that] in reading 'God's Word' in the presence of God, the community reaffirms its relationship with God. There is an analogy with what linguists call 'phatic communion', where we speak to someone else not in order to communicate information, ask questions, or give instructions, but simply to 'service' our relationship with them.

Defenders of the Latin Mass would certainly agree that a sense of divine mystery and transcendence is more important than the mere transfer of information in intelligible words – as would the adherents of other religions. Muslims indeed speak of an inherent sacrality in the very recitation of the Qur'an; for them, the original Arabic sounds are an utterance from God, regardless of how far such speech is comprehended. Yet for Christians the 'incarnational' principle must be borne in mind; namely, that we worship a God who has come alongside us and shared our human existence. This surely suggests a liturgy that resonates with our cultural forms of expression, even if it lifts us beyond them into new dimensions of divine experience. And this is actually the ancient Christian tradition, as Josef Jungmann observed in his study *The Early Liturgy* (1959):

> The local Churches... did not hesitate to absorb into the Liturgy certain purified solemn and festive cultic elements deriving from the pagan world. They were regarded as capable of moving the minds and imaginations of the people who felt drawn towards them.

Such an abiding principle is clearly affirmed in the 2nd Vatican Council Decree *Ad Gentes*:

> The faith should be... celebrated in a liturgy that is in harmony with the character of the people... The communion of the young Churches with the whole Church must remain intimate, they must graft elements of its tradition on to their own culture.

It remains a sensitive area where getting the right balance is not easy, and down the centuries the Church has sometimes oscillated between the opposite poles of rigidity and laxity.

Tensions can therefore sometimes be generated. A notorious struggle eventually developed, for example, in China where Jesuit innovators were challenged and in the end defeated by Dominican and Franciscan hardliners. The controversy centred on the policies of Matteo Ricci, an Italian Jesuit who reached China in 1582, where he joined Michele Ruggieri. Both of them were determined to adapt to the religious qualities of the Chinese: Ruggieri to the common people, among whom Buddhist and Taoist elements predominated, and Ricci to the educated classes, where Confucianism prevailed.

Matteo Ricci (on the left) and two Jesuit colleagues

Although they met with considerable success, a dispute developed that lasted for over a hundred years. This so-called Rites Controversy centred on Ricci's contention that the ceremonial rites of Confucianism and ancestor veneration were primarily social and political in nature and could be practised by converts. The Dominicans, however, charged that the practices were idolatrous; this kind of respect paid to one's forebears was nothing less than demon worship. The case was taken to Rome, where it dragged on and on, largely because no one there knew much about Chinese culture. The Jesuits themselves appealed to the Chinese emperor, but understandably he was confused as to why missionaries were attacking each other. The timely discovery in 1623 of an ancient Nestorian monument enabled the Jesuits to answer one common objection – that Christianity was, after all, a very new religion. Here was evidence that a thousand years earlier the Christian gospel had already reached China. This persuaded the emperor to expel those missionaries who opposed Ricci. This did not, however, end the struggle. Spanish Franciscans later persuaded Pope Clement XI that the Jesuits were making dangerous accommodations to Chinese sensibilities. So in 1704 he placed a ban on using Chinese terms such as *Shang Di* (supreme emperor) for God, and insisted that God should be dressed instead in European guise.

Related issues are in evidence in 18th century England. The Methodist revival, for example, was a response to the failure of the Church of England to embrace 'the common people' whom Ruggieri had reached in China. The Enlightenment was all very well for the educated classes, but there were many in the expanding population, not least in the newly industrialised towns, who needed pastoral care and spiritual ministry. They were like those on whom Jesus himself took pity:

> He saw a great throng, and he had compassion on them, because they were like sheep without a shepherd; and he began to teach them many things. [Mk 6.34]

So a small band of Anglican clergymen, especially George Whitefield and the Wesley brothers John and Charles, became itinerant preachers who met with a huge response. In John Wesley's own words: 'In every place where they came, many began to show such a concern for religion as they had never done before.' Although tensions arose within the established church, resulting eventually in the Methodist movement becoming a separate denomination, its influence became widespread; kindred spirits were found across the spectrum of churches who rejected the meagre theology and unabashed worldliness of the Hanoverian church in favour of fervent evangelical teachings. Quite often the patterns of worship that accompanied them were very different from inherited liturgies.

We should not forget that this was John Henry Newman's background. While he saw his own theological ideas develop, and thus also his church allegiance, his early evangelical instinct to bring the hearts and minds of the multitude into a deeper relationship with God never left him. It was as a Catholic later in life that he became more aware of issues like those that had faced Ricci in China – the dominance of Romish practices (*ultramontanism*, as it came to be called) – and so led him to become the standard bearer for a more appropriately *English* Catholicism. He wrote:

> If Christianity be a universal religion, suited not simply to one locality or period, but to all times and places, it cannot but vary in its relationships and dealings with the world around it, that is, it will develop. Principles require a very various application according as persons and circumstances vary, and must be thrown into new shapes according to the form of society which they are to serve.

Nor need development, he believed, always be shaped by the hierarchy. He never forgot his early study of the 4th century Arian controversy, when orthodox beliefs were retained more by the faithful than by some of the bishops. Thus he could write an article entitled *On*

Consulting the Faithful in Matters of Doctrine. He argued that no 'channel of tradition' – which included bishops, doctors of the Church and lay people – should be 'treated with disrespect'. He was wary of insensitivity towards the laity, considering that it is 'not the wise and powerful, but the obscure, the unlearned, and the weak' who constitute 'the real strength' of the Church.

He was alert to the many and various ways in which God prompts and nurtures faith, even at times from the unlikeliest of directions. He even suggested that God may on occasion speak to us through unbelievers or through the rites and customs of non-Christian people. Such ideas were radical for his day, but later proved particularly influential. In the 2nd Vatican Council's *Decree concerning non-Christian Religions* there are striking resemblances to the strategy he had once proposed: that, following St Paul's earlier lead, the missionary should 'seek some points in the existing superstitions as the basis of his own instructions, instead of indiscriminately condemning and discarding the whole assemblage of heathen opinions and practices'.

Hence, as a follow-up to Newman's thinking, I want now to review the practice of inclusivity in the African Church. Several new missionary congregations were established in the second half of the 19th century as opportunities presented themselves in Africa – precisely the period of Newman's mature writings. Without exception they were clear about the need for what has since been called 'inculturation'. Here is Cardinal Lavigerie of Algiers, who founded the Missionaries of Africa, better known as the White Fathers, in the 1850s:

> Missionaries must not only learn the local language in order to communicate with the people, they must speak it among themselves. The children they educate must be allowed to remain truly African and to keep their customs and their way of life.

Soon afterwards, Daniel Comboni launched the Verona Fathers and Sisters. His crucial idea was to regenerate Africa 'by means of Africa herself', with young Africans 'trained in their own environment, preserving their racial characteristics'. Trainees of the Holy Ghost Fathers were likewise reminded that the Christian religion had 'invariably to be established in the soil'. It has to be admitted that there were still contrary views within the Vatican, but in time these gradually weakened. Although (in 1890) Leo XIII instructed missionaries that their chief task was 'to bathe those inhabitants living in darkness and blind superstition with the light of divine truth', by 1919 Benedict XV laid more emphasis upon paving the way for a fully local Church; missionaries, he taught, should 'never despise nor disparage local people'. It was then Pius XII who made a landmark address in 1944 to the Pontifical Aid Societies, in which he began to discern a plurality of cultures. But it took John XXIII in *Princeps Pastorum* (1959) to flesh this out in a more radical concept of a multicultural Church:

> She does not identify herself with any one culture to the exclusion of the rest – not even with European and Western culture, with which her history is so closely linked... (She) is ever ready to recognise and acknowledge – and indeed to sponsor whole-heartedly – everything that can be set to the credit of the human mind and spirit.

In fact, his thinking stretched beyond the bounds of the Church:

> Wherever real values of art and thought are capable of enriching the human family, the Church is ready to encourage such work of the spirit.

This same perspective is embodied in the epoch-making documents of the 2nd Vatican Council:

> We... turn our thoughts to all those who acknowledge God and preserve in their traditions precious elements of religion and humanity. We wish that a frank dialogue may lead us all to welcome the impulses of the Spirit and to carry them out courageously.
>
> Liturgical reforms must ... be open to the genuine pastoral needs of the individual churches.

Most famously, it was Paul VI speaking after the Council to African bishops gathered in Kampala in 1969 who asserted, 'You may, and you must, have an African Christianity'. And his successor John Paul II made similar comments on his numerous visits to Africa. For example, he said in Lagos in 1982, 'The Church comes to bring Christ; she does not come to bring the culture of another race'. In Nairobi he was even more specific: 'Christ, in the members of his Body, is himself an African.'

We may ask, How far have these stirring ideas been implemented? What in practice might such inclusiveness actually look like? A friend of ours in Malawi, Bishop Patrick Kalilombe, once observed 'how, in the face of tremendous odds, Africans have developed a spirituality of joy: the song, the dance, the celebration' – which seldom feature prominently in Eucharistic liturgies in the West, but are endemic elsewhere. Various evaluations have been carried out of indigenous beliefs and practices, and there seems to be much indeed that is potentially compatible with Christian faith:

> The idea of a supreme Creator – evocative religious symbolism – belief in the afterlife – a sense of mutual belonging – the importance of the extended family – bonds between the living and deceased relatives – sacred shrines – times of festival and celebration such as harvest – rites of purification for individuals and communities (here the Eucharist may introduce an important healing dimension).

But there are notorious weaknesses and blind spots too. The bonds of 'community' or 'solidarity' are often still limited to one's own lineage or tribe, and need supplementing with a care for the individual, or the outsider, or those members of the community who may seem no longer effective or productive. Or again, there are superstitions connected with the afterlife that can lead to unhealthy fears of witchcraft or other malevolent influences. Traditional 'rites' may also include such harmful features as female genital mutilation, or rituals of sexual initiation.

Allowing for suitable discernment though, we may conclude that as the Christian mission has expanded worldwide, new gifts of the Holy Spirit have emerged which, while particularly important in a local culture, may actually enrich the whole Church – provided always that the rooting of the faith in a different environment guards carefully against fracturing the hard won unity of Christ's earthly body. (More than once, I recall explaining to African seminarians that, although bread and wine are seldom products of their native soil, to replace them with maize and a home-brew such as *joala*, would not be faithful to the Lord's instruction. If wine in particular is hard to obtain, it should be the responsibility of a world-wide *inclusive* Church to facilitate its availability, as a sign of our unity with each other and with our forebears in the faith. The use of local products could well signal a breach, just as some indigenous customs can also conflict with universal teaching.)

A reforming church

Development and change happen in the Church for all sorts of reasons, as we have seen. The location, the circumstances, the size and social composition of those who gather for worship call for suitably appropriate liturgy and forms of ministry. Their witness in the world will in turn need to be responsive to the prevailing culture and to the often changing issues of the day. Sometimes too a reforming element is required when corruption or abuses set in, when emphases are wrongly stressed, when pastoral sensitivity is forgotten, when ill-considered teachings are promoted, or when devotional habits distort the centrality of Christ himself. In fact, the Church must constantly be alert to the guidance of the Holy Spirit, whose intent is to make us all ever more Christlike.

Pope Francis pointed a couple of years ago to two opposite temptations:

- Some are tempted to close themselves within the written word, without allowing God to surprise them. They are walled in by 'the certitude of what they know and not of what they still need to learn and to achieve'.

- Then there are those with good intentions, but in facing new situations tend 'to bypass the roots, the causes, and treat only the symptoms'.

The obvious danger that can arise is a polarising of the Church into opposite camps, 'traditionalists' at war with 'progressives' – or so the media portrays them.

Nevertheless, unity has always been an essential concern for the Church, ever since our Lord prayed, 'Holy Father, keep them in thy name... that they may be one, even as we are one.' This was clearly a vital priority as the Church expanded in apostolic times, and there are many references to its importance in the New Testament. We have noted that when Paul wanted to allow greater freedom to his pagan converts, he did not do so unilaterally. He went to Jerusalem to lay his reforming ideas before the church leaders there. He explains to the Galatians that he did not want to 'be running in vain' on a path of his own devising. When divisions arose within the Corinthian church, he appealed that they should be 'united in the same mind and the same judgment'. He begs exactly the same when writing to the Ephesians:

There is one body and one Spirit, just as you were called to the one hope that belongs to your call, one Lord, one faith, one baptism, one God and Father of us all. [Eph 4.4]

In very practical terms too, the collection [2 Cor 8 cf. Rom 15.26] that he organised for the poorer brothers and sisters back in Judaea was an expression of the churches' belonging together in Christ.

When one realises that today there are tens of thousands of *different* churches across the world, it is clear that something has gone badly astray. Our Lord's expressed prayer on the eve of his crucifixion has been ignored, as if it matters very little. And yet in a seriously broken world what better witness could Christians offer than the example of their own commitment to dialogue, to reconciliation, and to unity – instead of the all-too-common pursuit of divisive agendas. Once again Newman's sane advice is apposite:

What the genius of the Church cannot bear is, changes in thought being hurried, abrupt, violent – out of tenderness to souls...

The great thing is to move all together and then the change, as geological changes, must be very slow.

But patience is not a modern virtue; we live in a much more 'instant' society when individuals and groups demand immediate action. Here, for example, is a list of urgent reforms proposed recently in a letter to *Time* magazine by an Australian lady:

No doubt Pope Francis genuinely endeavours to move the Roman Catholic Church into the 21st century. But unless he addresses the core issues of the modern world – such as ordination of women, marriage for priests, contraception, abortion, euthanasia, homosexuality – the church will remain marginalized, and membership, at least in the developed world, will dwindle rapidly.

My own response might run something like this:

Dear 'concerned', I understand that for you what counts is the developed world, which you also refer to as the modern world. That leaves rather a lot of people in the rest of the world who may not ascribe nearly as much importance to these issues – but then, if they're not as 'modern' as you and rather more undeveloped, you may not think their concerns matter so much. However, they're the ones who suffer violence and conflict on a daily basis, whose food security is minimal compared with yours, who also bear the brunt of climate change; and if trafficking and slavery are still carried on today, it's probably not so much on your home run in Australia. You may not be aware that Pope Francis has been campaigning strongly on their behalf because for him too these are actually today's most pressing issues.

Some further news: when I carried out a parish survey a few years ago as to why some Catholics had lapsed, none of them breathed a word of the supposed core issues that you mention. Instead, they fell away because mass times were inconvenient, because of mobility problems, because worship seemed uninspiring or because they were angry about a re-ordering of the church interior. Others had faced a personal crisis and felt that they were offered insufficient support; a few had been through a divorce and now felt excluded by the church on account of their remarriage; doctrinal doubts were raised by just two people. I suspect that elsewhere (such as Ireland) other factors might feature more prominently – clerical abuse of children or maybe the tyrannical attitudes of some priests.

But if you have evidence for the rapid dwindling of numbers as you predict, let us have it. Do you really think that if the Catholic Church ordained women, and promoted contraception, abortion, euthanasia and homosexuality, there would be a huge rush to grab a seat? Might there not be others, in any case, who would collide with them in the doorway as they left? As for married priests, little by little that seems to be happening anyway, but it would be strange if their promoters stayed away from mass when they're obviously calling for more masses.

PS Pope Francis hasn't forgotten your concerns: after holding two consultative Synods on what are broadly called 'family' issues, he has now issued Amoris Laetitia (The Joy of Love) in which he urges respect for individual consciences. In his words, 'Not all discussions of doctrinal, moral or pastoral issues need to be settled by interventions of the magisterium. Each country or region… can seek solutions better suited to its culture and sensitive to its traditions and local needs.' You may also be surprised to know that he challenges attitudes over 'leadership roles', which for him can certainly be exercised by women.

It may be helpful to recall an important discussion of church reform that was published by the Dominican Yves Congar in 1950 under the title *Vraie et fausse réforme dans l'Église*. He offered various suggestions that might enable genuine reform while avoiding schism (always the greatest hazard). He insisted that discussion must be serious and well-informed, certainly not losing touch with core beliefs and with inherited traditions. In the latter respect he called for a *reditus ad fontes*, a return to our roots. The goal is not to win an argument, but (in Paul's words) to 'build up the body of Christ'; so it is best to begin by focusing on what is held in common and not on what is contentious. He envisioned a Church where we talk *with* each other and not *at* each other, recognising that tradition is always open to development and is best done when a variety of perspectives work together. It can happen too that age-long disputes can be resolved in this way, with a growing realisation that different parties (or churches) have been stressing different facets of the same truth, using perhaps different nuances of language. It may be that varying church practices can be seen as complementary, with a potential for others suitably to adopt as well. Here one may recall that it took Catholics and Lutherans nearly 500 years to discover that their doctrinal disagreements were far less significant than had been assumed for most of that time: and that some Anglicans at least were sufficiently close to a Catholic ethos that a home (or Ordinariate) could be provided for them within the Catholic fold.

Congar perhaps did not realise that his own line of thinking resonated with the typical African point of view. Here I invoke the distinguished Catholic theologian Benezet Bujo and the insights in his book *The Ethical Dimension of Community*. The African perspective he unfolds is an important corrective to the prevailing individualism of the West. Bujo heralds its instinct for communitarianism, which is not 'a duel where defeat of the opposite adversary is aimed at... (but) a form of mutual assistance.' It is 'a process of talking and listening', a dialogue searching for the common good. He insists that it is more than rational discourse, for 'without communal relationship one can neither find his or her identity nor learn to think.' In Africa Descartes would have to modify his thinking and say, *Cognatus sum ergo sum* ('I am known, therefore I am' – I exist only in relation to others) for which there are many African proverbial equivalents, like the famous Zulu saying, *Umuntu ngumuntu nagabantu* ('a person is a person because of other people'). Such an expression surely reflects the Christian understanding of God as Trinitarian; it was Gregory of Nazianus in the late 4th century who observed that the 'persons' of the Trinity are named after their *mutual relationships*, one with another.

Africa has its own traditions of debate, as mentioned already. The *pitso* or palaver is a gathering to discover the common mind of a community, and it may seem more in keeping with the spirit of Christ than some procedures found today in the Church. For example, in the present soul-searching of the Anglican Communion, there can be fierce antagonism between liberal thinkers in America (and increasingly in England too) and the more conservative attitudes of Nigerians and Ugandans. Yet during my ten years serving on General Synod I do not recall speakers ever suggesting that the debate needed widening to include the views of Anglicans elsewhere. 'We decide for ourselves' was the prevailing mood. The fraternal spirit of the Lambeth Fathers, however, from 1867 onwards was always one of sympathetic consultation rather than for enacting hasty legislation, a tradition different from today's too frequent factional strife. Some have perhaps forgotten that the Greek word 'synod' means literally 'together on the way'. So a reminder is necessary that simply to achieve a voting majority may be far from discerning the truth in love, and that to work to a scheduled timetable is not quite the same as allowing the spirit to 'blow where he wills'.

Indeed, one may ask, how much conflict in the Church is born of impatience and intolerance? Even the sometimes argumentative Paul has room for the slower thinkers: 'Sinning against your brethren and wounding their conscience when it is weak, you sin against Christ' [1 Cor 8.12]. He necessarily practised self-restraint, as he explained: 'Am I not free?... Do we not have the right?... nevertheless, we have not made use of this right, but we endure anything rather than put an obstacle in the way of the gospel of Christ' [1 Cor 9.1, 4, 12]. His role model was Jesus, who was undoubtedly what an Asian theologian once termed a 'three mile an hour' God. He walked at a human pace, he spoke in earthy symbols, he resisted the devil's triumphalism, he rejected the royal road (the fast motorway) to success. He died as a minority of one, not even sure whether his closest friends had grasped the point. A bishop under whom I once served was wont to remind his flock that denying ourselves, and sometimes refusing to accede to popular demands, can be for a greater good, 'for the sake of the others': such was the motivation that led our Lord to his Cross. Before pursuing our own ends – in which I include any deeply held convictions – we need to ask, Will this promote the common good? Will others be blessed and enriched by this action, this decision, or will it sow confusion and discord? Will 'the little ones', as Jesus called them, be made to stumble? What is clear from the Gospels and the rest of the New Testament is that unity was more fundamental to Jesus and to his Church than some of our contemporary fashions and passions.

I am aware that I have cited the Anglican Communion as an example of how changes made too rapidly can lead to fractious disunity, with plans for a Lambeth Conference in 2018 having to be scrapped (admittedly with hopes of one taking place in 2020 instead). But the Catholic Church is not immune from unhealthy animosities of its own. For example, the transition to a vernacular liturgy was not a universal success, and some who objected split away from the main body under the leadership of Archbishop Lefèvre. More recently (as mentioned already in a footnote) there has been a new English translation of the Roman missal which has resulted in much disaffection. It was in effect imposed without adequate consultation – indeed, an agreed alternative that had been much more widely discussed was rejected on doctrinaire grounds. Equally, some of the recommendations of the 2nd Vatican Council have proved divisive, with a polarising of views between 'conservatives' and 'modernisers'.

Again, referring to those concerns of Pope Francis that I have already listed, the phrase 'a preferential option for the poor' reminds us that long-lasting tensions have only recently been resolved in Latin America. It was because of lurking fears of Marxism in the ranks of Catholic laity that the process of canonising Archbishop Oscar Romero was frozen for a long time. He was accused of promoting 'liberation theology', which did not go down well with some church leaders and others who supported the military government of San Salvador.

Nor was liberation theology at all popular in Rome for many years. The history of its rehabilitation is worth recalling. The so-called 'father' of this approach was the Peruvian Fr Gustavo Gutiérrez, who summarised it thus:

This is a theology which does not stop reflecting on the world, but which tries to be part of the process through which the world is transformed.

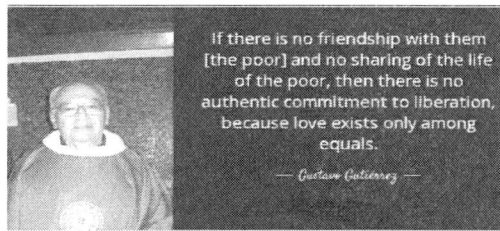

If there is no friendship with them [the poor] and no sharing of the life of the poor, then there is no authentic commitment to liberation, because love exists only among equals.

— Gustavo Gutiérrez —

It is a theology which is open – in the protest against trampled human dignity, in the struggle against the plunder of the vast majority of humankind, in liberating love, and in the building of a new, just, and comradely society – to the gift of the Kingdom of God.

The context of Latin America in which he was writing was particularly violent and bloody. For example, during the first 75 years after the Spaniards reached Mexico, the indigenous population fell from perhaps seventeen million to around one million – and only a percentage of deaths were the result of imported European diseases. The most renowned critic of Spanish ruthlessness was the Dominican Bartolomé de las Casas, who died in 1566. He campaigned tirelessly for the welfare of local people but alas! there were too few like him. Eventually most countries gained their independence; yet although by the early 20th century church and state were separate, there was still much conservative collusion between them. Then came the successful Cuban revolution in 1959 which became the great inspiration for insurgencies elsewhere.

It was about this time that a grassroots movement of 'base ecclesial communities' began to grow, particularly in Brazil, although a particularly famous one (eventually destroyed by government forces) was in Nicaragua led by the priest-poet Ernesto Cardenal. These were rooted in communal study of the Bible, and often sprang up on the fringes of cities or in rural areas that lacked priests. Their mainly lay leaders encouraged people to reflect on what they read in scripture and to discern what should be changed in their everyday life. Hence plenty of organised local action took place, which was unpopular with both the political and the religious authorities. An influential text was the groundbreaking book of the Brazilian Paulo Freire *The pedagogy of the oppressed*:

> We must never provide the people with programmes which have little or nothing to do with their own preoccupations, doubts, hopes and fears...
> Our role (the educationalists) is to dialogue with them.

You can see that there are clear links here with the idea of 'inculturation'. You can also appreciate why there were serious hesitations about these communities and the whole thrust of liberation theology among the church hierarchy. Freire's key text was published in 1970 and just over a decade later Cardinal Ratzinger as Prefect of the CDF (the Congregation for the Doctrine of Faith) published his famous critique. At the heart of it was the fear that the Christian faith was being distorted into a Marxist-inspired manifesto of revolutionary fervour. Liberation theology, he claimed, 'proposes a novel interpretation of both the content of faith and of Christian existence which seriously departs from the teaching of the Church and, in fact, actually constitutes a practical negation'. In a further move, Leonardo Boff was summoned to Rome to discuss his writings which were felt to criticise church authorities, and he was silenced for over a year.

The CDF critique did, however, remind its readers of existing responses by Latin American bishops, endorsed by successive Popes Paul VI and John Paul II. These went some way towards addressing the appalling social realities their people faced. There was a very important gathering of bishops in Medellín (Colombia) in 1968 which actually encouraged the base communities, at the same time pledging the clergy to adopt the simplest of lifestyles, to renounce 'honourable titles belonging to another era', to overcome the system of fees linked to the administration of the sacraments, to entrust the administration of church property to lay people, to look above all to the welfare of the neediest – if possible by living with them. 'No earthly ambition impels the Church', they said, 'only her wish to be the humble servant of all.' There was a further conference in 1979 at Puebla in Mexico which 'affirmed the need for conversion on the part of the *whole church* to a preferential option for the poor, an option aimed at their integral liberation'. The word 'integral' is extremely important, since it implies liberation from the inner forces of sin, from selfishness, from hatred and violent behaviour and so on, as much as (or even more than) social and political liberation.

By the time Cardinal Ratzinger became Pope Benedict XVI in 2005, the world had changed considerably, in that communism had largely collapsed and the fear of Marxism taking over Christian communities had disappeared altogether. In Latin America the challenge of an expanding Pentecostalism was by now far more significant, and environmental issues were much more to the fore. When the bishops across the continent met in 2007, liberation theology was firmly established, and was now also embracing so-called 'Indian theology', meaning the traditional myths and wisdom of the indigenous Indian population. Benedict attended the conference and affirmed this development, which he said led to a fortunate 'synthesis between traditional cultures and the Christian faith.' He applauded 'the rich and profound popular synthesis, in which we see the soul of the Latin American peoples.' One aspect of indigenous spirituality which he appreciated was the awareness of a creator God gifting life in its many and varied forms.

The future Pope Francis, who lived through all the upheavals I have described, was also present, and it is clear that his priorities reflect his Latin American experience. I want to illustrate this from his 2013 encyclical *Evangelii Gaudium* (the Joy of the Gospel). He appreciates the need for appropriate decentralisation in the Catholic Church:

I do not believe that the papal magisterium should be expected to offer a definitive or complete word on every question which affects the Church and the world. It is not advisable for the Pope to take the place of local bishops in the discernment of every issue which arises in their territory.

Even in a bishop's own diocese (or territory), he urges something similar:

[The bishop] will sometimes go before his people, pointing the way and keeping their hope vibrant. At other times, he will simply be in their midst with his unassuming and merciful presence. At yet other times, he will have to walk after them, helping those who lag behind and – above all – allowing the flock to strike out on new paths.

All bishops, he insists, should open up 'means of participation' so that he can hear the full range of voices, and not just those who tell him what they think he'd like to hear. The aim is 'the missionary aspiration of reaching everyone'. In a changing world he wants the Church to stay in touch and to be as responsive as possible. So he notes the impact of urbanisation:

This challenges us to imagine innovative spaces and possibilities for prayer and communion which are more attractive and meaningful for city dwellers. Through the influence of the media, rural areas are being affected by the same cultural changes, which are significantly altering their way of life as well.

You may now appreciate why I began this (quasi-historical) review by recalling how the locus of worship was once very different and has a history of its own, which needs to be borne in mind when we consider current problems faced by (say) rural churches and clergy shortages. Pope Francis encourages us to be boldly creative. Once again this includes the readiness to welcome the 'positive values and forms' of other cultures, which can 'enrich the way the Gospel is preached, understood and lived'. 'We in the Church', he warns, 'can sometimes fall into a needless hallowing of our own culture, and thus show more fanaticism than true evangelising zeal.' Strong words indeed! Yet in implementing his advice, we need not be hasty. We should not, he says, be 'obsessed with immediate results'. We may have to be patient in the face of 'difficult and adverse situations, or inevitable changes in our plans'. We have to attend 'to the bigger picture' and be concerned 'for the long run', adding a reminder of Christ's teaching on the subject:

> The Lord himself, during his earthly life, often warned his disciples that there were things they could not yet understand and that they would have to await the Holy Spirit.

A final example of the Church's growth in understanding may be found in the Synod on the Family that took place in October 2015. The German language group, one of thirteen, included the following in its report:

> It became clear to us that, in many of our discussions, our thinking was too static and the personal-historical dimension was given little thought. The Church's teaching on marriage developed and deepened over time. Initially it was a case of humanising marriage, which led to the conviction that marriage was monogamous. In the light of Christian faith, the personal dignity of spouses was recognised more deeply and the image of God in human beings was perceived in the relationship between husband and wife. In a further step, the ecclesial dimension of marriage was extended and marriage was understood as a house church. And finally the Church became explicitly aware of the sacramentality of marriage... We request the insertion of this additional aspect in the finalised (Synod) text: every impression that Sacred Scripture only serves as a source of quotes for dogmatic, legal or ethical convictions should be avoided... The written word is to be integrated into the living word residing via the Holy Spirit in the heart of man.

That particular view has now been endorsed by Pope Francis himself, in his subsequent Apostolic Exhortation, *Amoris Laetitia*. Thereby he exemplifies what he teaches about the nature of the Church itself. The 2015 Synod is not to be regarded as an exceptional occurrence, since the Church – as he insisted at the time – must strive to 'become synodal': this means always *listening* to one another and to the voices of the faithful. Indeed, *The Tablet* rightly concluded in its editorial of 16 April 2016:

> The idea that general rules in the Catholic church are set in concrete for all time, never to be questioned let alone changed, is the major casualty of this (synodal) exercise.

When visiting Mexico soon after the Synod, Pope Francis reminded the bishops there to avoid 'the harsh rhetoric of elite discourse, clericalism, cold distance and princely conduct'. He stressed that only by sympathetic, careful listening do we begin to discern where the Holy Spirit is leading us – and thus what initiatives and what changes need to be undertaken. (Indeed, during the same visit, not only did he endorse the use of local languages in the Mass, he assured the indigenous peoples that the rest of the world had much to learn from them, especially at the present time about how to interact harmoniously with nature, 'our common home and an altar of human sharing'.)

Following the publication of *Amoris Laetitia* the bishops of England and Wales embarked at their 2016 post-Easter gathering upon their own 'synodal' journey of 'sympathetic, careful listening' and proposed a path of pastoral discernment for those whose marriages no longer reflected the traditional Christian norms:

> The Holy Father... notes the acute difficulty of judging difficult situations and calls priests to be close to these families and understanding of the reality of their lives, however 'untidy' these may be... In the particular case of the divorced and civilly remarried, there is a need to consider both those elements which can lead to a greater openness to the gospel of marriage in its fullness and those factors which may limit a free response to the Gospel in order to understand the subjective situation of a person before God. 'Hence it can no longer simply be said that all those in any irregular situation are living in a state of mortal sin and are deprived of sanctifying grace' (Amoris Laetitia 301). Through this spiritual discernment they should feel confident in the promise of God's mercy, the love of the Church and discover the next step in their response to God.

* * * * * * *

Little by little, therefore, Christians from the very beginning until the present day have learnt how to lend their individual ears and their collective mind to 'hear what the Spirit says to the churches' [Apoc 2.29] – whose continuing mission is in Jesus' words 'to take what is mine and declare it unto you' [Jn 16.14-15]. The worldwide challenge to the Church thus remains that of 'rediscovering' the apostolic experience, being formed as a community of disciples who live in the presence of the Lord, and who reach out to the whole of humankind.

God and the World

EXPLORING THE MYSTERY OF LIFE

The march of science

It is hardly necessary to draw attention to the remarkable advances in scientific understanding, accompanied by many technological innovations, which have taken place since the dawn of civilisation – but particularly in the last two hundred years. What we too easily overlook, however, is that the benefits are very unevenly shared across the world; that there can be side-effects, sometimes of alarming proportions; that knowledge can be put to malevolent purposes; that some supposedly 'scientific' approaches can be dehumanising; and that science itself does not always live up to the ambitious claims sometimes made for it.

To begin to justify each of these caveats would take separate lecture courses or a bulky tome, so I will merely offer a few brief illustrations.

- While many of us in Western countries appreciate the availability of clean running water, electricity and gas supplies, good communications, medical facilities, a high degree of food security and so on, these advantages may well be at a premium in the so-called 'developing' world. In Lesotho in the 1980s there was not a single dentist. Twenty years later the local hospital in Malawi often had no wipes or clean towels, and drugs were in short supply. In many places there is still no borehole for water. The electricity supply has become even more erratic – perhaps six hours a day in Zomba, but the bulk of the population, who live in rural areas, continue to be unconnected to the grid. Yet naïve forecasts imagine that everyone will soon be on the internet.
- Climate change is an established reality, and there are very few sceptics left who are in denial about global warming. Although long term temperature fluctuations can be traced back over thousands of years, and the activity or otherwise of sun spots may be a contributory factor, most scientists today agree that the vast increase in greenhouse gases is having an adverse effect: hence the recent

scramble to negotiate targets aimed at limiting future emissions. Since these are linked even more to modern consumer needs and demands than to the growth of populations, there are now warnings that the biggest environmental threats facing us will come from the increased use of technology (even if to some extent developments here may mitigate the harmful side effects).

- In Britain (as elsewhere) the lion's share of governmental investment in research is spent on defence projects. Devising new and deadlier forms of weaponry is a priority; selling them abroad is also one of the chief planks in the government's strategy for the maintenance of high employment figures. Yet, even where ethical considerations may rule out certain potential customers, once the product is sold there is little to prevent it reaching other less 'trustworthy' hands. A Nigerian member of St Teresa's in Ashford commented sadly that quite a few of the bullets used by Boko Haram might well bear the label 'Made in Britain'. In a more threatening scenario, what is to rule out other terrorist groups or unprincipled countries gaining access to enriched uranium or to toxic chemicals and acquiring the expertise to employ them?

- Quite apart from such destructive public uses of technology, biochemical developments that have led to certain 'recreational' drugs have also resulted in many individual lives (and those of their families) being wrecked. A recent example is fentanyl, a synthetic opioid many times more powerful than heroin. The drug trade too can indirectly help to fund criminal gangs and terrorist groups abroad, although it is seldom pointed out very robustly to users that their personal habits increase the threat to international security.

- In modern health care, statistics plays an important part. Quite often a correlation may be established between an ailment and a particular life style, or between a symptom and a medication with some success in its alleviation. The correlation, however, is seldom anything like one hundred per cent, and in any case the underlying explanation isn't necessarily clear. But it is quicker for a doctor to utilise such (possibly inconclusive) research – 'categorising' the patient or the symptom (or both) – rather than taking time to investigate factors that may sometimes be more significant. So treatment becomes less holistic, and the resulting prescription is unfortunately often liable to lead to unwanted side effects. These in turn may need further medication in a potentially regressive spiral. Another unwelcome consequence can be that medical personnel come to regard patients as clinical objects rather than as human beings. Sixty years ago, doctors were encouraged to listen to their patients: 'If you'll let them talk to you, they'll tell you what's wrong with them' – words of a long-serving GP in Wye.

- The dramatic discoveries of past decades have placed science on a pedestal in the public mind. It is, however, as fallible as any other human enterprise; theories need correcting or refining, mistakes need to be identified. It may be slightly unfair to single out the weather forecast, but I still recall that, following several winters of particularly snowy conditions in the 1970s, we were then warned of an impending Ice Age (alarming because we were also told that oil fields would be exhausted by the millennium); and in 1976, when no rain fell at all for several summer months, the prediction was made that reservoirs would take three years to refill – whereas in fact it took a mere three weeks of heavy September storms for them to be overflowing.

At a more theoretical level, it is also clear that as time progresses flaws may be found even in a widely accepted theory; this may have provided an explanatory framework satisfactory for most existing observations, but then further research makes discoveries that fall outside its predictions. So Newton's laws of gravity hold good until an Einstein demonstrates that (special or general) relativity gives a better account of certain phenomena. Both men are hailed as outstanding thinkers, but neither would claim omniscience. In Newton's words, 'I do not know what I may appear to the world, but to myself I seem to have been only like a boy playing on the sea-shore, and diverting myself in now and then finding a smoother pebble or a prettier shell than ordinary, whilst the great ocean of truth lay all undiscovered before me.' He was ready to pay tribute to those who had paved the way before him: 'If I have seen further, it is by standing on the shoulders of giants.'

Many issues arise just from the few examples cited above, but our focus must remain upon the human instinct to explore (and maybe exploit) the intricate mysteries of life: what moral accountability is required of those who research these matters, and how far may such explorations take us? The 2nd Vatican Council document *Gaudium et Spes* comments here:

Man is becoming aware that the forces he has unleashed are in his own hands, and that he himself must either control them or be enslaved by them.

More encouragingly, however, it also notes:

> Far from considering the conquests of man's genius and courage as opposed to God's power, as if he set himself up as a rival to the creator, the Christian ought to be convinced that the achievements of the human race are a sign of God's greatness and the fulfilment of his ineffable design.

Fortunately much wisdom may be gained from biblical and other religious sources, and under the guidance of rationality itself.

Biblical insights

A familiar, but misleading, reading of the opening chapters of Genesis pits its creation narrative against the scientific understanding of evolution over billions of years. Literalists of course reject the latter as contrary to their belief in the inerrancy of scripture, but biblical hermeneutics has also evolved into more plausible and fruitful methods of interpretation.

The Genesis account of creation is a post-exilic blend of two radical elements of Jewish thought. The earlier one, whose origins seem to lie in the emergence of Israel as a people chosen to follow a distinctive calling under Yahweh, is the institution of the *Sabbath*. Whereas there are natural cycles of time (the day, the month, the year) which in various ways have led to corresponding rituals in most primal religions, the artificial demarcation of time into a week of seven days is a deliberate cultural assertion which reflects the needs and responsibilities of human society. The oldest textual references to the Sabbath seem to be in the 8th century BC prophets Amos, Hosea and Isaiah, although tradition ascribes its institution to Moses; in the Book of the Covenant (later incorporated into the Pentateuch) we read:

> Six days you shall do your work, but on the seventh day you shall rest; that your ox and your ass may have rest, and the son of your bondmaid, and the alien, may be refreshed. [Exod 23.12]

An injunction to this effect is of course included in the Decalogue (the Ten Commandments) found in slightly different versions in Deuteronomy 5 and in Exodus 20. Each of these attempts to justify it, but for different reasons: it is because of God's liberation from slavery in Egypt that Israelites have now achieved their dignity as human persons and so should celebrate both his mercy and their own freedom from endless drudgery, which should be extended to all other people and indeed to the animals who serve them [Deut 5.14-15]; but again, it reflects the pattern of creation itself, when the Lord 'rested the seventh day' [Exod 20.11].

The latter explanation is firmly embedded in the creation narrative [Gen 1.1-2.3], which was the work of priests and scribes *universalising* what had been learnt through the years of captivity in Babylon. This radically enlarged their understanding of Yahweh's sovereignty in the world. ('Deutero') Isaiah expressed eloquently how he had not abandoned Israel during their period of exile, and indeed had enabled them to return to their homeland through the agency of a foreign ruler. Surprisingly, Cyrus whom he called the Lord's 'anointed' (that is, *Messiah*) is the first person to be so named.

> Thus says the Lord to his anointed, to Cyrus, whose right hand I have grasped, to subdue nations before him and ungird the loins of kings, to open doors before him that gates may not be closed: 'I will go before you and level the mountains, I will break in pieces the doors of bronze and cut asunder the bars of iron, I will give you the treasures of darkness and the hoards in secret places, that you may know that it is I, the Lord, the God of Israel, who call you by your name. For the sake of my servant Jacob, and Israel my chosen, I call you by your name, I surname you, though you do not know me. I am the Lord, and there is no other, besides me there is no God; I gird you, though you do not know me, that men may know, from the rising of the sun and from the west, that there is none besides me; I am the Lord, and there is no other. I form light and create darkness, I make weal and create woe, I am the Lord, who do all these things.' [Isa 45.1-7]

The phrase here concerning 'light' and 'darkness' is clearly suggestive of God's activity on 'day one' of the creation story, in which other details also relate to what has gone before:

- The lights in the firmament are 'for signs and seasons' [Gen 1.14]: this appears to be an insistence upon their function within the Jewish religious framework, and a rejection of astrological interpretations that would have been prominent in contemporary Babylon.

- The repeated use of the introductory words 'And God said' occurs ten times in all, echoing the ten clauses of the Decalogue. The implication is that this text, which as the Prologue to all that follows takes theological precedence as well, offers fundamental teaching to the whole of mankind.
- As already suggested, embracing the whole of creation within the framework of a week is a literary contrivance, whose aim was to enhance the importance of the Sabbath by tracing its origin back to God himself. To read it as a 'scientific' account is to miss its main theological purpose: indeed, one should recall other texts which specifically reject over-ambitious claims – as in the rebuke to Job, 'Where were you when I laid the foundations of the earth?' [Job 38.4]

The opening narrative of Genesis therefore does not stand alone, but needs to be read in the context of Israel's developing history. In particular, the later verses of chapter 1 which refer to men 'subduing' the earth, having 'dominion' over every living thing and the right to consume every seed-bearing form of vegetation, must be taken in conjunction with Sabbath ordinances. Indeed, it is not only 'your ox and your ass' who should be allowed proper rest every seven days, but the land itself should be left to lie fallow every seventh year:

For six years you shall sow your land and gather in its yield; but the seventh year you shall let it rest and lie fallow, that the poor of your people may eat; and what they leave the wild beasts may eat. You shall do likewise with your vineyard, and with your olive orchard. [Exod 23.10-11]

So there should be regard for the needs of the poor – a point hammered home in many other texts, especially those of the prophets – and for wild creatures as much as for domestic animals. In modern terminology this would come under the heading of 'justice, peace and the integrity of creation'. A detail very relevant to our contemporary world is the above mention of 'seed-bearing' plants or trees: the intention lying behind this restriction is obviously to enable vegetation to reproduce itself for the benefit of future generations. By extension, there is no scriptural warrant for the elimination of any species, animate or inanimate, nor for the poisoning of the atmosphere by greenhouse gases, nor for polluting the oceans (or anywhere else) with unwanted debris, nor for leaving barrenness behind; the destruction of life is specifically ruled out in the Decalogue.

It is nonsense therefore, when so much stress is given in the Bible to an ethic of responsible 'stewardship' of the earth's resources, to criticise church leaders for drawing attention to such teaching. The prophets of old – and Jesus himself – did not hesitate to make plain how God intended life on earth to be lived, and when necessary to rebuke those who thwarted these intentions. Some adverse comments were recently directed at Pope Francis for issuing his encyclical letter *Laudato Si'* (2015) which bears the subtitle *On care for our common home*; it was described as 'politically' motivated by those who were themselves inspired perhaps rather more by commercial interests. A reference to an address made by the Orthodox patriarch Bartholomew seems to summarise the thrust of the encyclical, which in many respects would command support from environmental groups and secular organisations concerned likewise about the future of the planet:

> Bartholomew has drawn attention to the ethical and spiritual roots of environmental problems, which require that we look for solutions not only in technology but in a change of humanity; otherwise we would be dealing merely with symptoms. He asks us to replace consumption with sacrifice, greed with generosity, wastefulness with a spirit of sharing, an asceticism which 'entails learning to give, and not simply to give up. It is a way of loving, of moving gradually away from what I want to what God's world needs. It is liberation from fear, greed and compulsion'.

A similar point was made over sixty years ago at the 2nd Vatican Council. It is once again in *Gaudium et Spes* that we read:

Technical progress is of less value than advances towards greater justice, wider brotherhood, and a more humane social environment.

> Technical progress may supply the material for human advance, but it is powerless to bring it about.

One further comment on the biblical presentation of our shared ethical responsibilities may be helpful. Although the book of Genesis itself opens with the words 'In the beginning God created the heavens and the earth' (a view shortly to be examined further), elsewhere in the Hebrew scriptures a significant variation is often found – with a reminder of the rationality underlying the whole plan of creation. There is an important stress upon God's 'wisdom':

> But the Lord is the true God... It is he who made the earth by his power, who established the world by his wisdom, and by his understanding stretched out the heavens. [Jer 10.10, 12]

> O Lord, how manifold are thy works! In wisdom hast thou made them all; the earth is full of thy creatures. [Ps 104.24]

> The Lord by wisdom founded the earth; by understanding he established the heavens. [Prov 3.19]

These references are fully amplified in the 'personification' of Wisdom later in the book of Proverbs:

> The Lord created me at the beginning of his work, the first of his acts of old. Ages ago I was set up, at the first, before the beginning of the earth. When there were no depths I was brought forth, when there were no springs abounding with water. Before the mountains had been shaped, before the hills, I was brought forth; before he had made the earth with its fields, or the first of the dust of the world. When he established the heavens, I was there... [Prov 8.22-27 cf. Sir 24.9; Wisd 9.9]

There is an insistence that, however the universe evolved after its early beginnings it was not a haphazard process – even if, as scientists may now argue, 'randomness' was an inherent part of it. We should note that the sequence of events in the Genesis narrative certainly envisages *developments* occurring in the variety and complexity of the created order, and classic commentators on the final verse of the text [Gen 2.3] explain the Hebrew word *la'asot* found there as meaning *evolve*: in other words, the world was created in such a way that 'it would continue to create itself' (as Jonathan Sacks expresses it in *The Great Partnership*).

The discerning mind will discover 'signs' in the natural world, therefore, that point to its divine origin: certainly its beauty and wonder make a spiritual impact upon most people, causing them to catch their breath and pause for a moment of contemplation. This is equally true in other religious traditions as well: the Qur'an, for example, often directs attention to the 'signs' that may be observed in the order and fruitfulness of creation, which testify to their origin in a single beneficent God:

In the creation of the heavens and the earth... there are signs in all these for those who use their minds. [Q 2.164]

Watch their fruits as they grow and ripen! In all this there are signs for those who would believe. [Q 6.99]

This language is reminiscent of the Fourth Gospel. There is no compelling proof of the universe's foundation in God's creativity, just as Jesus' miracles do not compel belief in his divine origin; but to those with open hearts and minds there are 'signs' that lead us to that conclusion. Newman summarised the logical dilemma in his *Essays Critical and Historical* (1870), 'The visible world is the instrument, yet the veil, of the world invisible'.

Searching for truth

For now we see in a mirror dimly, but then face to face. Now I know in part; then I shall understand fully, even as I have been fully understood. [1 Cor 13.12]

Despite St Paul's admission of our human limitations, there have been times when Christian theologians have claimed too much for their formulation of God's truth. The tendency towards dogmatic certainties is a weakness shared universally, even among some scientific disciplines: thus, in 1895 Thomson Kelvin made a definitive pronouncement that 'heavier-than-air flying machines are impossible', but only thirty years afterwards the Wright brothers proved him wrong. It is generally easier for scientists, however, to admit the shortcomings of their theories than for religious propagandists to hear alternative points of view. The fact that the Church has canonised, not just one, but four Gospels which offer varying interpretations of Jesus' life and ministry is surely an important reminder of the many-sided nature of truth – and therefore of the needful readiness to be open to fresh insights under the guidance of God's Spirit [Jn 16.13].

While some fixed tenets of belief are fundamental to the Church's very existence, the present generation is wary of what has become known as a 'grand narrative'. Too many memories persist of the ill effects of totalitarian ideologies, whereby individual freedom of choice and the creative instinct have often been suppressed. For many today their preferred creed is that of 'individualism', tempered only by the (sometimes grudging) recognition that other people too have their own rights to self-expression. Hence any idea of absolute truth is abhorrent, and even the dictates of reason are questionable. Among the younger generation in Britain today 'no religion' is the majority position, while others will dabble in experimental creeds collectively bracketed as 'New Age' (including a revival of Druidism, witchcraft, astrology and multiple therapies). A glance at the shelves of British bookshops offers ample confirmation: yards of books on 'alternative' beliefs contrast with little more than a foot of those relating to Christianity. The surprising element here is the abandonment of rationality in favour of emotional experiences, sometimes bracketed as 'self-spirituality': this suggests that, whereas science and religion are often posited to be in opposition to each other, in the contemporary world they are much needed partners in the search for well-grounded truth.

Well-known clashes have of course occurred in the past, where the names of Galileo and Darwin spring to mind. One should remember that in Galileo's case, however, the Church – in which the Pope in the early 17th century was more concerned with his personal authority than with the truth – removed most restrictions on Galileo's writings within a hundred years, and has since expressed regrets (and indeed its own errors) in the handling of the affair.

As for Darwin, much of the response to *The Origin of Species* was favourable when it was published in 1859, and it was later distortions – especially what came to be known as Social Darwinism – that aroused serious opposition. The last lines of his work remind us that, if not in later life a practising Christian (because of doubts about the authority of the Bible, its attribution of vindictiveness to God and its naive portrayals of the miraculous), Darwin remained a theist, a firm but (in his own word) 'muddled' believer in God:

There is grandeur in this view of life, with its several powers, having been originally breathed by the Creator into a few forms or into one; and that, whilst this planet has gone on cycling on according to the fixed law of gravity, from so simple a beginning endless forms most beautiful and most wonderful have been, and are being, evolved.

THE ORIGIN OF SPECIES

BY MEANS OF NATURAL SELECTION.

PRESERVATION OF FAVOURED RACES IN THE STRUGGLE
FOR LIFE.

By CHARLES DARWIN, M.A.

LONDON:
JOHN MURRAY, ALBEMARLE STREET.

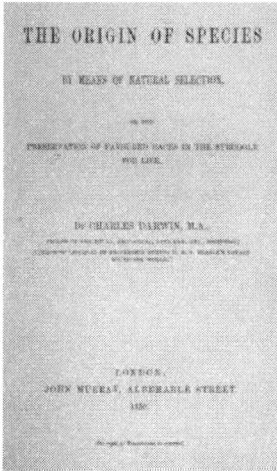

The year after the book's publication, the British Association for the Advancement of Science debated it during its annual meeting in Oxford. Darwin was unwell and unable to be present, but read the Bishop of Oxford's critique. 'I have just read the *Quarterly*,' he wrote to a botanist friend, reporting that he found Wilberforce's assessment 'uncommonly clever; it picks out with skill all the most conjectural parts, and brings forward well all the difficulties'. Elsewhere he admitted that 'geology assuredly does not reveal any such finely graduated organic chain'.

His theory of natural selection was not challenged by Wilberforce on theological but scientific grounds. When Frederick Temple, then Headmaster of Rugby School but destined to be Archbishop of Canterbury, preached the official sermon for the Association's gathering, he supported Darwin in principle; he argued that God's activity in the world could be discerned through the working out of the underlying scientific laws. An Oxford botanist, Aubrey Moore, suggested that, although Darwinism appeared to some 'under the guise of a foe', yet it 'did the work of a friend' to the Church and to Christian theology; 'the facts of nature,' he insisted, 'are the acts of God.' Within twenty years or so the idea of evolution was part of mainstream science, and accepted by most educated Christian thinkers.

Charles Darwin did, however, damage his reputation by incorporating the phrase 'survival of the fittest' into the 1869 edition of his work. This was the unfortunate influence of the English polymath Herbert Spencer, who in 1864 coined the phrase as a way of claiming Darwin's ideas in support of his own. Spencer was opposed to a generation of 'spurious philanthropists' who encouraged 'the multiplication of the reckless and incompetent by offering them an unfailing provision' – by which he meant those who were 'unhealthy, imbecile, slow, vacillating [and] faithless'. Under the natural order of things society would 'excrete' them. Spencer certainly failed to appreciate that (for Darwin) natural selection was about 'biological reproduction'; but those who knew themselves to be comparatively 'unfit' – in other words, the general public – naturally were not in favour of Spencer's *Social* Darwinism, which would justify their continued oppression by the elite. In time, many other isms attempted similarly to misrepresent Darwin's work in their self-promotion, claiming as 'the latest' to be also 'the fittest'.

A recent publication *Darwin's Sacred Cause* (by Adrian Desmond and James Moore), which utilises previously unknown documentation, argues convincingly that, whereas leading apologists for slavery in Darwin's day proposed that blacks and (superior) whites had originated as separate species, part of the motivation behind *The Origin of Species* was his own strong commitment to the abolition of slavery: hence *evolution* was consciously a theory in favour of *emancipation*. The family ethos in which he had grown up was indeed 'abolitionist', and when he moved from Edinburgh University to Cambridge he found it very much an anti-slavery stronghold. But it was in the 1830s on the *Beagle's* long voyage that he personally met many 'natives' and encountered the horrors of slavery for himself. He noted in his journal, 'I never saw anything more intelligent than the Negros, especially the Negro or Mulatto children', and later confided that he who fights slavery is helping to relieve 'miseries perhaps even greater than he imagines.' Years later his son William wrote of Darwin's 'intense detestation of slavery'.

Although *The Origin of Species* does not discuss the evolution of humans – Darwin was hesitant to stir up too much controversy – those who reviewed the book were in no doubt about its implications. It was not until 1871 that he published *The Descent of Man*, which states his anti-racist position quite clearly:

All the races agree in so many unimportant details of structure and in so many mental peculiarities, that these can be accounted for only through inheritance from a common progenitor; and a progenitor thus characterised would probably have deserved to rank as man.

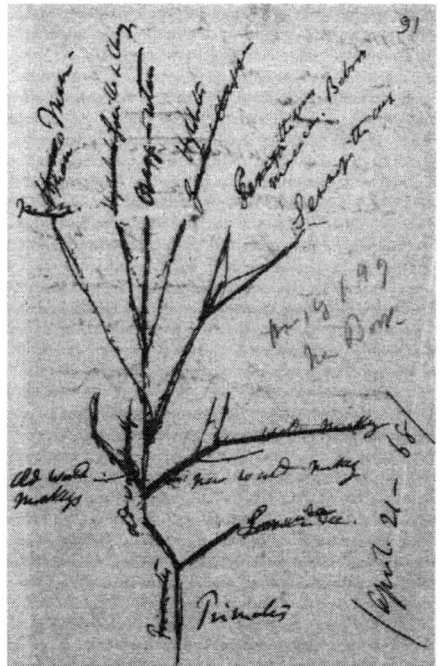

His tree showing the descent of man

Darwin was aware, as we have seen, of difficulties and conjectural elements in his theory. Some consider that fossil evidence for some of the intermediate life-forms that were predicted is still inadequate. 'Intelligent design' (commonly abbreviated as ID) has been popularised over the past thirty or so years, and claims that only supernatural intervention can account for the complex structures of some living things. This is really an argument akin to 'the God of the gaps' and is steadily being eroded as biologists continue to fill those gaps, as in the following news bulletin of 2016:

A string of underwater expeditions has found more species of Xenoturbella. Gregg Rouse, of the Scripps Institution of Oceanography in the US and lead author of a paper published in Nature, said: 'By placing Xenoturbella properly in the tree of life we can better understand early animal evolution.' The new examples allowed further genetic analysis, offering insights into the evolution of organ systems, such as guts, brains and kidneys, in animals.

Biologists have also discovered what appear to be 'design flaws', such as the blind spot in the retina, which argues in favour of gradual evolution – whereas it would be reasonable to suppose that an 'all-knowing designer' would surely have removed such errors from his master plan.

Another criticism of Darwinism has focused on the importance of 'chance' in its theory of evolution. Yet its contribution to the process has not always been properly realised: biologists speak here of 'convergence', meaning the repeated evolution of the same biochemical pathway or structure in different life-forms. Conway Morris, Professor of Palaeobiology at Cambridge, has explained that, although 'the evolutionary routes are many', nevertheless 'the destinations are limited' – in other words, natural selection acts as a tight filter on the random mutations within any DNA:

The constraints of life make the emergence of the various biological properties (such as intelligence) very probable, if not inevitable.

Perhaps the most difficult question for Christians who accept Darwin's theories is why the outcome of some genetic mutations is apparently the opposite of life-enhancing, with less satisfactory results – diseased organisms, pain, suffering – making evolution a wasteful as well as a fertile process. It was certainly an issue for Darwin himself, which he experienced personally in the early deaths of three of his children. Science by itself is unlikely therefore to provide all the answers to our questions, and any 'teleology' (the understanding of life's purpose) will need to interact with faith's own quest.

A further religious problem for Darwin, which has continued to attract a great deal of attention ever since[6], is summed up in the word 'altruism' – and to what extent this can be favoured in the evolutionary process. Since 'self-denial' can sometimes lead to a shortening of one's life in contrast to a more selfish, or at least self-centred, approach which may prolong one's days, it is by no means obvious that it is beneficial in the Darwinian sense.

Darwin caricatured in 1871

Ten years before Darwin's main thesis was published, Alfred Lord Tennyson had drawn attention to the issue in his In Memoriam A.H.H. (1849). He testifies here to his friend Arthur Hallam's faith...

Who trusted God was love indeed
And love Creation's final law
Tho' Nature, red in tooth and claw
With ravine, shriek'd against his creed.

Tennyson was responding particularly to the evolutionary ideas circulating after the anonymous publication in 1845 of Robert Chambers' work entitled Vestiges of the Natural History of Creation. Darwin also read this book, and found it lacking in scientific rigour:

The author apparently believes that organisation progresses by sudden leaps, but that the effects produced by the conditions of life are gradual. He argues with much force on general grounds that species are not immutable productions. But I cannot see how the two supposed 'impulses' account in a scientific sense for the numerous and beautiful co-adaptations which we see throughout nature.

---

[6] Books of particular interest include Richard Dawkins' *The Selfish Gene* (1976) and Elliott Sober's *The Nature of Selection* (1980). Much of the complex debate depends upon whether it is the gene or the organism that is more significant.

Aware of the mixed public reaction to Vestiges, Darwin seems to have delayed publishing his own account in The Origin of Species until he was confident that it offered a more convincing scientific analysis. Yet he continued to be less certain that it properly addressed the dichotomy raised by people such as Tennyson, and touches on it subsequently in The Descent of Man. While altruism may inspire be a source of inspiration to others to do likewise – as Tertullian put it so memorably in the late 2nd century, 'the blood of the martyrs is the seed of the Church.' But Darwin expressed his Church' – it is by no means obvious that it carries any evolutionary value. So in the Descent he first gave expression to the well-aired doubts, followed by his own 'selectionist' doubts in his 1871 work The Descent of Manclarification:

It is extremely doubtful whether the offspring of the more sympathetic and benevolent parents, or of those who were the most faithful to their comrades, would be reared in greater number than the children of selfish and treacherous parents of the same tribe. He who was ready to sacrifice his life, as many a savage has been, rather than betray his comrades, would often leave no offspring to inherit his noble nature. The bravest men, who were always willing to come to the front in war, and who freely risked their lives for others, would on average perish in greater numbers than other men.

Darwin thought he had an answer:

It must not be forgotten that although a high standard of morality gives but a slight or no advantage to each individual man and his children over the other men of the same tribe, yet that advancement in the standard of morality and an increase in the number of well-endowed men will certainly give an immense advantage to one tribe over another.

Subsequent analysis suggests that, while this is not invariably the outcome, it may hinge on the proportion of 'well-endowed men' reaching a critical ratio – which may not often occur?

The Bible perhaps stubbornly reminds us that 'Christ crucified' is 'a stumbling block to Jews and folly to Gentiles' [1 Cor 1.24]. In the Gospel tradition there is even the suggestion that life on earth will get much worse before it gets any better:

When you hear of wars and rumours of wars, do not be alarmed; this must take place, but the end is still to come. [Mk 13.7]

So the possibility remains that 'Nature, red in tooth and claw' will continue to thwart the human race's optimism about its own evolutionary ascent. Will humanity in general ever reach a shared vision that transcends narrow self-interest? Will 'altruism' ever prevail?

A theory of everything?

Darwin as a young man had spent five years travelling the world on the surveying ship *Beagle* with the opportunity to study many geological formations and of course an abundance of wild life. For the rest of his life, he was mainly concerned to account for the development of such variety within an all-embracing theory. In the 20th century it was the turn of astronomers, cosmologists and fundamental physicists to extend evolutionary ideas beyond planet earth to the vast array of stars and galaxies. They too were not necessarily lacking in sympathy for religious instincts. Here, for example, is a brief reflection of Albert Einstein:

Science can only be created by those who are thoroughly imbued with the aspiration towards truth and understanding. This source of feeling, however, springs from the sphere of religion... The situation may be expressed by an image: science without religion is lame, religion without science is blind.

Indeed, although this may be an unfounded exaggeration, cosmologists often seem to have a greater sense of awe and mystery as they contemplate the far-off reaches of the universe than, let us say, laboratory-based scientists with the ability to 'manipulate' or even 'control' biochemical substances much closer at hand.

A depiction of the destruction of a binary star system – stars orbiting one another with accelerating rapidity, generating gravitational waves as they lose energy.

Guy Consolmagno noted: 'The discovery of gravitational waves confirms Einstein's insight that creation is stranger and more wonderful than the clockwork universe imagined by Enlightenment scientists... It shows what humans can achieve when we join together for a common cause.'

Although it took the talents of many people over many years to uncover this outstanding advance in understanding reality, it has been the heroic mind of Stephen Hawking, so severely handicapped, that has brought 'black holes' and the goal of 'a theory of everything' firmly into the public mind. The very phrase occurs in the title of a biographical film about him. His own background was much less religious, however, than that of Charles Darwin, who was at one time an Anglican ordinand. Two years older than me, Hawking attended the same school, which had daily prayers including morning worship every Monday and Thursday in St Albans Abbey[7]. Whereas Hawking's sisters were also in the same Methodist Sunday school, the only other link I had with him was in our shared left wing views. Yet God does feature from time to time in his scientific deliberations, although here – as in other of his pronouncements – he wavers. A theory of everything might tell us how the universe works, but in *A Brief History of Time* (1988) he wondered:

What is it that breathes fire into the equations and makes a universe for them to describe?... Why does the universe go to all the bother of existing?

In *The Grand Design* (2010), written jointly with Leonard Mlodinow, these questions are broken down further, with some partial answers, but the unanswered teaser is still 'Why is there something rather than nothing?' The book met with a singular lack of critical enthusiasm, and even the accusation of 'Godmongering'. Subsequently therefore Hawking modified his stance:

Perhaps science has revealed that there is some higher authority at work, setting the laws of nature so that our universe and we can exist. So there is a grand designer, who lined up all the good fortune? In my opinion, *not necessarily.*

---

[7] N.B. Sir Francis Bacon, widely regarded as the father of 'scientific method', once lived at Verulam House, very close to St Albans.

His grand designer begins to look now like a 'God of the gaps', to be evoked should science fail to provide the answers. Yet even if a theory combining the macro-world of relativity with the micro-realm of quantum physics were to be acclaimed, Vlatko Vedral has pointed out in *Decoding Reality*:

> Physics is a very dynamic activity, and as soon as we are set on a model to describe reality, along comes an experiment that completely challenges our view. In this way, physics evolves through time.

My own apprehension of this truth was reinforced by a season spent at Herstmonceux in 1963, when I realised that astronomical observations were in various ways *refracted* to planet Earth not only through atmospheric gases but also through intergalactic space containing as yet much unexplored 'dark matter'. Much more still needs to be known about this elusive feature of the universe, as well as (for example) about the distribution of black holes before astrophysical conclusions can be reached with any degree of confidence. Until then, theories can only be tentative and provisional.

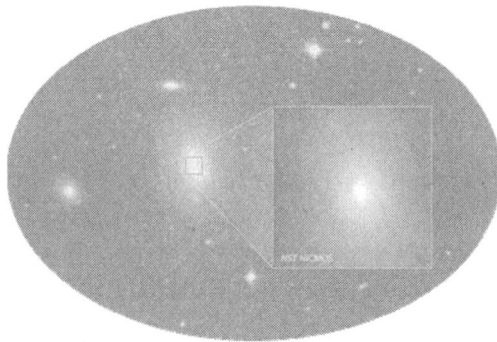

A sky survey image of the massive galaxy NGC 1600, and a Hubble Space Telescope closeup of the bright centre of the galaxy where a 17-billion-solar-mass black hole has unexpectedly been found. Black holes are probably 'the most mysterious objects' in the cosmos, according to research astronomers.

Even then, as Pope John Paul II once set out very clearly, there are questions that are beyond the scope of science:

Every scientific hypothesis... leaves unanswered the problem concerning the beginning of the universe. By itself science cannot resolve such a question: it requires human knowledge which rises above the physical, the astrophysical, what we call the metaphysical; what is required above all is the knowledge which comes from the revelation of God.

What should also be recalled is that a physicist's *theory* is (in Hawking's own words taken from *The Nature of Space and Time*) 'just a mathematical model and it is meaningless to ask whether it corresponds to reality. All that one can ask is whether its predictions agree with observation.' It is indeed essential to appreciate that the language of physics is mathematics, and to take notice of what has been called 'one of the most important advances in logic in modern times'. This appeared through the ground-breaking work of the Austrian mathematician Kurt Gödel in 1931, whose paper carried the forbidding title *On Formally Undecidable Propositions of Principia Mathematica and Related Systems.* An introduction to this highly technical work was published by Ernest Nagel and James Newman in 1959, which made it a regular topic of conversation during the early 1960s when I studied mathematics at Cambridge – and concluded with others that a 'grand cosmological theory' was logically an impossibility.

A summary of what Gödel established is as follows. Mathematics is built on axioms, with theorems derived from those axioms (the choice of which needs justification from without). Gödel demonstrated, *first*, that it is impossible to prove, using the methods available within many important areas of mathematics (including elementary arithmetic), that any set of axioms is *consistent* – meaning that conclusions drawn from them could never lead to contradictions; *second*, he showed that even if it were possible to prove consistency for a particular system, it would remain *incomplete* – meaning that there would be true statements contained in it whose truth could not be established by means of the axioms alone, but only by meta-mathematical reasoning. It is this inherent *lack of completeness* that would inevitably arise in any mathematical system modelling the universe, leaving any grand theory unable to explain every truth found in the universe. The goal of a complete 'theory of everything' is therefore unattainable.

But if the crude claim that science can 'disprove' the need of a Creator is false, Gödel's work is certainly not a knock-down proof of his existence. It points us to a 'source' underlying the particular physical laws of the universe which cannot be fully formalised by the human intellect. If we know that source as God, what we may say about 'him' comes from his own revelation appropriated in acts of faith, as indeed Pope John Paul pointed out. Yet given the ingenious subtleties of Gödel's own constructions, one's first response to God might well be the humble recognition of his even more wondrous wisdom, as heralded in our biblical sources.

It would be a mistake to imagine that those who acknowledge a Creator have thereby acquired their own 'theory of everything'. St Paul has memorably reminded us of our human limitations:

> Now we see in a mirror dimly, but then face to face. Now I know in part; then I shall understand fully, even as I have been fully understood. [1 Cor 13.12]

So too John Henry Newman wrote in his *Essay in Aid of a Grammar of Assent*, just a decade after the publication of Darwin's great work:

> Our image of (God) never is one, but broken into numberless partial aspects, independent each of each. As we cannot see the whole starry firmament at once, but have to turn ourselves from east to west, and then round to east again, sighting first one constellation and then another, and losing these in order to gain those, so it is, and much more, with such real apprehensions as we can secure of the Divine Nature. We know one truth about Him and another truth – but we cannot image both of them together; we cannot bring them before us by one act of the mind.

These theological limitations are well illustrated in the Nicene Creed itself. Jesus Christ is '*begotten*, not *made*': although these two words are virtually synonymous, the point is that a *different* term is needed to describe the origin of our Lord's existence from that of ourselves – but otherwise its meaning remains unfathomable. Likewise, the Holy Spirit is described in the Creed as the one who *proceeds*, which thus serves as a *contrast* with what is said of the Son – and so again has symbolic value.

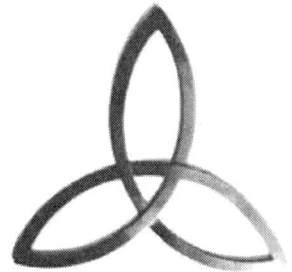

A Trinitarian heart of love

Facing the future

Theological boundaries are thus established, but not an explanation of God's mysteries, which human thought is incapable of penetrating – any form of language or symbolism takes us only so far. When St John the Divine attempted to describe 'the voice from heaven', he could only do so in evocative imagery, suggesting it was 'like the sound of many waters'. Our own response too must likewise begin with awe and wonder.

A related warning on the limitations of human explanation came recently from Daniel Kahneman, Nobel Laureate in Economics (and an expert in detecting fallacious certainties):

The line that separates the possibly predictable future from the unpredictable distant future is yet to be drawn.

Yet while the future of the universe remains unresolved as between the different scenarios sketched by scientists, our own planet seems well-nigh certain to reach the point where human habitation must cease. The thought of this once led the philosopher Bertrand Russell to reflect:

That all the labours of all the ages, all the devotion, all the inspiration, all the noonday brightness of human genius, are destined to extinction in the vast death of the solar system, and that the whole temple of Man's achievement must inevitably be buried beneath the debris of a universe in ruins – all these things, if not quite beyond dispute, are yet so nearly certain, that no philosophy which rejects them can hope to stand.

At the present time there is a growing body of opinion that the only future for humankind is a mass emigration to some other – as yet unspecified – destination within our galaxy. Meanwhile, Hawking's latest suggestion in his 2016 Reith Lectures is an energy source, in the form of so-called 'Hawking radiation' from a black hole, to keep planet earth going until emigration plans are finalised (others look to solar power or to nuclear fusion):

A black hole of the mass of the sun, would leak particles at such a slow rate, it would be impossible to detect. However, there could be much smaller mini black holes with the mass of say, a mountain. A mountain-sized black hole would give off X-rays and gamma rays, at a rate of about 10 million megawatts, enough to power the world's electricity supply. It wouldn't be easy however, to harness a mini black hole. You couldn't keep it in a power station, because it would drop through the floor and end up at the centre of the Earth. If we had such a black hole, about the only way to keep hold of it would be to have it in orbit around the Earth. People have searched for mini black holes of this mass, but have so far not found any.

The scientific layman begins to wonder at this point whether we have now reached the realm of science fiction, especially as a couple of months later Hawking helped launch a new project, outlined in the following (edited) press report, to send a spacecraft to the nearest stars, emphasising the crucial importance of it being no more than featherweight.

Breakthrough Starshot will test the knowhow and technologies necessary to send a featherweight robot spacecraft to the Alpha Centauri star system, at a distance of 4.37 light years. A 100 billion-watt laser-powered light beam would accelerate a "nanocraft" to the three nearest stars at 60,000km a second. Professor Hawking said: "Earth is a wonderful place, but it might not last forever. Sooner or later we must look to the stars. Breakthrough Starshot is a very exciting first step on that journey."

New advances in nanoscience mean that fabrics with unique properties can be made to order. And advances in laser technology mean that huge power can be generated at relatively low costs. The headlong miniaturisation of microelectronics means that it might be possible to pack the entire control system onto a tiny silicon wafer, and mount it on an ultra-thin sail weighing only grams, that would respond to the pressure of light. Spacecraft could become ever smaller and lighter: they could be launched by the thousand from a mothership and then driven by the proposed Light Beamer, a billion-watt laser array, mounted somewhere high and dry such as the Atacama desert in Chile. This could multiply the radiation pressure, and accelerate the space sailors to a significant fraction of light speed. This would reduce such a journey to the timescale of one human generation.

Since the range of focus of a big laser on a small target would be no more than a million kilometers, the fragile spacecraft must reach terminal speed in just two minutes, and survive an acceleration of 60,000 times the force of gravity. The big challenge would be to transmit the information across a distance of more than four light years to a receiving station on a planet already far away and long ago.

Speaking at the project's launch, Hawking said transcending our limits was what made humans unique. "Gravity pins us to the ground but I just flew to America. I lost my voice but I can still speak thanks to my voice synthesiser. How do we transcend these limits? With our minds and our machines. The limit that confronts us now is the great void between us and the stars. **But now we can transcend it.**"

Freeman Dyson, the American physicist and writer, said that in the quest to find life elsewhere, humans should focus not just on planets, but on asteroids, comets and even the dust clouds that hang in interstellar space. "The huge advantage is that it's easier to get off one object and move to another," he said. "You can hop into space, fly over to your neighbour's, have a cup of tea, and come back again."

Some of the ideas expressed in that report are distinctly ambitious, but no doubt feed a strong public interest in the existence of life elsewhere in the universe, either in the form of aliens or of locations where humans themselves might relocate. There is a steady trickle of news items that space probes have discovered unexpected 'signals' as well as revealing some of the constituent elements that enabled life on earth to develop. Thus, in the middle of 2016 the European space agency's mission to comet 67P/Churyumov-Gerasimenko, launched in 2004, reported its latest finding:

> Scientists on the Rosetta mission claim to have found building blocks for life in a cloud of gas and dust around comet 67P. They now believe that life on earth was created by what are dubbed 'dirty snowballs' smashing into our planet. And if it did that here it is likely to have created life elsewhere.

There is certainly potential in exploring these hints much further, but it is often forgotten that there is a huge gap between learning more about the possible origins of our own planetary existence and the (as yet far from proven) hypothesis that this is 'likely' to have been replicated, albeit in variant form, elsewhere.

Nor can I resist quoting a little of Craig Brown's commentary on the related subject of aliens. This was written in 2004 when strange signals were picked up by a giant radio telescope in Puerto Rico and were ascribed by several astronomers, including the Astronomer Royal (Martin Rees), as plausibly emanating from aliens:

> Rees argues that if these strange signals were indeed transmitted by aliens, they would have taken quite a time to get here, since they would have travelled nearly 183 trillion miles across space to reach us. This means that whatever it is that they are trying to tell us would now lack zip... But Sir Martin Rees remains buoyant... 'Any two-way exchange would take decades at least, so there would be time to plan a measured response... In the long run a dialogue could develop, but not snappy repartee.'

It is therefore quite a relief to turnreturn to classical Christian writings which recognise that the creation is driven by more than a set of mathematical equations or even the brain-storming of imaginative scientists., and that the concept of a Creator God is more readily defensible than the idea of aliens in outer space. Thus Pope Leo the Great (in the 5th century) returns our thoughts to thatinvokes a sense of wonder in one of his sermons:

> The heavens and the earth, the sea and all within them, proclaim the goodness and the almighty power of their maker. The wonderful beauty of these inferior elements of nature demands that we, intelligent beings, should give thanks to God.

As intelligent beings we recognise too that the universe continues to evolve, revealing more of its mysteries to us. Indeed, in Paul's words, 'The creation waits with eager longing for the revealing of the sons of God' [Rom 8.19]; to which St Ambrose adds the comment in one of his letters that 'creation... awaits the glory of our adoption and redemption, giving birth to that spirit of salvation, *yearning to be freed from slavery to what is devoid of meaning.*' He reminds us thereby that as human beings we are not concerned just about *what* the future of the universe – and more particularly of our planet – may be like, but much more about *the meaning and purpose* of its existence.

When St Augustine meditated upon the creation in the concluding books of his *Confessions*, what struck him most forcibly was its emergence from 'darkness' – a being 'without form' [Gen 1.2] – into its proper 'definition' resulting from the illumination of God's light. Evolution, in his terms, may be seen as a process of *conversion*, in which all that exists comes to fulfil its destiny by God's grace. Understanding such purpose can only be disclosed to us by the Creator himself – a 'metaphysical' revelation.

Once again words from Job are apposite; the following extract is the version used in William Boyce's famed anthem:

> Whence cometh wisdom, and where is the place of understanding? Seeing it is hid from the eyes of all living. God understandeth the way thereof, and He knoweth the place thereof... And unto men He said, Behold, the fear of the Lord, that is wisdom, and to depart from evil is understanding. [Cf. Job 28]

Nor was God's revelatory truth imparted only at the beginning of time, as Enlightenment thinkers (contemporary with Boyce) were prone to claim in the 18th century. William Paley then popularised the analogy they used between God as Creator and a watchmaker, who, having made his clock and wound it up, left it to run by itself. A more scientific expression of determinism was given by Pierre-Simon Laplace in 1814:

> We may regard the present state of the universe as the effect of its past and the cause of its future. An intellect which at a certain moment would know all forces that set nature in motion, and all positions of all items of which nature is composed, if this intellect were also vast enough to submit these data to analysis, it would embrace in a single formula the movements of the greatest bodies of the universe and those of the tiniest atom; for such an intellect nothing would be uncertain.

This analysis was proffered a century before Heisenberg discovered his Uncertainty Principle, and thus before the probabilistic character of quantum mechanics and of chaos theory was known. Equally, Paley's description of God ignores the testimony of his lively interaction with believers down the centuries:

> In many and various ways God spoke of old to our fathers by the prophets; but in these last days he has spoken to us by a Son, whom he appointed the heir of all things, through whom also he created the world. [Heb 1.1-2]

Although religious minds are open (given a 'probabilistic future') to the possibility of God continuing to express himself in physical terms – beyond the birth, life, death and resurrection of his Son still enabling the 'miraculous' to occur? – it is always the case that such manifestations need in the end to be understood and appropriated by human beings. At a popular level, miracles can support belief in divine powers that appear to surpass natural processes and can thus help to generate faith; but sometimes such interpretations are based upon scientific ignorance, and in any case there is a danger of seeing the miraculous solely as a form of alternative medicine. Of the four evangelists it is St John who presents miracles particularly as *signs* of a greater reality (and prompts us to perceive that a change of heart is as much, or even more, of a miracle than recovery of sight by the blind.)

But revelation is by no means confined to such 'unusual' events, and can happen in a variety of ways, as John Henry Newman insisted: 'People are variously constituted; what influences one does not influence another.'

The medicines necessary for our souls are very different from each other.
Thus God leads us by strange ways.

Much depends, he explained, upon the 'antecedent probability' of our hearts and minds being responsive to the stimuli that God provides – he thus anticipated the quantum physicist's use of the word *probability* by providing a *complementary* religious meaning. Undeniably, the wonders of science are one such potential stimulus, but even here it is worth heeding Newman's account in his *Tamworth Reading Room*:

> Science gives us the grounds or premises from which religious truths are to be inferred; but it does not set about inferring them, much less does it reach the inference;—that is not its province. It brings before us phenomena, and it leaves us, if we will, to call them works of design, wisdom, or benevolence; and further still, if we will, to proceed to confess an Intelligent Creator. We have to take its facts, and to give them a meaning, and to draw our own conclusions from them.

Where the ancient biblical tradition had always stressed the needful readiness of our ears to hear and our eyes to see, Newman draws out the truth that the promptings of God's love, whether through the mysteries of his creation or the artistic insights of poets and musicians or the myriad kindnesses exchanged between fellow human beings, will only be effective when our minds are receptive and our hearts are sufficiently open.

My personal testimony is that it is in the quiet prayerful spaces of the day that fresh appreciation of life's blessings awakens unbidden ideas and new resolutions: this is, *so I believe*, when God is able to address me personally. Given the scientific debate over the multi-dimensional realities of space and time, I would further add that my experience does suggest something of a 'triune' relationship: there are promptings that embrace the widest possible concerns of humanity (a 'Father-like' impulse); those too that concern the immediate network of family, friends and neighbours (a pastoral 'Christ-inspired' focus); together with the sense of needing to search further and move forward (the influence of 'the Spirit'). Indeed, in the evolution of church buildings, these three aspects have come to play a valuable symbolic role for all Christians: their starting point may be the intimate space where the church community meets with their Lord, but even there one finds valuable reminders of God's ineffable mystery and his ultimate purposes in (for example) soaring arches and steeples; hence the Church is not an introspective gathering, but one that looks beyond the altar into the developing needs and challenges that lie ahead (indeed, in some early churches – as at Dura-Europos or at Qalb Lozeh in Syria – a window or doorway positioned here was an opening to the outside world). If the architecture of space and time matters to scientists, this is no less true for Christian believers[8] – although for us it is deeply symbolic of a world to come. As the Angel reminded Gerontius in Newman's poem:

Thou livest in a world of signs and types...
Thou art wrapped and swathed around in dreams,
dreams that are true, yet enigmatical;
for the belongings of thy present state,
save through such symbols, come not home to thee.
And thus thou tell'st of space, and time, and size,
of fragrant, solid, bitter, musical,
of fire, and of refreshment after fire...
How, even now, the consummated Saints
see God in heaven, I may not explicate.

---

[8] It is worth recalling that, when Theodore and Hadrian came to Canterbury after fleeing from an expanding Islam in the later 7th century, they imported intellectual property with them and inaugurated the study of 'ecclesiastical arithmetic' in the schools they founded. The outstanding mathematician of these 'dark' centuries was Bede, who wrote *On the Nature of Things* and *On Time*, works which 'had a strong hold on understandings of chronology and cosmology up till modern times' (Scott DeGregorio). His *Commentary on Genesis* too carries profound reflections on the creation of the universe and on the spiritual meaning of time.

Joining the ranks of heaven

LIFE AFTER DEATH

Human yearnings for immortality

From the dawn of time, the fact of human mortality has attracted a range of responses, sometimes held in uneasy conjunction with each other. Acceptance of the finality of death has usually been one of the less popular options, at least until modern times; but even this has been tempered by the idea that a person 'lives on' in his offspring, which has meant that barrenness is seen in many societies as a misfortune of tragic dimensions. More commonly, though, the human spirit has reacted against the prospect of personal extinction, being less than satisfied with the notion that the survival of the clan, the tribe, the nation or the human race as a whole is paramount. For some, reincarnation, which offers a new earthly life in some bodily shape or form, has been the answer. For others, the migration of the soul to some heavenly abode or to a paradisal dwelling has seemed more plausible. Yet realism has also suggested that, if the soul or spirit in some way survives the death of the body, its continuing existence may be but a shadow of what it once knew on earth. Is it but a feeble copy of real life, perhaps just a temporary flicker dependent upon being remembered by surviving kith and kin? Or is it a dormant period, akin to sleep, before some further, more dramatic, transformation occurs? If resurrection is one such outcome, will it be in a body brought back to life, or as part of a newly recreated order? How far do these different possibilities imply the importance of safeguarding, and perhaps provisioning, a person's mortal remains? Would a 'physical' resurrection be frustrated if the corpse were to be cremated rather than interred?

Further questions arise as to whether a person's fate depends upon moral qualities exhibited here and now. Is survival universal; and, if so, do prospects for life beyond the grave vary according to the good or the evil committed this side of it? How far in fact is 'immortality' ingrained in the nature of our human being, and how much does it reflect our standing before God or the gods, who dispose of our future at their discretion? And if there are divine powers not indifferent to us, could it be that 'out of the body', and therefore as more 'spiritual' beings, we may become closer to them, with the potential for more powerful intercession and hence increased influence over human life? Could there then be some contact between the living and the dead, to the possible benefit of the former, as, for example, knowledge of things yet to come, or enhanced vitality of some sort? The opposite, of course, might also be true, that the dead are to be feared, as being vengeful for injuries once received or for lack of proper respect. But if there is intercourse with the spirit world, how is it manifest? Is there any residual power in ancestral bones or body parts?

A long and detailed essay would be needed to plot the factors which have predisposed each culture or religion to make particular teachings their own. Yet there are surely certain common experiences: alongside the acceptance of death as a 'natural' aspect of creaturely existence, a deeply ingrained human rebellion against it sees it as 'unnatural' and sometimes unjust. The bitter pain of relationships being sundered in a moment of radical discontinuity cries out for healing and restoration. Beyond that, memories persist, and it is not uncommon for the bereaved to have 'intimations of immortality' when the dead still address them in dreams, or even (as may happen in the months immediately following a death) in waking visions. Genetic factors too can play a part when a new generation exhibits characteristic features of the dead, making the past more visible and the future more hopeful.

Yet a key question still remains to be addressed: is there any substantial evidence to support these varied beliefs, other than a human instinct that of all the creatures on this planet we are somehow fitted for a fulfilment that lies beyond our span of years? Here it is arguably the Christian faith that leads the field, being based on the testimony of many witnesses that two thousand years ago Jesus of Nazareth was seen alive after his cruel death by crucifixion. In itself that might only indicate that life after death is a viable possibility. Whether or not it is universal in its scope is another matter; perhaps only a select band of mortals are qualified to share the same experience – after all, in a number of cultural traditions the expectation of any afterlife tends to be limited to those regarded as suitably worthy or indeed 'heroic'.

Cultural practices and religious traditions from around the world

In recent centuries archaeologists have discovered human remains from many cultures around the world; the manner of their burial has sometimes revealed a good deal about the beliefs that were once held about the afterlife. What follows is a small sample drawn from different continents.

An excavation took place in 1900 of a grave in southern Egypt. It contained the body of a man, together with various clay items – a red-striped baton, a small red box, leg bones of a small animal, several pots and a stand of four cows grazing on simulated grass. The grave, which lies within the cemetery of El Amra, has been dated to about 3500 BC, long before the age of the pharaohs and a thousand years before embalming or mummifying were practised. The local village would then have been one of the many small farming communities living along the Nile Valley. The artefacts surrounding the corpse are termed his 'grave goods', items quite unlike the photographs or flowers that mourners sometimes bury alongside a coffin these days. The latter are mementoes of the deceased's life on earth, or tokens of the affection in which he or she was held. But in ancient Egypt what accompanied the person who had died were items considered important for his coming journey into the next world. What role did the cattle play? Here other excavations have uncovered the remains of ancient animal enclosures in the same region, with some evidence that cattle were eaten. However, many cattle bones proved to be those of well-aged beasts, suggesting that in fact – as with the Dinka people today – cattle were used less for meat than to provide essential protein in the form of blood. Milk too has been suggested, but this is quite unlikely since it is only more recently that the human gene has adapted sufficiently for the majority of people to absorb it – and a significant minority are still unable to do so. The miniature clay models thus represent what in those distant times was thought to offer vital sustenance for one who had not simply perished, but was making a transition into a new phase of existence.

The later practice in Egypt of mummifying corpses maintained this ancient custom of including grave goods, but with added sophistication. It was in 1825 that one very impressive mummy came to light. The coffin holding it has an elaborately decorated inner case with various hieroglyphic inscriptions. They tell us that the corpse's name was Hornedjitef, a priest in the Temple of Amun at Karnak during the reign of Ptolemy III. The mummy therefore dates from the late 3rd century BC, well over 3000 years after the El Amra burial. Close inspection of the coffin's contents revealed that Hornedjitef's internal organs had been packaged carefully before being replaced inside him, along with expensive resins to act as preservatives. There were also amulets, jewellery and charms underneath the wrappings to protect him on his onward journey; evidently each of these were positioned very precisely in order to enhance their magical effect and to cover every eventuality. The underside of the coffin's lid was discovered to be decorated with spells, together with images of various gods and a map of star constellations. By now the afterlife was considered to be fraught with hazards; whatever ultimately lay ahead was to be reached only after meticulous preparations had been made. It was unlikely, therefore, that ordinary mortals would ever succeed – only the wealthy or those with the insider knowledge of a priest could plan ahead in sufficient detail and with artefacts of sufficient potency and durability.

Hornedjitef's inner coffin

Another ancient culture is of course that of China. Grave goods mattered here too, and perhaps surprisingly continue to matter to this day: thus, practical items such as money, food, water – even smartphones – are still sometimes buried with the deceased. Nor has ritual feasting died out: holding banquets with and for the ancestors has for centuries been part of Chinese life. Sometimes these feature regularly in the life of ordinary families. The underlying belief is that if food and drink are properly prepared, they will nourish the dead who in turn will continue to look after their descendants. There are many bronze containers specially made for such ritual purposes that survive from three thousand or more years ago. A number of them were for domestic use, but some of the grander ones would have been for more public ceremonies in which Chinese emperors sought to enlist the aid of their own predecessors and indeed of the gods who watched over them. To depart from this life was not necessarily to fade away into insignificance, but was rather to achieve some closer form of contact with the powers that rule the universe.

If bronze was the treasured material that honoured the dead in China, its equivalent in early Peruvian culture was the carefully embroidered textile in which mummified bodies were wrapped. Accompanying it were offerings of animal skins, bird feathers and shell necklaces, along with food stuffs such as maize and peanuts. But it is the strange illustrations on the cloth – figures of bared teeth who clutch daggers and severed heads in their clawed hands – that fascinate most of all. Their interpretation remains a mystery; a process of human transformation may be what they portend, but they hint too at themes of blood sacrifice. Here we are in the realm of mythic beliefs which cannot easily be clarified in the absence of texts and of any similar tradition that has endured to the present day. So-called Latin America suffered huge losses through the conquistadors' invasion, as did other parts of the world when colonial expansion reached their shores.

Traditional burial in Ivory Coast

Yet primal religion (as scholars term it) remains alive throughout much of Africa, still remarkably influential alongside the vigorous impact both of Islam in the north and of Christianity further south. Generally speaking, the concepts of 'life' and 'death' are not seen as mutually exclusive; there are levels of life and of death, so that human existence is understood more as a process in which the life-force may fluctuate. When, for example, a person is sick, an expression such as 'he is living a little' may be used – in other words, there is considered to be a diminution of vitality. Death is not the end of an individual's life span, but an event that changes the conditions under which he exists. He enters upon a deeper relationship with the created order, in which there is potentially more interaction between the visible and the invisible worlds. Although life as lived in the present is the focus of much African religion, it is also possible to say that life's goal is to become an 'ancestor' after death. This depends upon two factors: first, that the person has already shown himself to be sufficiently worthy in life, particularly by the extent of his care and provision for those around him; secondly, that he receives an appropriate burial, accompanied by whatever ceremonies are customary in his tribe or religious culture. Not all, therefore, will be venerated as ancestors after they die; and those denied the proper funeral rites may remain as wandering ghosts, unable to enter the realm of the departed and so a continuing danger to their family or their village. Since there can be an element of doubt as to whether their obsequies have been fully satisfactory, there can be an ambivalence in people's attitudes to the recent dead. Yet potentially, as in other cultures, if their transition to the next world is properly achieved, the ancestors who are now closer to the gods (or in a Christian or Muslim context to God himself) will be able to access divine blessings for the benefit of those they have left behind.

Only the most renowned of ancestors who died long ago are likely still be remembered, so what is termed 'the veneration of ancestors' involves mainly the 'living-dead', those who were actually known to older members of the population. As mediators between God and the living, they receive offerings and prayers, particularly at their graveside. No immediate response is expected, but in the following days people take special note of dreams, apparitions, and possible omens. These may well need further interpretation, which could involve recourse to an experienced diviner. At times of sickness, so-called 'medicine men (or more commonly women)' may take the initiative in invoking spiritual aid from their patient's ancestors: healers will often use drumming, clapping or rhythmic dancing to summon up the ancestral spirits, who perhaps are the only ones who can help. Thus, in different ways their 'earthly' concern for their relatives is considered to be enhanced in the afterlife, along with their role as guardians of tribal tradition and as a source of wisdom. Certain issues arise here of course – as with other ancient beliefs – about possible incompatibilities with Christian teaching, and indeed about the centrality of Christ's own role. These we may consider later; but for now, it may suffice to use a phrase of John Paul II, whereby he described some alternative religious traditions as being 'open to the Gospel', 'open to the truth'.

Whereas the beliefs of Africa, China and Peru were of no consequence in the development of biblical thought about life and death, Israel's long association with the Mediterranean world of Greece and Rome is quite a different matter. These classical civilisations display a considerable range of beliefs, including the philosophically sophisticated ideas that emerged in later centuries. In more ancient times there were multiple burials in chamber tombs, but also some individual graves; there were cremations, with the use of bronze urns to preserve the ashes of warriors. But even heroes had little to hope for: it was generally held that the *psyche* (the dead person's spirit) was a helpless shade, existing in the subterranean shadow-land of Hades where 'life' (such as it was) was entirely purposeless. As Achilles expressed it in Homer's 8th century writing *Odyssey*, 'I would rather be a day-labourer on earth working for a man of little property than Lord of all the hosts of the dead.' There was, in other words, no consolation in being dead; the only possible solace might be for one's name to live on.

It was, however, in this work that the name Elysium first appeared; it was initially conceived as a paradise at the ends of the earth where privileged humans (the 'heroes') might in death enjoy an easy 'god-like' life. There is increasing evidence from the 8th century BC onwards of hero cults in which sacrificial offerings were made to win blessings and favours, and to ward off any harmful influence the heroes might exert through malevolent gods. It was usually only their opposite numbers, the grossest of sinners, who were thought to receive punishment beyond the grave. When Homer described Odysseus' visit to the underworld, it was certainly a dark, dank place, but there was little evidence of rewards and punishments being generally meted out. For most people, therefore, there was no fear of the afterlife. In the 5th century BC the lyric poet Pindar wrote in his *Olympian Odes*:

> In company with the honoured gods, those who joyfully kept their oaths
> spend a tearless existence, whereas the others endure pain too terrible to
> behold.

> But those with the courage to have lived three times in either realm, while keeping their souls free from all unjust deeds, travel the road of Zeus to the tower of Kronos, where ocean breezes blow round the Isle of the Blessed, and flowers of gold are ablaze.

The latter are the great heroes who have been rewarded for their courage, whose future is considered more blessed than the mere 'tearless existence' of ordinary upright folk – but in total contrast to the fate of the truly wicked. In Plato's *Republic* the argument is proposed that 'being just' is reward enough in itself.

In later centuries the delights of Elysium (otherwise 'The Isle of the Blessed') began to be seen as more widely available. Various 'afterlife texts' inscribed on gold leaves have been unearthed from 4th century BC tombs in both Calabria and Thessaly:

> When your soul leaves the light of the sun, go on the right-hand path,
> taking careful note of everything... Travel on this right-hand path to the
> holy meadows and the groves of Persephone.

263

Now you have died and now you have been born, thrice lucky one, on this day... You have the wine of good fortune... The rites which other blessed ones have await you beneath the earth.

What though was the *psyche* that survived bodily death? In earlier usage it meant a somewhat insubstantial image of the one who had died, but by the 5th century BC it suggested rather more his or her essence, which was capable of surviving the body. Socrates seems to have thought along these lines, although remaining agnostic on the issue of survival. Plato, however, offered repeated arguments for the soul's immortality, allowing for the possibility of its transmigration into another human (or even animal) body. The primary philosophical connotations of *psyche* were reckoned as life, consciousness and self-caused movement. Not all Greek sages followed him: Epicurus a century later insisted that a person's life depended on the liveliness of atoms in his body; after death no feeling remains, hence for him the soul died along with the body; what happens after death as before birth, he said, is 'nothing to us'. This point of view had little popular following: various cults (once unhelpfully described as 'mystery' religions) attracted individuals who aimed above all at transcending the constraints of everyday existence by becoming – at least temporarily – members of a privileged community of bliss. They were initiated into esoteric teachings that might not be divulged and experienced ecstasies which held the promise of even greater fulfilment beyond the realm of death.

All this is a far cry from the more austere attitudes of the Romans, at least until Hellenistic ideas and practices overtook them. In their traditional approach death was seen as a blemish: it struck the deceased's family and risked affecting others too – neighbours certainly, but also priests and their sanctuaries. Cypress branches were used to warn people away from the deceased's house. Tombs were built outside the boundaries of habitation, with the poor sometimes disposed in huge open pits. However, by the 1st century BC cremation had become the norm, and urns containing the ashes were often placed together in barrel-vaulted brick tombs. Sacrifices were offered for the dead, but funeral rituals were no gateway into eternal felicity. Rather, they enabled those who had died to be included among the *di manes*, the collective community who were remembered in the Parentalia cult held each February; this began with days of family devotions and concluded with a public ceremony. When there was no longer any one to offer sacrifices for the dead, in effect they ceased to survive. A late innovation borrowed from the Greeks was the deification of exceptional individuals: elevation to the status of a god became the rule for emperors and some members of their families. At about the same time, verse epitaphs suggest that speculative thoughts regarding the afterlife (if indeed there was any) were also gaining ground – but these were scarcely well-grounded beliefs that shaped a person's moral outlook. The popular following throughout the Roman Empire of Stoicism, which held that 'virtue is sufficient for happiness', suggests that the focus often remained on life in this world rather than in any other.

Changing attitudes today

The variety of attitudes to the afterlife in this brief survey of different cultural traditions around the world would seem to justify the description of most of them as speculative thinking. Such a description might in the past have been firmly resisted, although back in 5th century BC Athens it would surely have been applauded by the Sophist philosopher Protagoras, who wrote:

> Concerning the gods, I have no means of knowing whether they exist or not or of what sort they may be. Many things prevent knowledge including the obscurity of the subject and the brevity of human life.

In the present-day Western world, if perhaps not elsewhere, Protagoras' agnosticism would scarcely cause a ripple, and might be applied equally to the issue of life after death.

It remains of course a convention that when people die, they receive plaudits for their time on earth, usually (but not always) accompanied by the expression of religious aspirations to meet again in heaven. Even the increasing number of secular funerals use language borrowed from the Christian tradition. Waiting in the wings at a crematorium on one such occasion, I noted how the officiant addressed the deceased as if she herself was alive (but surely not in the coffin?) and indeed listening intently: 'Sally, we want to say how much you meant to us.' Curiously too, in more religious settings, the custom is steadily evolving for the deceased to be cremated quickly and privately prior to a public memorial service being held in a church. Thanks to modern sound systems, this latter event is likely to include one or more of the deceased's favourite songs, irrespective of their conformity with Christian teaching (a development accelerated by the presence of Elton John in 1997 at Princess Diana's funeral, when Westminster Abbey side-stepped the liturgical norms); there is usually a token Bible reading, but secular sources such as romantic poems may also be used; one or more so-called 'eulogies' will be offered reviewing the deceased's past life. The focus, in other words, will be almost exclusively on what has gone before, celebrating the life that has now ceased while allowing for expressions of solidarity with the mourners. Modern tendencies therefore avoid any awkward issues concerning the deceased's future. The officiating priest or minister will strain his ears for a congregational Amen if he ventures to pray for God's mercy upon the departed soul, although such a prayer may by now have been abandoned in some Christian churches.

In more devout circles the older customs prevail and these still have the power to be moving occasions for believer and unbeliever alike. Yet again, as we shall explore, even believers may have an uncertain grasp of orthodox teaching. Is the afterlife a natural progression from earthly existence – that is, do we believe in the immortality of the soul, or does life beyond the grave depend upon an act of God's grace in which we may be resurrected? In either scenario, do we ever face a moment of judgment? And what of the future of the human race, indeed of the whole created order – is it moving to some climactic Last Day, or is the universe fated to final extinction? These, and many other questions, are ones which are too often avoided in our natural preoccupation with the life that has to be lived and endured in the present.

I suspect, however, that growing uncertainty about the sustainability of things as they are, fostered by climate change, depletion of resources, and the spread of global violence, will force us all to think more soberly about what lies in store for us both as individuals and as a human community. In the aftermath of the 1st World War the novelist Virginia Woolf gave birth to a consciously 'modern' novel. In one place her heroine *Mrs Dalloway* reflects upon her own future, with any idea of an afterlife being totally abandoned:

What she loved was this, here, now, in front of her; the fat lady in the cab. Did it matter then, she asked herself, walking towards Bond Street, did it matter that she must inevitably cease completely; all this must go on without her; did she resent it; or did it not become consoling to believe that death ended absolutely?

A similar question remains open for all of us to answer: how much difference does it make to our present lives if we believe that death is not the end?

The background of Jewish thought

For much of the Old Testament period it was largely the future of God's people Israel that was the focus of concern. Only passing references were made to the fate of individuals who had died. It was generally accepted that a dead person went to sleep with his or her ancestors, as, for example, Solomon with 'his fathers' [1 Kgs 11.43]; and also that the land of departed spirits, known as Sheol or the Pit, was below ground [Gen 37.35, or more graphically Num 16.30]. It was a place of no return:

We must all die, we are like water spilt upon the ground, which cannot be gathered up again. [2 Sam 14.14]

The shades could yet be roused to speak to new arrivals –

You too have become as weak as we! You have become like us! [Isa 14.10]

And the fierce condemnation of necromancy [Deut 18.11-12], which was once Saul's desperate ploy [1 Sam 28], suggests a popular belief that, while the departed were necessarily enfeebled, it was still possible for the living, through a medium, to communicate with them. It may be, of course, that his reported contact with Samuel was only feasible because of Samuel's exalted status as a former 'hero' (to use a classical term) or as what Africans would regard as a true ancestor. Yet even those who survived in a much more enfeebled existence were necessarily not beyond God's reach:

If I make my bed in Shed, thou art there! [Ps 139.8]

Such comfort as that affords might be mitigated by the prospect of needing to render account for any misdeeds in life, from which death is no escape:

Though they dig into Sheol, from there shall my hand take them. [Amos 9.2]

A fire is kindled by my anger, and it burns to the depths of Sheol. [Deut 32 22]

In fact, evildoers will find that the Lord will 'cut off the remembrance of them from the earth' [Ps 34.16], in complete contrast to the righteous who 'will be remembered for ever' [Ps 112.6].

However, other texts are less hopeful. The long years of exile in particular, when God's people were far removed from their ancestral land and burial places, may have contributed to the pessimism found, for example, in Book III of the Psalter. The uncertainties associated with the destruction of Jerusalem are clearly reflected in the lament of Psalm 74, and this seems to be personalised in the psalmist' own sense of disorientation:

> My life draws near to Sheol, I am... like those whom thou dost remember
> no more. [Ps 88.3,5]

The psalm uses the term Abaddon, literally a 'place of destruction', as synonymous with Sheol. This occurs in later writings too [Prov 15.11, 27.20, Job 26.6, 28.22] where there is also a sense of death's finality. Life ends in dust [Job 17.16], which is the fate of man and beast, the righteous and the wicked alike:

> All go to one place; all are from the dust, and all turn to dust again.
> [Eccles 3.20]

Nor is Qoheleth ('the Preacher') to be drawn on what may have been contemporary discussion about the destiny of a person's spirit [3.21]: if it 'returns to God who gave it' [12.7], this is no indication of a further phase of life, for this too is 'vanity' [12.8].

There are in the Hebrew scriptures, though, a few intimations of an afterlife, featured in those rare individuals whom God preserved from death's decay. As in other cultural traditions, outstanding ancestors might be considered exempt from the human norm. Enoch 'walked with God; and he was not, for God took him' [Gen 5.24]. Elijah was taken bodily into heaven [2 Kgs 2.10-11]. And, with the mystery surrounding Moses' burial place – 'no man knows the place of his burial to this day' [Deut 34.6] – later speculation concluded that he too had made his home with God. Apart from these few, the main reward for the ancestors seems to have been a much extended lifespan on earth. A number of these are listed in Genesis 5, with Methuselah's 'nine hundred and sixty-nine years' beating the previous record. Among the patriarchs Abraham achieved 'a hundred and seventy-five years' [Gen 25.7].

Although the imagery of resurrection is itself used in several Old Testament texts, it occurs mainly as a metaphor. Just as the word 'death' could be used figuratively of any diminution of life, so a favourable turn of events could encourage poetic licence in the opposite sense. Recovery from deep distress or from sickness, or a revival in the nation's fortunes, might all be described as being released from Sheol [Ps 16.10, 49.15], as being nearer to God [Ps 17.15, 73.25], even as being raised up [Hos 6.2, Ezek 37.12, Isa 26.19]. If there is sometimes an implied recognition of the worth of the individual, nevertheless the chief focus remained on Israel herself: first and foremost Jewish eschatology looked to the realisation of God's kingship over Israel and the nations. At quite a late date ben Sira thought it sufficient to say of Israel's heroes that

Their line will endure for all time... and their name lives for ever [Sir 44.13-14] since what continued to matter was the survival of the nation.

Yet it was the Maccabaean heroes, who had died fighting in God's cause to save his people, who provoked the question whether this was sufficient, or indeed just. The one text in the Old Testament that unequivocally asserts belief in life beyond death seems to be a response to their situation:

Many of those who sleep in the dust of the earth shall awake, some to everlasting life, and some to shame and everlasting contempt. [Dan 12.2]

This may not have been an entirely novel belief since a couple of Psalm verses seem to hint that for a few at least there may be a more vigorous life beyond the grave than exists in Sheol itself:

God will ransom my soul from the power of Sheol, for he will receive me. [Ps 49.15]

Thou dost guide me with thy counsel, and afterward thou wilt receive me to glory (or honour?). [Ps 73.24]

While it is of course possible (or even quite likely) that ideas from neighbouring cultures may have had some influence on Jewish thinking, it seems that it was above all these 2nd century BC martyrdoms that were the catalyst for the remarkable development expressed in the book of Daniel. In time, the reward of everlasting life came to embrace others besides the martyrs – the 'wise' are mentioned, and 'those who turn many to righteousness' [12.3], that is, the outstanding leaders of God's people. A later text makes the same assertion in more spirited language, addressed to Antiochus Epiphanes:

> Fiend though you are, you are setting us free from this present life, and
> the King of the universe will raise us up to a life everlastingly made new,
> since it is for his laws that we are dying. [2 Macc 7.9]

Whereas Daniel depicts the righteous enjoying eternal life as 'like the stars' [Dan 12.3], here a bodily resurrection is certainly envisaged, since one of the tortured brothers tells the king [2 Macc 7.10] that he expects to receive back intact any severed limbs. By contrast a work of much the same period, the Wisdom of Solomon, which also speaks of the virtuous having 'a sure hope of immortality' [3.4], betrays something of the growing impact of Greek philosophy – yet without necessarily questioning the future resurrection of the body.

The possibility of a future life, through these and other inter-testamental and apocalyptic writings, was thus entering the mainstream of Judaism. Josephus mentions [Ant 18.1] that both Pharisees and Essenes held that souls could survive death – and there is corroborative evidence of the latter's belief among the Dead Sea Scrolls e.g. *4Q385*, known as *Pseudo-Ezekiel*, paraphrases Ezekiel 37, while in *4Q521* (the so-called *Messianic Apocalypse*) the raising of the dead is included among the anticipated events of the end-time. Nevertheless, there were others such as the Sadducees who retained the old beliefs about the finality of death, a fact of which Paul was fully aware:

> 'Brethren, I am a Pharisee, a son of Pharisees; with respect to the hope
> and the resurrection of the dead I am on trial.' And when he had said this,
> a dissension arose between the Pharisees and the Sadducees; and the
> assembly was divided. [Acts 23.6-7]

One later work *2 Esdras*, perhaps contemporary with New Testament writings, has a detailed account of the soul's fate after death. A privileged few gain access to heaven 'without ever tasting death' [6.26]; others may have a brief foretaste of what lies in store beyond the Last Judgment when final separation of the righteous and the wicked will take place. For the present, the righteous wait in an abode of 'undisturbed peace' [7.85], but the wicked 'wander in torment, endless grief, and sorrow' [7.80]. Pending God's verdict on their lives none of the departed are accessible to the living, nor can prayer win any favours for them [7.102-105] – unlike 2 Maccabees 12.40-45 where atoning sacrifice may be efficacious. Yet God was known to be compassionate:

Without his continued forgiveness there could be no hope of life for the world and its inhabitants [7.137]

In the end, however, 'only a few will be saved' [8.3].

To summarise: in general, Jewish hopes centred upon 'that day' when God would restore the fortunes of his people, either here on earth (which would be of little benefit to the departed) or – latterly in apocalyptic thinking – in a radically new order which would include the righteous who had died already.

God's judgment

In the Old Testament, 'the book of remembrance' appears a number of times – for example:

At that time your people shall be delivered, every one whose name shall be found written in the book. [Dan 12.1 cf. Ps 40.7; 56.8; 69.28 Isa 34.16; Mal 3.16]

The following verse, as we have seen, adds that of those who 'sleep in the dust of the earth' others will awake 'to shame and everlasting contempt'. So this book is a ledger which includes the names of all who will inherit God's final reward. They are evidently a select company.

In fact, the emphasis of many 'pseudepigraphic' writings from this late period, which was seen by now as an evil age in which God's righteous are but few in number, is upon the judgment that awaits all human souls. Precise dating of these texts is difficult, but parts of *1 Enoch* (still counted as scripture in the Ethiopian Church) may go back to the early 2nd century BC, not long therefore before the book of Daniel. It combined several traditions about the coming end-times, whose overarching theme was the reward of the righteous and the punishment of sinners:

There shall be a judgment upon all, including the righteous. And to all the righteous he will grant peace. He will preserve the elect, and kindness shall be upon them. They shall all belong to God and they shall prosper and be blessed; and the light of God shall shine unto them. Behold, he will arrive with ten million of the holy ones in order to execute judgment upon all. He will destroy the wicked ones and censure all flesh on account of everything that they have done, that which the sinners and the wicked ones committed against him. [1 Enoch 1]

If this passage was early enough to have been known to the author of Daniel (which is uncertain), its influence seems to have bypassed his contemporary ben Sira ('no questions are asked in Hades'). But other Jewish writings began increasingly to express a similar perspective, sometimes reflecting ancient Near Eastern motifs; for example, (1) *The Testament of Abraham* has (along with a fiery ordeal) a vision of angels weighing souls in the balance, which was depicted in Egyptian art as far back as the 2nd millennium BCE; while (2) *The Testament of Benjamin* asserts that the patriarchs will rise first to take their place at God's right hand, after which 'all men will rise, some to glory and some to disgrace' – a staggered process found also in the New Testament in the Apocalypse of John. Again, in *The Apocalypse of Zephaniah* the prophet's journey takes him to the underworld where he sees Eremiel, the angel who guards all the souls 'imprisoned' in Hades until the time of their judgment:

'This is the one who accuses men in the presence of the Lord.' I looked and saw him with a manuscript in his hand. He began to unroll it... I found that all my sins which I had committed were written into it. [Apoc Zeph 7]

The text then reveals that a second scroll, evidently recording his good deeds, is discovered, and so the prophet is absolved and leaves the underworld in a boat – perhaps a reminiscence of Greek mythology. Regardless of the imagery, however, the belief that one's earthly deeds had eternal consequences became the dominant view in the late Second Temple period: thus, the fate of those who walk 'in the spirit of light' was contrasted at Qumran (in *1QS4*) with that of others who live 'in the spirit of darkness'. Such ideas became the norm of both rabbinic and Christian thinking.

Eventually, in further apocalyptic writings, the punishments of hell begin to be described in lurid detail, with apparent relish: thus, *The*

Apocalypse of Ezra (4th century) depicts dogs ripping sinners apart before fire consumes them. Imagery of this sort is found in both Christian and Jewish texts, with *The Apocalypse of Peter* (dating from the first half of the 2nd century) being particularly influential. This portrays both heaven and hell quite graphically:

(Heaven) is exceedingly bright with light, and the air of that place illuminated with the rays of the sun, and the earth itself flowering with blossoms that do not fade, and full of spices and plants, fair-flowering and incorruptible, and bearing blessed fruit. [Apoc Pet 16]

By contrast, idolaters are visualised being burnt by everlasting fire, blasphemers are seen hanging by their tongues – and adulterers, depending on their gender, by their hair or their thighs – while abortionists sit up to their necks in a lake of excrement (etc). Such descriptions fuelled the imaginations of many later writings e.g. *The Questions of Bartholomew*, which also mentions the idea of hell as 'a bottomless pit'.

The main issue calling for clarification is how literally these more developed notions are to be taken. It is one thing to believe that the righteous will be resurrected to live forever, but quite another to contemplate any future life at all for the unworthy. Is not oblivion a sufficient fate, which may in any case be accounted 'condemnation' without compounding such 'punishment' with scenes of everlasting torture? The latter descriptions seem to have arisen when religious belief was under severe threat itself, and may have served to warn the faithful against apathy or, even worse, apostasy. In such a context they can be seen as emotive words serving to heighten the importance of maintaining a true confession and an upright life. This is apparently the thrust of the explanatory comment in the Apocalypse, following a vivid description of the everlasting torment of those who 'worship the beast' [Apoc 14.9-11]:

Here is a call for the endurance of the saints, those who keep the commandments of God and the faith of Jesus. [Apoc 14.12]

Arguably too this explains the appearance of such language in the Gospels, recorded as the teaching of Jesus himself:

Gather the weeds first and bind them in bundles to be burned, but gather the wheat into my barn. [Matt 13.30]

The harvest is the close of the age, and the reapers are angels. Just as the weeds are gathered and burned with fire, so will it be at the close of the age. The Son of man will send his angels, and they will gather out of his kingdom all causes of sin and all evildoers, and throw them into the furnace of fire; there men will weep and gnash their teeth. Then the righteous will shine like the sun in the kingdom of their Father. [Matt 13.39-43 cf. 13.49-50]

Cast the worthless servant into the outer darkness; there men will weep and gnash their teeth. [Matt 25.30]
Then he will say to those at his left hand, 'Depart from me, you cursed, into the eternal fire prepared for the devil and his angels.' [Matt 25.41]

The most graphic account comes in the parable of Dives and Lazarus:

The poor man died and was carried by the angels to Abraham's bosom. The rich man also died and was buried; and in Hades, being in torment, he lifted up his eyes, and saw Abraham far off and Laz'arus in his bosom.

And he called out, 'Father Abraham, have mercy upon me, and send Laz'arus to dip the end of his finger in water and cool my tongue; for I am in anguish in this flame.' But Abraham said, 'Son, remember that you in your lifetime received your good things, and Laz'arus in like manner evil things; but now he is comforted here, and you are in anguish. And besides all this, between us and you a great chasm has been fixed, in order that those who would pass from here to you may not be able, and none may cross from there to us.' [Lk 16.22-26]

Since Luke has already incorporated a series of 'woes' that contrast with Jesus' promised blessings, one interpretation of this passage (likewise the parables in Matthew 25) is to see it as a vivid reiteration of his teaching; that is, whereas the rich have 'received their consolation' *already*, the poor will inherit the infinitely greater reward of blessings in God's kingdom [Lk 6.20, 24]. The emphatic Semitic language used here does not necessarily demand a literal reading that implies any future 'hell' in store for the heartless and the wicked, beyond their failure to attain 'heaven', as in Luke 11.52:

Woe to you lawyers! for you have taken away the key of knowledge; you did not enter yourselves, and you hindered those who were entering.

There is therefore a debatable question as to how far Jesus is endorsing existing Jewish views of heaven and hell by his use of familiar imagery (or is so represented by the evangelists) and how far, as Luke Timothy Johnson expresses it in his commentary on Luke, 'the obvious use of such conventions... whether or not it derives from (Jesus') historical mission is also marked by the experience of the early Church as it confronted its near and bitter rival within developing Judaism, the Pharisaic party.' In the evolution of Christian thought did the early Church sometimes neglect Jesus' own emphasis upon a merciful and forgiving outreach to those who opposed him in favour of a more strident need to condemn the opposition they sometimes faced?

The role of heavenly intercessors

Alongside the idea of everlasting life for the righteous there is a further theme that begins to appear in the so-called Common Era (CE, now often used instead of the more familiar AD), namely, intercession by the righteous on behalf of sinners. In the Jewish tradition, it is Abraham especially, and to a lesser extent other patriarchal figures, whose compassion for souls in torment is seen as effective. In the Talmud, the advice was given:

> If there is someone ill in your house, go to the wise man of the city and ask that he should pray for him. [Baba Batra 116a]

Talmudic teaching [Sotah 34b] linked this with the visit of Caleb to Abraham's burial place in Hebron [Num 13.12] while reconnoitring the land of Canaan; by extension this was seen to justify seeking help from any *tzadik*, the righteous whose goodness abounds for others too. No doubt the story in Genesis 18, where Abraham sought to avert the destruction of Sodom, was influential here – but, with increasing interplay between Jewish and Christian ideas, so too was the account in 1 Peter of Christ's 'descent into hell' when 'he went and preached to the spirits in prison' [1 Pet 3.19].

In the letter to the Hebrews Christ's intercessory role is given prominence:

> [He is our] great high priest who has passed through the heavens. [4.14]

He is able for all time to save those who draw near to God through him, since he always lives to make intercession for them. [7.25]

The bond between Christians and their Lord is, however, so close that those who have passed to glory with him have a share in his priestly role even now:

Thou... hast made them a kingdom and priests to our God. [Apoc 5.10]

[Those martyred for their 'testimony to Jesus and for the word of God'] shall be priests of God and of Christ. [Apoc 20.6]

Hence, the Church's tradition of seeking the 'priestly' intercession of the saints in glory appears firmly rooted in New Testament theology.

A careful distinction does, however, need to be drawn between Christ as divine intercessor and the saints whose prayers are joined with the Church's prayer on earth. Although at times, the veneration of the saints may have overstepped the mark, the conviction of the saints' intercessory role in heaven reflects a deep sense in the human psyche that those who have lived good lives and have cared for others in their lifetime (in Jewish terms, the *tzadik*) will surely not cease to be equally compassionate in the afterlife. This is much akin to the role of ancestors as venerated in African and other cultures. The clearest difference is that, whereas 'the ancestors' are seen as promoting the welfare of their family or their tribe, Christian saints fulfil a universal role in God's worldwide family. Since there is insufficient room for all of them to be listed in the Church's calendar, in practice some will receive devotional attention just from particular dioceses or regions. Yet the transmission of relics, particularly in the Middle Ages, was of considerable significance in enabling the virtues of such locally renowned saints to become more widely known.

Life in Christ

The outstanding question remains: what is the blessedness of the afterlife, which some fail to attain? Here we turn to the fate of the dead in Christian understanding. The tension between the two poles of Hebrew thought (the fate of Israel as a people *versus* the issue of individual survival) is present in the New Testament as well.

On the one hand, the individual is of inestimable worth to God. For example, 'even the hairs of your head are all numbered' [Mt 10.30], while in the parables of Luke 15 there is a strong emphasis upon the lost one who is sought or prayed for until found. This emphasis came to undermine any narrowly ethnic dimension of salvation, enabling Peter to declare:

> Truly I perceive that God shows no partiality, but in every nation any one who fears him and does what is right is acceptable to him. [Acts 10.34-35]

On the other hand, there is a strong corporate identity to Christian existence, expressed by Jesus in the symbolic appointment of the Twelve and then, for example, by Paul in his image of the body.

> We, though many, are one body in Christ, and individually members one of another. [Rom 12.5]

The Fourth Gospel uses the related analogy of a vine and its branches, with further emphasis in Jesus' farewell discourse upon mutual indwelling.

Both these strands are present in **Paul**'s thinking too. In what is probably his earliest extant letter, *1 Thessalonians*, there is concern about Christian brothers and sisters who have already died [4.13], whom Paul describes as being 'asleep'. On the day of the Lord's coming, however, they will be the first to rise, and then all will meet the Lord 'together' [v17]. The Christian's final destiny is to be in a community that will 'always be with the Lord'.

1 Corinthians has features in common with 1 Thessalonians. Those who have died are 'asleep' [15.20], awaiting God's action at the coming of Christ, when 'those who belong to Christ' will be raised [v23] as 'spiritual' (God-related cf. 2.13ff) rather than as 'physical' beings [v44]. Paul retains the word 'body' here, which indicates the relational aspect of existence, but avoids the dualistic language of a soul or spirit 'having' a body. Clearly, whatever the 'spiritual body' may be like, it has ceased to be of a fleshly nature. The word soul (*psyche*) seems to be its equivalent elsewhere in the New Testament, often translated as the 'self' [e.g. Mt 10.28; Heb 13.17; Jas 1.21; 1 Pet 1.9]. But Paul is flexible in his imagery: thus, he can liken the human person to a seed, first buried in the ground before emerging in quite different guise [1 Cor 15.36-38]. Or again, our destiny is to 'bear the image of the man of heaven' [v49], that is, to become like Christ. He speaks here of change 'in a moment, in the twinkling of an eye [v52], when the dead will be raised 'imperishable'.

In *Philippians* the issue of his own future presses upon Paul, who is now in prison. It would certainly help the understanding of Paul's theological development to be able to locate this imprisonment either in Ephesus in the middle of the 50s, or else in Rome at the end of that decade – in other words, to know whether or not Philippians preceded his Corinthian correspondence: there is however no definitive evidence. With his hope of release remaining uncertain [Phil 2.24], he reflects upon the two possible outcomes:

To me, to live is Christ, and to die is gain. [1.21]

I am hard pressed between the two, my desire is to depart and to be with Christ, for that is far better. But to remain in the flesh is more necessary on your account. [1.23-24]

So Paul now conceives that if he dies he will have left behind 'the flesh' and will at once be 'with Christ', as the penitent thief was promised in Luke 23.43 (although this verse is absent in some early manuscripts, suggesting it raised certain debatable questions). This surely indicates more than a state of sleeping: faced with the imminent prospect of his own death, Paul's thought has developed very considerably. Nevertheless, in the same letter he reminds his readers that collectively their hope is still some way in the future [Phil 3.20-21]. Christ will come from heaven, which is where Christians have their true politeuma or 'citizenship', so as 'to change our lowly body to be like his glorious body'. Beyond death then, it would appear that while Paul anticipates being himself 'with Christ', full participation in the life of heaven must somehow await further divine action.

In *2 Corinthians* 4.13-5.10 he offers the aspiration (akin to that of Philippians 1.21) of being 'away from the body and at home with the Lord'. He speaks of being 'further clothed' with the life that comes from

God. Paul affirms that a 'guarantee' of this has already been experienced in the gift of the Spirit, so he does not envisage sharp discontinuity between this world and the next. His belief that 'God will raise us also with Jesus and bring us with you into his presence' [4.14] argues for resurrection being a corporate experience; Christians, however, will face Christ's judgment seat [5.10] with confidence:

> We all, with unveiled face, beholding the glory of the Lord, are being changed into his likeness from one degree of glory to another. [3.18]

Once again, the final goal is presented as being 'like Christ'.

Such assurance is evident too in *Romans*, written not many months later than 2 Corinthians. Paul often refers to the existential bond of being 'in Christ', and here explains further:

> If we have been united in a death like his (in baptism), we shall certainly be united with him in a resurrection like his. [Rom 6.5]

He adds later that, though 'each of us shall give due account of himself' before God's judgment seat [14.12], yet in both life and death 'we are the Lord's' [14.8]. In 2 Timothy, whether by Paul or (more likely, in view of the less Christocentric language) by one of his followers, the note of confident anticipation recurs:

> Henceforth there is laid up for me the crown of righteousness, which the Lord, the righteous judge will award me on that day, and not only to me also to all who have loved his appearing. [2 Tim 4.8]

What then of the **Johannine tradition**? In the *Fourth Gospel* the raising of Lazarus features prominently. The question is asked:

> Could not he who opened the eyes of the blind man have kept this man from dying? [Jn 11.37]

Roman sarcophagus c. 300

Indeed, Martha herself asserts:
> Lord, if you had been here, my brother would not have died. [Jn 11.21]

Jesus had in fact delayed his visit by two days [Jn 11.6], seemingly in order to allow the death to be firmly established, so that no doubt could be entertained about the reality of the resurrection that then ensued. The episode is another 'sign' in this Gospel, here anticipating both the death and resurrection of Jesus himself and also of those loved [Jn 11.5] by him.

The delay may prompt thoughts here of the Last Day that is still awaited:

For this is the will of my Father, that everyone who sees the Son and believes in him should have eternal life; and I will raise him up at the last day. [Jn 6.40]

The promise is made to the disciples that they will follow where Jesus leads the way [Jn 13.36]. He is 'leaving the world and going to the Father' [16.28] where he will prepare a place [14.2-3 cf. Heb 11.16]: such *monai* (abiding places) feature also in the writings known as *1 and 2 Enoch*. The fulfilment of Jesus' promise is partially anticipated in the present world:

If a man loves me, he will keep my word, and my Father will love him, and we will come to him and make our home (abide) with him. [Jn 14.23]

There is thus the same dichotomy in the Fourth Gospel as in Paul's letters:

- final resurrection will take place on 'the last day':

He who eats my flesh and drinks my blood has eternal life, and I will raise him up at the last day. [Jn 6.54]

- believers will never (truly) die – they will remain safe with Christ.

He who believes in me, though he die, yet shall he live, and whoever lives and believes in me shall never die. [Jn 11.25-26 cf. 8.51-52; 10.28]

In the *Johannine letters* the two aspects converge:

(Since) he who abides in love abides in God, and God abides in him... we may have confidence for the day of judgment. (1 Jn 4.16-17).

It is here too that perhaps the deepest insight into the resurrection experience is expressed, concerning our needful transformation:

Beloved, we are God's children now; it does not yet appear what we shall be, but we know that when he appears we shall be like him, for we shall see him as he is... No one who abides in him sins. [1 Jn 3.2, 6]

In the *Apocalypse*, it is the Christian martyrs who form the vanguard. Even now these have a place in heaven [Apoc 6.9-11], wearing white robes of perfection and victory. Any who die for their faith will be similarly rewarded [6.11; 11.12]. For the time being, the martyrs are 'resting' from their labours [cf. 14.13] before coming fully to life [20.4]. 'Over such the second death has no power'; hence they have nothing to fear at the last judgment, and so may be described as already reigning with Christ [20.6], thus anticipating the glorious future that awaits all of God's faithful.

In his final vision the Seer remains true to the Johannine understanding of God's abiding presence with his people. Not only is the new Jerusalem seen as 'coming down' [3.12; 21.2, 10], but God himself dwells in it [21.3]. As Christ's risen body replaced his earthly body, which was seen no more, so the holy city has now replaced whatever was once on earth, which has 'passed away' [21.1-4]. There is a parallel passage in Hebrews:

Now he has promised, Yet once more I will shake not only the earth but also the heaven... (This) indicates the removal of what is shaken, as of what has been made, in order that what cannot be shaken may remain. Therefore let us be grateful for receiving a kingdom that cannot be shaken. [12.26-28]

So what is the Christian's hope? Jesus himself urges his disciples, not to celebrate their own achievements, but rather to 'rejoice that your names are written in heaven' [Lk 10.20]. Paul mentions 'the book of life' in Philippians 4.3; and there are those who are 'enrolled in heaven' in Hebrews 12.23. But it is John the Seer who mentions the 'book' most frequently [Apoc 3.5; 13.8; 17.8; 20.12,15; 21.27]. While some texts imply that God has a record of persons and their deeds, reference to 'the Lamb's book' must surely witness to the wider saving work of Christ, and so to the embrace of God's mercy and forgiveness. According to Colossians 2.14, 'the bond' or record which stood against us was cancelled when − metaphorically − it was nailed to the cross. Hence the faithful who turn to Christ, as emphasised across the New Testament, need 'have no anxiety' [Phil 4.6] so long as hearts and minds remain 'in Christ Jesus' [v7]. Nor is death to be feared, for it is Christ who holds 'the keys of death and Hades' [Apoc 1.18]. Always in the New Testament the focus of Christian hope is Christ himself, and it is the believer's relationship with him that governs the heavenly perspective.

Afterlife in the Qur'an

The teachings revealed to Muhammad in the early decades of the 7th century reflect many biblical ideas, including of course the key concept of judgment on the Last Day. The Qur'an has its own account of heaven and hell, but accepts that the resolution of differences between Muslims and the People of the Book (as it termed those who were faithful Jews and Christians) will rest with God:

> Say, 'God is our Lord and your Lord − to us our deeds and to you yours, so let there be no argument between us and you − God will gather us together, and to Him we shall return.' [Q 42.15]

> On the Day of Resurrection, your Lord will judge between them regarding their differences. [Q 45.17]

How then is the qur'anic vision of the afterlife to be summarised?

> Bear in mind that the present life is just a game, a diversion, an attraction, a cause of boasting among you, of rivalry in wealth and children... So race for your Lord's forgiveness and a Garden as wide as the heavens and earth, prepared for those who believe in God and His messengers. [Q 57.20-21]

There are abundant references to the Last Day, regarded as a key doctrine governing the full accountability of human life, alongside verses explicitly directed to those who are sceptical about the idea of resurrection. The latter are reminded of the many natural phenomena which in one way or another display God's creative powers and his ability to bring or restore life where there was none before.

As for Paradise, it is frequently depicted as a garden:

God has promised the believers, both men and women, Gardens graced with flowing streams where they will remain; good, peaceful homes in Gardens of lasting bliss; and – greatest of all – God's good pleasure. [Q 9.72]

They will enter perpetual Gardens, along with their righteous ancestors, spouses, and descendants. [Q 13.23]

Another *sura* spells out the meaning of 'righteous', which may entail hardships:

Any who direct themselves wholly to God and do good will have their reward with their Lord... Do you suppose that you will enter the Garden without first having suffered like those who passed away before you? [Q 2.112, 214]

Repentance is expected of any 'who neglected prayer and were driven by their own desires' [Q 19.60] – or who sought 'superiority on earth or spread corruption' [Q 28.83].

The accoutrements of Paradise are then elaborated imaginatively, in language that seems to derive ultimately from pagan burial imagery of earlier centuries – bucolic landscapes that certainly appealed to some Christian authors too:

They will have Gardens of lasting bliss graced with flowing streams. There they will be adorned with bracelets of gold. There they will wear green garments of fine silk and brocade. There they will be comfortably seated on soft chairs. [Q 18.31]

The people of Paradise today are happily occupied – they and their spouses – seated on couches in the shade. [Q 36.55-56]

But those mindful of God will be in a safe place amid Gardens and springs, clothed in silk and fine brocade, facing one another: so it will be. We shall pair them with maidens with beautiful eyes. [Q 44.51-54]

The text here has obviously become a little less chaste, with its switch from 'spouses' to 'beautiful-eyed maidens', repeated in further *suras*:

They are comfortably seated on couches arranged in rows; We pair them with beautiful-eyed maidens. We unite the believers with their offspring who followed them in faith. [Q 52.20-21]

For those who are aware of God there is supreme fulfilment: gardens, vineyards, maidens of matching age. [Q 78.31-32]

And there is a further development in which Paradise is subdivided according to one's faith and works. It has an upper and a lower heaven, both of which are contrasted with hell, a scenario similar to those found in later Jewish and Christian apocryphal writings:

Then you will be sorted into three classes. Those on the Right—what people they are! Those on the Left—what people they are! And those in front—ahead indeed! For these will be the ones brought nearest to God in Gardens of Bliss: many from the past and a few from later generations. On couches of well-woven cloth they will sit facing each other; everlasting youths will go round among them with glasses, flagons, and cups of a pure drink that causes no headache or intoxication; any fruit they choose; the meat of any bird they like; and beautiful-eyed maidens like hidden pearls: a reward for what they used to do. [Q 56.8-24]

For those who fear (to) stand before their Lord there are two gardens... [Q 55.46]

A wall with a door will be erected between them (the believers and the hypocrites): inside it lies mercy, outside lies torment. [Q 57.13]

Ultimately though, even if the pious anticipate their reward in the shape of delightful gardens and couches, with 'rivers of water forever pure', 'milk forever fresh', 'wine a delight for those who drink', 'honey clarified and pure', with 'fruit of every kind' [Q 47.15], such imagery is only a symbol for their acceptance with God:

The final return is to God. [Q 3.28]

They will find forgiveness from their Lord. [Q 47.15]

These more restrained *suras* may remind us of biblical verses. For example, we read of the Psalmist's longing:

As a hart longs for flowing streams, so longs my soul for thee, O God. My soul thirsts for God, for the living God. When shall I come and behold the face of God? [Ps 42.1-2]

Or there is the quotation from Isaiah that summarised the Pauline understanding of a heaven beyond all human imagination:

What no eye has seen, nor ear heard, nor the heart of man conceived, what God has prepared for those who love him. [1 Cor 2.9]

Or again, two centuries later when the martyr Perpetua envisaged her own arrival in heaven, she dreamt that those who met her there would welcome her with the words 'Enter in and *greet the Lord.*'

A complex of issues

It will be clear by now that thinking about life after death underwent considerable elaboration in the centuries that both preceded and followed the time of Christ. The fate of an individual after death certainly needs to be seen in the context of God's purposes for the world as a whole, hence many factors must be taken into consideration: the future (if any) of that person (whether a 'believer' or not) alongside that of the faith community, of the human race in its entirety, of planet earth and of the cosmos to which all belong. The interaction between time and eternity also remains a 'mystery' [cf. 1Cor 15.51], despite the various revelations vouchsafed through God's prophets and above all through the person of Christ. Sacred scriptures provide many divinely-given insights, including the Christian claim that God's new age has already begun in the Lord Jesus and in those who follow him. Biblical sources indicate that the fulfilment of God's purposes for his creation is a developing process, in which human beings themselves pass through different stages; the language of change is employed, which describes not merely a transition from one state of being to another, but has moral and spiritual implications that affect a person's relationships with other people and with God himself. Thus, in Paul's letters and implied in the Johannine conviction is the idea that we shall be purified and made into the likeness of Christ. Yet alongside this aspect of *discontinuity* in Christian writings must be set a strong emphasis upon the *continuing presence* of the risen Lord, who accompanies the believer both in this life and in the world to come. So the concluding words of Matthew's Gospel, 'Lo, I am with you always, to the close of the age' [Matt 28.20] stand alongside the pain of being in some sense 'away from the Lord' (as Paul expressed it) in this present age. Citing Paul's words to the Philippians, St Ambrose, reflecting on the death of his brother Satyrus, could urge therefore that for the Christian 'death is a gain and life a penalty'.

Over succeeding centuries we have noted how each of the Abrahamic traditions continued to develop their ideas of the afterlife. For Christians, the notion of purgatory became more and more prominent from about the 5th century onwards – whereas today both it and even the concept of hell have largely disappeared from view, at least among the general public of the Western world who retain but vague ideas of a universally benign afterlife. It is only in religious circles that teaching about death and beyond remains considerably more qualified, although 'hell-fire' preachers as such are now few and far between. The medieval elaboration of such teachings is a vast subject, but a brief survey of their 'rise and fall (or at least their current decline in popularity)' is worth attempting.

The idea of purgatory

'I will raise you up on the Last Day' was Jesus' promise to his disciples, but by the end of the 1st century the faithful who had shed their blood in martyrdom were reckoned to have already received their reward. Since martyrdom was essentially a potent expression of Christian witness, other saints might also be counted alongside them – in advance of the final judgment. There was, however, a lack of clarity – indeed an ambiguity – about what happened to others between their time of death and the Last Day.

Even from early Christian times prayers were said for the dead, which would be *unnecessary* if the souls were already saved and *fruitless* if the souls were already lost. There is a passage in the New Testament which seems to be such a prayer:

> May the Lord grant mercy to the household of Onesiph'orus, for he often refreshed me; he was not ashamed of my chains, but when he arrived in Rome he searched for me eagerly and found me (may the Lord grant him to find mercy from the Lord on that Day) and you well know all the service he rendered at Ephesus. [2 Tim 1.16-18]

It is not explicitly stated that Onesiphorus has died, but the contrast with the 'greetings' sent to various living Christians at the end of the same letter rather points that way.

Otherwise there is much evidence that may be cited. Thus, the late 2nd century tomb of the Christian Abercius of Hieropolis in Phrygia carries the inscription 'Let every friend who observes this pray for me'. The Roman catacombs bear similar witness to the practice, by the occurrence of such inscriptions as 'Mayst thou live among the saints' (3rd century); 'May God refresh the soul of . . .', 'Peace be with them'. Among Church writers Tertullian, who died in 230, is the first to mention prayers for the dead as a duty:

The widow who does not pray for her dead husband has as good as divorced him.

Subsequent writers make incidental mention of the practice; it was evidently prevalent, and went undisputed until the heretical Arius challenged it towards the end of the 4th century.

An important element in the Christian liturgies both East and West consisted of the diptychs (lists of names of the living and the dead) commemorated at the Eucharist. To be inserted in a diptych was a confirmation of one's orthodoxy, although canonisation gradually evolved beyond such (often spontaneous) local recognition. The occurrence of diptychs and accompanying prayers for the dead in all parts of the Christian Church by the 4th and 5th centuries suggests that they originated early on. At this stage the prayers asked only for rest and freedom from pain and sorrow.

It was during the 3rd century that bishops such as St Cyprian of Carthage began to offer firm teaching about the purging of one's sins in the afterlife. He writes in *Letter 51*:

It is one thing, when cast into prison, not to go out thence until one has paid the uttermost farthing; another thing at once to receive the wages of faith and courage... It is one thing, in fine, to be in suspense till the sentence of God at the day of judgment; another to be at once crowned by the Lord.

Although saintliness (being 'at once crowned by the Lord') was recognised in the witness of martyrs, by the 4th century martyrdom had for the time being largely ceased and a broader assessment of sanctity was needed. Thus, *The Life of St Antony* written by Athanasius around the year 360 gave prominence to his *ascetic life*, and encouraged the growing emphasis upon the virtues of renunciation and celibacy.

Most Christians would, however, need to find alternative routes to heaven, and would remain 'in suspense' before their lives were weighed in the balance. Here the most influential writing was probably that of St Augustine who in his magisterial *City of God* gave careful scrutiny to the notion of a purgatorial fire, testing souls in the interval between death and one's final destiny. His argument in Book 21.26 rests on a passage of St Paul:

> According to the grace of God given to me, like a skilled master builder I laid a foundation, and another man is building upon it. Let each man take care how he builds upon it. For no other foundation can any one lay than that which is laid, which is Jesus Christ. Now if any one builds on the foundation with gold, silver, precious stones, wood, hay, straw - each man's work will become manifest; for the Day will disclose it, because it will be revealed with fire, and the fire will test what sort of work each one has done. If the work which any man has built on the foundation survives, he will receive a reward. If any man's work is burned up, he will suffer loss, though he himself will be saved, but only as through fire. [1 Cor 3.10-15]

The essential requirement for ultimate salvation, as Augustine saw it, was the foundation of faith in Christ. It was the superstructure built on this which would be tested by fire, implying that on 'the Day' there would be a purging experience for all. (The terminology of 'the Day' has no temporal implications since – as we know – 'with the Lord one day is as a thousand years', although for those who have built with gold, silver or precious stones the 'fire' would in truth pass them by). Augustine rightly observed that this purging fire is distinct from the 'everlasting' fire of permanent separation from Christ, experienced by those who lack all love for him.

His near-contemporary St John Chrysostom urged his congregation to do all that they could for the departed who would soon face such a trial:

> Let us weep for these; let us assist them according to our power; let us think of some assistance for them, small though it be, yet still let us assist them. How and in what way? By praying and entreating others to make prayers for them, by continually giving to the poor on their behalf... Not

288

in vain did the Apostles order that remembrance should be made of the dead in the dreadful Mysteries. They know that great gain results to them, great benefit; for when the whole people stands with uplifted hands, a priestly assembly, and that awful Sacrifice lies displayed, how shall we not prevail with God by our entreaties for them? And this we do for those who have departed in faith.

Yet the efficacy of such prayers and rituals was not taken for granted. Not long before Augustine published his *City of God* (426), he was challenged by an educated correspondent, Laurentius, in Rome: did rituals for the dead 'work' – and if so, how? In his reply *Enchiridion* (422), he explained that they were not needed for the *valde boni* (the altogether good, the saints), nor were they relevant to the *valde mali* (the altogether bad); it was those who were neither one nor the other – probably the large majority of people – who could be helped by the offerings of those still living. Augustine remained reticent, however, on the question of *how*: that, he implied, rests with the mysterious workings of God's mercy and grace.

In the following centuries these ideas circulated across the whole Church. St Gregory the Great based his thinking upon one of Jesus' sayings:

As for certain lesser faults, we must believe that, before the Final Judgment, there is a purifying fire. He who is truth says that whoever utters blasphemy against the Holy Spirit will be pardoned neither in this age nor in the age to come. From this sentence we understand that certain offences can be forgiven in this age, but certain others in the age to come. [Cf. Mt 12.31]

He also referred to the Matthaean parable of the sheep and the goats – a straightforward twofold division. In *De Virtutibus Sancti Martini* he envisages himself among the goats:

And when, at the Last Judgment, I am to be placed on the left hand, Martin will deign to pick me out from the middle of the goats with his sacred right hand. He will shelter me behind his back, as the angels tell the King, 'This is the man for whom St Martin pleads.'

For Gregory, therefore, it seems that the *non valdi mali* and the *valdi mali* are not quite as Augustine had seen them. It is only on the day of reckoning itself that judgment will be made, and the prayers of the saints themselves might yet tip the balance in someone's favour. What they needed to bring about above all, he suggested, was the miracle of repentance, when 'tears at last flow loose and genuine remorse follows... sighs rise from the bottom of the heart, and guilty breasts are beaten.' This might not lead to a full share in heavenly glory, but 'at the very least' Gregory hoped to gain God's forgiveness for himself.

Thereafter, the popular imagination went to work: in Peter Brown's summary, not many generations passed before the focus shifted from Gregory's reliance upon the saints to the vital role of those still living to pray for the dead before ever they reached the judgment seat. There were increasingly dire descriptions of their prospects in the purgatorial landscape (which Augustine would have dismissed as speculative and certainly 'not necessarily true'; in fact, pagan undercurrents of fear about the underworld and about 'raging Tarturus' continued to influence people's ideas for centuries). Certain visions of the afterlife were recounted: for example, Bede in his *Ecclesiastical History of the English People* tells of Dryhthelm's vision, and in the late 12th century the story of St Patrick's Purgatory was often repeated. The latter legend reckoned the entrance to purgatory was on an island in Lough Derg. (When I visited this place I was stung by a bee that flew onto my head and became trapped by my hair, so I can attest there are certainly punishments lurking there.) The most famous of all descriptions is Dante's *Il Purgatorio*: in summary, he observes how, for each of the seven deadly sins, the 'punishment' fitted the 'crime' that had been committed.

Although these many depictions must have served as a powerful warning to those who strayed from the 'narrow' paths of righteous living, their inbuilt weakness lay in their too literal readings of biblical language whose meaning is arguably of a more spiritual nature. To give but a couple of examples: 'pain' does not have to mean any kind of physical torture, but is equally descriptive of mental and emotional distress; while the word 'fire' is certainly used of the energy associated with divine love.

The fate that awaited the dead was, however, a major preoccupation of the late medieval Church. Profound pessimism about the afterlife was generally the order of the day, and salvation for the departed was considered as nothing less than a miracle. Relatives prayed for deceased family members; the wealthiest founded chantries; sometimes these were separate chapels staffed by a 'chantry priest' paid solely to offer masses for one or more individuals. Charities were created to assist the poor in the hope that this ongoing work of mercy would not only bring the departed some relief from purgatorial suffering but might also earn merit for the donors. Underlying these practices was the commendable sense that Christians are one family in God, called to support one another in this life and in what lies hereafter.

Rogier van der Weyden's Last Judgment (in the hospital at Beaune)

Yet corroding influences were also at work — the over-literal interpretation of the 'pains' and 'punishments' as seen, for example, in graphic paintings and descriptive writings, or as recounted in people's dreams and visions, together with the tendency to quantify the penalties by the degree of suffering they inflicted or the supposed length of time they had to be endured. Plainly life beyond the grave can only be sketched in figurative language and time has no meaning in the realm of eternity. To preach or teach as if earthly valuations still obtain in the afterlife begins to distort the gospel itself, so there were rightly individuals (and indeed religious movements) who protested against this. So-called 'virtue ethics' which challenges the Christian to consider the kind of person he or she is becoming, and his or her relationship with Christ himself, is threatened when the ecclesiastical mind becomes too legalistic or presumes to dispense mercy according to man-made formulae that measure one's sins.

One noteworthy popular reaction against the increasingly rigorous teaching of the Church about punishment and damnation occurred in the late 11th century with an upsurge of devotion to the Blessed Virgin Mary. She was venerated as a mediator with God: her compassion for the weak and the wayward was believed to be effective in winning a reprieve for those whom justice, whether human or divine, had condemned. The office of the Virgin sung in churches hailed her as 'the mother of mercy, who took pity on Theophilus (who in a legend had sold his soul to the devil, but had come to regret it) and saved him from the trough of sin and misery'. If church authorities were seen as harsh, the Virgin was yet the ordinary man's advocate in God's court of appeal – hence the popularity of her many shrines.

Refocusing the church

'When a coin in the coffer clings, a soul from purgatory heavenward springs.' These are words famously attributed to the 16th century German friar Johann Tetzel who sold 'indulgences' to help finance the construction of St Peter's Basilica in Rome. The practice of granting indulgences grew steadily between the 12th and 16th centuries; it reflected the belief that pastors can apply the superabundant merits of Christ and the saints (the so-called 'treasury of the Church') to reduce a sinner's time in purgatory, or to apply the same grace to one who is already deceased. The idea of an 'indulgence' can of course claim some biblical precedents. God is often seen as exceptionally 'merciful':

> Who is a God like thee, pardoning iniquity and passing over transgression for the remnant of his inheritance? He does not retain his anger for ever because he delights in steadfast love. [Mic 7.18]

Or again, 'forgiveness' and 'mercy' are prominent in Christ's own example:

> Jesus looked up and said to her, 'Woman, where are they? Has no one condemned you?' She said, 'No one, Lord.' And Jesus said, 'Neither do I condemn you; go, and do not sin again.' [Jn 8.11]

However, to speak of a 'treasury' of grace is treading on potentially treacherous ground, opening the way to an unbiblical 'spiritual economy' – indeed ultimately to cash transactions. Since indulgences attached to the churches that could offer them varied in the remissions thus gained, and since pilgrims and penitents brought financial gain to those churches, fierce competition eventually sprang up between them to win as much custom as possible. Rome, for example, saw itself in the early 14th century outclassed in popularity by Jerusalem: the Roman churches therefore attempted to revive their fortunes by hugely boosting the indulgences they offered.[9] Thus, Leopold, an Augustinian prior from Vienna, noted in 1377 that ascending each step outside St Peter's brought him seven years remission, and prayer at each of the eighty altars inside gained at least four times as much as that. Before the *sudarium* of Veronica he reported:

> I, Leopold, unworthy sinner that I am, spent three sessions of twenty-seven hours in prayer. For you must know that for every hour that a Roman looks on this image of the Lord he gains an indulgence of three thousand years; the Italian gets nine thousand years, and the foreigner twelve thousand years.

But at least Leopold made the journey and said his prayers. Those unable to travel were not, however, deprived of the benefits – provided they paid for them. As soon as the Roman Jubilee Year of 1390 was over, Pope Boniface IX set up an elaborate organisation to sell the Jubilee indulgence north of the Alps, and succeeded in extracting large sums 'from the rich and simple-minded' (who were merely required to undertake some small local act of piety). To dispense indulgences for cash was so obviously an abuse akin to simony that it is surprising it needed Martin Luther's vigorous protest in the year 1517 (the 500th anniversary on 31st October 2017 is the eve of All Saints, when it was customary for 'miraculous' relics to be displayed). Nevertheless, it took a little time before the Council of Trent, which met in the mid 16th century, came to outlaw the selling of indulgences.

Even then, another 400 years elapsed before the 2nd Vatican Council met and included a review of indulgences on its agenda. First of all, a

---

[9] In today's world, there has arisen a perverse Muslim equivalent to the indulgence as a fast-track into heaven viz. the notion that suicide bombers will automatically be rewarded with all God's promised rewards. It is, however, made abundantly clear in the Qur'an that Paradise is reserved for 'the righteous', and that if one takes up arms against aggressors it must be done 'in God's way'. If disbelievers cease aggression, 'then God is most forgiving and merciful' [Q 2.192]. There is a reminder that 'God does not love those who overstep the limits' [Q 2.190], which, according to Abdel Haleem, is widely 'agreed that it includes prohibition of starting hostilities, fighting non-combatants, disproportionate response to aggression, etc.' The righteous are described elsewhere as those 'who restrain their anger and pardon people' [Q 3.134].

Martyrs are mentioned in *sura 3*, as those who have died in the 'struggle for God's cause' by remaining steadfast to their faith. Self-harm is specifically ruled out: 'Do not contribute to your destruction with your own hands, but do good, for God loves those who do good' [Q 2.195].

commission which had been set up by Paul VI produced a position paper which aimed to link an indulgence with a change in the believer's interior attitude and any resulting outward action. Calculating supposed 'days' in purgatory was to be totally banned. When the final session of the Council considered these proposals, there was no unanimity. The Melchite Patriarch wanted indulgences to be abolished altogether, arguing that they were 'not only without theological foundation but the cause of innumerable grave abuses which had inflicted irreparable evils on the Church.' The Archbishop of Munich concurred, pointing out that the concept of a 'treasury of the Church' led all too easily to 'materialistic, even quasi-commercial' ideas. The outcome was a further papal commission, followed in 1967 by an *Apostolic Constitution*; this was a disappointment to those who shared the Patriarch's views, but at least used much more personal language and stressed how important was the attitude of one's heart.

With a vocal minority of traditionalists it is never easy for the Catholic Church to change direction too radically; the 1994 *Catechism of the Catholic Church* still retains the term 'punishment', while stating that this is not God's vengeance but has rather the nature of a self-inflicted injury. St Thomas Aquinas used a similar description, when he wrote in his *Summa Theologiae* of 'the penalties of purgatory due to personal defects'. Likewise scriptural commentators often agree today that the rewards and punishments mentioned in the Gospels are best interpreted as the *intrinsic* consequences of a person's life, rather than imposed extrinsically by God.

The continuing debate of bishops and theologians probably seems remote from the day-to-day attitudes of lay Catholics, the majority of whom seldom give indulgences a second thought – or, if they do, find the theology justifying the concept 'barely intelligible' to quote Eamonn Duffy. Indeed, he comments:

From the outset, theologians puzzled to explain how indulgences worked.

Pope Francis, as always much less medieval than some of his predecessors, offers the core of what we really need to understand in *Misericordie Vultus*:

From the heart of the Trinity, from the depths of the mystery of God, the great river of mercy wells up and overflows unceasingly. It is a spring that will never run dry, no matter how many people draw from it. Every time someone is in need, he or she can approach it, because the mercy of God never ends.

We might add the explicit footnote, 'which embraces our existence both here and hereafter'.

Protestant churches, if they can be regarded as the heirs of Luther, have no particular need to engage in the technicalities of this debate, although it is worth recalling how related teachings about heaven and hell stirred strong feelings a century earlier. Two names in particular caused perhaps the greatest uproar. First, that of F.D. Maurice, who was discharged from his teaching post at King's College, London in 1853 after publishing his *Theological Essays*. In the concluding essay, '*On Eternal Life and Eternal Death*,' he argued that these terms refer to a state of being, that is, to one's relationship with God. He saw alienation from God as sufficient punishment in itself; it is the sinful self at the centre of existence which is the worst torture for the convicted soul, worse than any external legal penalty. We might suitably recall Paul's experience on the Damascus road when a voice from heaven addressed him: 'It hurts you to kick against the goads.' Maurice stopped short of denying the possibility of a never-ending hell but hinted that the infinite love of God must be greater than human corruption: 'I am obliged to believe in an abyss of love which is deeper than the abyss of death.' Secondly, there was also the controversial J.W. Colenso, Anglican Bishop of Natal. The missionary movement (which had by now reached Zulu territory) had certainly opened the eyes of Europe to the diversity of cultures and religions in the world and, for some, made hellfire preaching not only morally objectionable but unrealistic and ineffective. Hence Colenso in his *Commentary on the Letter to the Romans* entertained 'the hidden hope that there are remedial processes, when this life is ended, of which at present we know nothing, but which the Lord, the Righteous Judge, will administer.' He cited St Paul in support of his idea that purgation experienced in the afterlife would effect a growth or progress toward spiritual enlightenment.

It would appear that, while not claiming unanimity across the Christian churches, there is nevertheless considerable convergence of thought, even if the theological niceties used to express it can be somewhat opaque, open to misunderstanding and perhaps liable to bypass ordinary lay Christians. The key texts, such as those already cited, must certainly be scriptural; it is their interpretation that on occasion has failed to be sufficiently contextual. There are indeed biblical passages worthy of further reflection which may have been underestimated in previous debates.

The role of Christ

The impression that can sometimes result from particular church pronouncements is that, once a person has died, the only support he or she is likely to receive in pursuing any heaven-bound journey will come from friends on earth or saints in heaven who offer prayers and intercessions. Yet the New Testament is quite insistent (as previously observed) that Christ himself will never abandon his people. Even though Matthew's Gospel takes his abiding presence only as far as 'the close of the age' [Mt 28.20], the interpretation that it therefore stops at that point, so that even those closest to him will then be on their own to face God's judgment, does not accord with passages elsewhere. Thus, there is in John's Gospel the reassurance that Jesus is to 'come again and will take you to myself, that where I am you may be also' [Jn 14.3]. Indeed, he is 'the way, and the truth, and the life; no one comes to the Father, but by me' [Jn 14.6]. There is a bond between Christ and those who follow him:

> In that day you will know that I am in my Father, and you in me, and I in you. [Jn 14.20]

> Father, I desire that they also, whom thou hast given me, may be with me where I am. [Jn 17.24]

If there are trials still to be faced in the afterlife, the *Letter to the Hebrews* speaks powerfully of Christ's active intercession on our behalf:

> We have this as a sure and steadfast anchor of the soul, a hope that enters into the inner shrine behind the curtain, where Jesus has gone as a forerunner on our behalf, having become a high priest for ever after the order of Melchiz'edek. [Heb 6.19-20]

> He is able for all time to save those who draw near to God through him, since he always lives to make intercession for them. [Heb 7.25]

> Christ has entered, not into a sanctuary made with hands, a copy of the true one, but into heaven itself, now to appear in the presence of God on our behalf. [Heb 9.24]

It was in fact Christ's self-offering on the Cross which has brought about our own salvation:

By that will we have been sanctified through the offering of the body of Jesus Christ once for all... by a single offering he has perfected for all time those who are sanctified. [Heb 10.10, 14]

We have therefore a 'new and living way which he opened for us' into the holiest of places – our 'advocate with the Father' [1 Jn 2.1].

Whether or not Christ's supportive, intercessory role is universally appreciated is another matter, but it suggests that the Gospels' depiction of him as the shepherd who is forever seeking the lost and those who have strayed is not confined to the present life. All individual people, in whatever circumstances they find themselves, continue to be of the utmost concern to him: he goes 'after the one which is lost, until he finds it. And when he has found it, he lays it on his shoulders rejoicing' [Lk 15.4-5]. Our God, we may say, is not punitive but merciful; and above all, desiring the restoration of relationships with himself whenever and wherever human beings have wilfully damaged or more carelessly neglected them, he never fails to take initiatives of love towards us. One obvious example of Jesus continuing to act as a shepherd of lost souls is found in the Apostles' Creed, where the clause 'He descended to the dead' is affirmed. This once again is derived from the New Testament:

Early 16th C Russian icon

He went and preached to the spirits in prison, who formerly did not obey... The gospel was preached even to the dead, that though judged in flesh like men, they might live in the spirit like God. [1 Pet 3.19; 4.6]

Those in Sheol (the place of the departed in Jewish thought) are in fact deprived of the vision of God whether they are evil or righteous; by the time of Christ the latter, such as the poor man Lazarus in the well-known parable, were conceived as awaiting salvation in Abraham's bosom'.

As the Catholic catechism expresses it, this descent of Christ into the nether world 'brings the Gospel message of salvation to complete fulfilment'. It spread 'Christ's redemptive work to all men of all times and all places.'

In the Orthodox Church the portrayal of this descent has become the festival icon of Easter, symbolising God's supreme triumph over death in whatever guise it is found, whether in this world or the next.

Allegorical paths to heaven

If heaven is to be a vastly better place for us than life on earth, we must be vastly better people to dwell there. Obviously, therefore, most of us are far from ready when we die, and significant changes must occur in our priorities and our personalities. C.S.Lewis wrote a story in the mid 1940s entitled *The Great Divorce* which highlights the shock some of us would experience if we were suddenly dropped into Paradise. It clearly drew some inspiration from Dante's *Divine Comedy* and from Bunyan's *Pilgrim's Progress.*

The narrator finds himself in a grim and joyless city, the 'grey town', which is either hell or purgatory depending on how long one stays. He subsequently finds a bus to take some sojourners there on an outing. When they reach their destination, which turns out to be the foothills of heaven, the passengers on the bus – including the narrator – are discovered to be ghosts. Although the country is the most beautiful they have ever seen, every feature of its landscape (including streams of water and blades of grass) is unyieldingly solid compared to themselves: it causes them immense pain to walk on the grass, and even a single leaf is far too heavy for any to lift.

Shining figures, men and women whom they have known on earth, come to meet them, and urge them to repent and enter Heaven proper. They promise that as the ghosts travel onward and upward, they will become more solid and thus feel less and less discomfort. These figures, called 'spirits' to distinguish them from the ghosts, offer to assist them on the journey towards the mountains and the sunrise.

Almost all of the ghosts, however, choose to return instead to the grey town, giving a variety of reasons. These excuses have an all-too-familiar ring, but although outwardly plausible they are patently thin and self-deceiving. The ghosts prefer to retain their old way of life, and thus throw away their chance of everlasting bliss.

Lewis suggests that a choice is necessary: if we want the blessings of heaven, we must conform to the life we find there, and prefer the company of those who live there. They are to be counted among the ones who will help us to change.

Two decades earlier a longer, and (for me) more powerful, novel was written by Elizabeth von Arnim, and can be read as a parable of the heavenly transformation that can occur. The authoress was an Australian writer, whose unhappy marriage to a domineering German count eventually ended when he died in 1910. Her first novel *Elizabeth and her German Garden* was a semi-autobiographical reflection on her marriage, and in fact most of her later writings were based on various personal experiences. This is certainly true of *The Enchanted April*, which drew upon an idyllic month's holiday she enjoyed on the Italian Riviera. Not long after its publication in 1922 it was turned into a Broadway play, and in 1991 it became a film directed by Mike Newell (whose parents promoted much drama in St Albans where I grew up). It was not intended to be a theological narrative, but the many references to heaven and several to the saints certainly encourage one to see it in religious terms. As a human narrative it is entertaining, if perhaps a little sentimental and too implausible: but read as an allegory of how heaven's own environment can work wonders it is certainly thought-provoking.

Four very different women respond to an advertisement in the Times appealing to 'those who appreciate wisteria and sunshine' to rent a small medieval Italian castle for a month. Mrs Wilkins and Mrs Arbuthnot, the original two respondents, are joined in their act of escape by the youthful Lady Caroline, whose beauty and general melodiousness have become something of a burden to her, and the formidable Mrs Fisher, who insists that everyone think of her 'just as an old lady with a stick' as she sets about imposing her will on the rest. Each one is vaguely unsatisfied with their lot and Mrs Wilkins and Mrs Arbuthnot are both miserable in their marriages. The latter is conventionally devout and suffers in silence; so Mrs Wilkins rightly observes, 'I can see you've been good for years and years, because you look so unhappy', while Mr Briggs, the generous owner of the castle, discerns her true inner goodness – 'there's [a Madonna] on the stairs really exactly like you'.

On arrival at the castle Mrs Wilkins lies in bed on her first morning wondering what she would see out of her window: 'A shining world, or a world of rain? But it would be beautiful: whatever it was would be beautiful.' She tells Mrs Arbuthnot later, 'I daresay when we finally reach heaven – the one they talk about so much – we shan't find it a bit more beautiful.' Mrs Arbuthnot too appreciates 'the simple happiness of complete harmony with her surroundings.' Meanwhile Lady Caroline is experiencing 'a violent reaction against beautiful clothes and the slavery they impose on one.' Mrs Fisher continues to 'behave as if [the castle] belonged only to her'. Yet in Mrs Wilkins' view, 'I'm quite sure that we've got to heaven, and once Mrs Fisher realises that's where she is, she's bound to be different... Why, I shouldn't be surprised if we get quite fond of her.'

Von Arnim has an eye for small human failings, the pettiness and selfishness in which most people indulge. She is perceptive about the way people misread one another's good (and not so good) intentions, and the early chapters read like a comedy of miscommunication. She also – perhaps not surprisingly, given her famed German garden – revels in the descriptions of the castle grounds and their beauty and colour. The climate and the castle eventually start to have an effect on the four women. Their attitudes shift and they wake up to the love in their lives. 'I had planned a holiday in Italy leaving [Mellersh, her husband] at home. He has every reason to be angry and hurt,' says Mrs Wilkins, so she invites him to share their good fortune and advises Mrs Arbuthnot to follow her example. For her part, Mrs Fisher finds that she can almost trot along without using her stick, while her personality mellows at the same rate. Lady Caroline is won over by Mellersh's impeccable courtesy in the immediate aftermath of his disastrous attempt to take a bath. 'Having choked the laughter down and got her face serious again, she said as composedly as if he had all his clothes on, "How do you do." The incident induces 'a sense of broken ice', a relaxed feeling of intimacy throughout the house that even includes the once frosty Mrs Fisher.

The happy ending is no less magical for its predictability. Thomas Briggs arrives for a short visit, as – quite unexpectedly – does Mr Frederick Arbuthnot. Lady Caroline by now has owned up to her own past disposition and admits what she really was – 'a spoilt, a sour, a suspicious and a selfish spinster'. The other ladies too are aware of the real lack of concern they had for each other's well-being when they first arrived. The marriages are mended, and the book ends with a new one in the offing – Mr Bridge and Lady Caroline. **The message is clear: this heavenly dwelling can produce more saintly people fit to occupy it, as little by little their kindnesses to each other begin to multiply.**

A hint of Paradise
- but 'greatest of all, God's good pleasure' [Q 9.72]

'When, on the first of May, everybody went away, even after they had got to the bottom of the hill and passed through the iron gates out into the village they still could smell the acacias.'

It may well be that what von Arnim was describing was more akin to purgatory than to heaven: that is to say, it seems to tell us of a process of healing, in which not only were relationships restored but also the participants came to greater self-awareness and learnt from their interaction with others how they themselves had sinned and needed to amend their lives. If our pilgrimage to heaven is not one enforced upon us but a path which we discover for ourselves – admittedly not without setbacks and mistakes – then the most important influence upon us is surely the love and support of the One who journeys with us, Jesus Christ himself. Nor can the prayers of the saints be discounted, for their own 'communion' is incomplete without us.

St Paul affirmed that 'we shall all be changed' [1 Cor 15.51], but the key issue is appreciating that spiritually that must mean our personal reformation. I began by citing evidence from the distant past in other religions and cultures, and here a quotation from Classical Greece, whose wisdom has much in common with Christian morality, is also apposite. There are elements in pre-Christian traditions around the world which may be recognised as *preparatio evangelii*. Some (but by no means all) ideas about human fulfilment in the afterlife may be included, but there is a telling fable of Aesop too which illustrates the power of Christian love to effect change. Aesop is believed to have been a slave who gained renown for telling the stories that bear his name. Various Greek authors refer to him – Herodotus suggests that he won his freedom by telling such stories. The evidence now is that some of them go back much further; for example, there are Sumerian fables remarkably similar to some of his that were discovered on cuneiform tablets dated to around 1800 BC.

The Aesop fable that suggests how people can best be brought to *metanoia* (the gospel term for 'a change of heart') tells of a competition between *the Wind and the Sun*:

The Wind and the Sun were disputing which was the stronger. Suddenly they saw a traveller coming down the road, and the Sun said: 'I see a way to decide our dispute. Whichever of us can cause that traveller to take off his cloak shall be regarded as the stronger. You begin.' So the Sun retired behind a cloud, and the Wind began to blow as hard as it could upon the traveller. But the harder he blew the more closely did the traveller wrap his cloak round him, till at last the Wind had to give up in despair. Then the Sun came out and shone in all his glory upon the traveller, who soon found it too hot to walk with his cloak on.

Exposed to the glory of the Lord, and the overwhelming fire of heavenly love, who would not want to respond? In fact, the imagery of both wind and fire is found in the Bible. The *burning bush* inspired Moses to his redemptive mission; and in the New Testament the *Pentecostal flames* alighted upon the apostles together with a *rushing mighty wind* driving them out of their safe haven to embark upon hazardous ventures of faith. On each occasion a (disruptive) divine influence was thus able to spread hope and joy in the world.

There is yet another biblical symbol of the way God works: the *dove* that descended upon Jesus was no bird, but the gentleness of the Spirit breathing mercy and compassion.

If these divine attributes are experienced here below, may we not expect complete fulfilment in the eternal domain?

Soul Mountain

'There's a mountain even higher,
and it's called Heaven'
(Samuel, aged 4)

THE WAY AHEAD

A palm cross

*carried one Friday afternoon
along the way of the Cross
in Jerusalem*

**now a sign of witness
when the churches of Wye
process together in Holy Week**

The Jerusalem palm was the original souvenir of a completed pilgrimage, long before the scallop shell came to rival it. St Peter Damian writing in the 11th century describes it as the 'customary' symbol of faith's victory over sin. It is nonetheless very fragile...

Yeshua bar Abba

THE MAN FOR OTHERS

Waiting on the father

For most of his life Jesus lived in obscurity:

When he began his ministry [he] was about thirty years of age, being the son (as was supposed) of Joseph. [Lk 3.23]

There were no doubt good reasons why he had remained quietly in Nazareth until this particular juncture. The last specific mention of Joseph is when Jesus at the age of twelve visited Jerusalem with both his parents for the feast of Passover, as was their custom. It seems clear enough in the gospel records that, once his peripatetic ministry had begun, the only surviving parent was his mother Mary; the presumption is therefore that Joseph had died some time earlier, perhaps when Jesus was a teenager and then took upon himself the role of bread-winner for the household. Caring for his mother was always important to him, hence at the point of his own death he commended Mary into the keeping of 'the disciple whom he loved':

He said to the disciple, 'Behold, your mother!' And from that hour the disciple took her to his own home. [Jn 19.27]

In Mark's Gospel, generally thought to be the earliest extant record, Jesus is indeed described as 'the carpenter' of Nazareth:

Is not this the carpenter, the son of Mary and brother of James and Joses and Judas and Simon, and are not his sisters here with us? [Mk 6.3]

Matthew alters this slightly, describing him as 'the carpenter's son', but there is no suggestion even so that the long-serving village carpenter Joseph is still alive. And certainly none of the Gospels give any indication that Jesus had previously stood out as an 'exceptional' figure in his village; the reaction to his teaching is one of 'astonishment', that so ordinary a person could utter such wisdom. The exaggerated stories that appeared in the much later 'infancy gospels' – such as bringing a clay bird to life, or causing a playmate who crossed his path to drop dead – may therefore be totally ignored.

At what point, we may wonder, did his self-awareness begin to include the uniquely intimate relationship with God that motivated his future ministry? Not many clues are available to us, but Luke's account of his childhood visit to Jerusalem indicate that by the age of twelve he was extremely well-versed in the Hebrew scriptures, more than able to hold his own with learned scribes in the Temple, who were 'amazed' at his understanding. Luke also tells us of his lifetime habit of attending the synagogue each Sabbath day [Lk 4.16], and of his evident literacy. Each recorded episode indicates that he had thoroughly absorbed the underlying scriptural meanings, interpreting them in very personal terms. On the earlier occasion he speaks of the Temple as 'my Father's house', while eighteen years later in Nazareth he announces himself as the one upon whom Isaiah's prophesied 'Spirit of the Lord' has indeed descended. It is exactly the same when, on the day of his resurrection, he explains recent events to Cleopas and his friend as they walk to Emmaus:

> Beginning with Moses and all the prophets, he interpreted to them in all the scriptures the things *concerning himself.* [Lk 24.27]

In the coming centuries, it was of course the same principle that Christ's followers adopted in their readings of the Old Testament: 'Christ' was the key to its interpretation. Nor was St Jerome speaking out of turn when he commented that 'ignorance of scripture is ignorance of Christ.' It was not, however, the apostles or the early Church Fathers who initiated this insight; it evidently derived from the Lord's own years of quiet reflection on God's word addressed through scripture to himself.

Why though – apart from his family responsibilities – did Jesus begin his public ministry at the particular age of thirty? In Jewish tradition that was usually regarded as the stage in life when a person's full strength was reached – as exemplified in both Joseph and King David:

> Joseph was thirty years old when he entered the service of Pharaoh king of Egypt. [Gen 41.46]

> David was thirty years old when he began to reign. [2 Sam 5.4]

Hence, although the 'legal' age of maturity was variously estimated as eighteen or twenty, *wisdom* was not achieved so readily; a person reckoned as inexperienced might not be too well regarded. By the time Jesus delivered his message, he was by contrast acclaimed as 'one who had authority, and not as the scribes' [Mk 1.22].

Yet the key to Jesus' emergence from the obscurity of Nazareth at this age actually seems to have been the much publicised preaching of John the Baptist in the Jordan valley. In all four Gospels Jesus' ministry begins with his baptism by John; indeed it actually features in the *opening* verses of Mark's Gospel. The implication seems to be that Jesus saw John's ministry as a divine signal beckoning him into the public arena himself; John was challenging people to turn again to God, in Mark's words taken from Isaiah, as 'one crying in the wilderness: prepare the way of the Lord.' It provided moreover a golden opportunity for Jesus to make his first public gesture: not a statement and certainly not a sermon, but a 'parabolic action' – his humble acceptance of baptism at John's hands. This was his self-identification: the one who came to be among people, whose mission was to share their lot; the one whose readiness to love and serve might enable John's worthy exhortations to be fulfilled. In self-references throughout the Gospels, the language which he generally used was the simple phrase 'the Son of man'. While others sometimes suggested grander (messianic) titles, he made no such claims but stressed the humility and humanity of his role.

The accounts of Jesus' baptism are (as with other episodes recorded in the Gospels) not entirely consistent. In John's Gospel, probably the latest to be written, John the Baptist emphasises that 'I myself did not know him.' He also claims to have seen 'the Spirit descend as a dove from heaven' which 'remained on him'. In the other Gospels it appears to have been Jesus himself who experienced this moving spiritual endorsement, and to have been reassured of his own divine Sonship. In the Fourth Gospel there is no mention here of a voice from heaven, but the Baptist expresses a similar testimony in his own words: there appears to be a reference to this later in the Gospel, when Jesus speaking to 'the Jews' notes that they 'sent to John, and he has borne witness to the truth' [Jn 5.33]. However, one should not forget that in the Synoptic Gospels, John the Baptist – now in prison – dispatches messengers to Jesus asking, 'Are you the one who should come, or shall we look for another?' [Mt 11.3 cf. Lk 7.20], which expresses a note of uncertainty in contrast to the ready recognition offered earlier [Mt 3.14]. This is consistent with the growing doubts expressed by others, including disciples of Jesus, that this 'Christ' is not quite the figure they had been expecting.

For his part, Jesus is recorded as paying remarkable tribute to John himself, in words that suggest it may indeed have been his mission centred on the waters of the Jordan that triggered the commencement of Jesus' own ministry:

> Truly, I say to you, among those born of women there has risen no one greater than John the Baptist; yet he who is least in the kingdom of heaven is greater than he. [Mt 11.11 cf. Lk 7.28-30, which emphasises the *popular response* to John in contrast to his rejection by Jewish authorities]

If the baptism itself was the very first expression of Jesus' role as 'the Son of man' (a theme to be pursued later), how should the signs from heaven be interpreted? The Spirit 'descending... like a dove' [Mk 1.10] and the voice from above [Mk 1.11] would seem to be how Jesus felt personally 'affirmed' at that critical stage of his life by his (heavenly) Father. In Luke's version Jesus was actually praying [Lk 3.21] when 'heaven was opened'. His bold move, plunging into the river Jordan in an act of humble solidarity with God's people, was thereby spiritually endorsed as indeed the right way forward. We can surely only know of the signs − of which he alone was truly aware, in his innermost being − because he later made reference of them to his disciples.

How they subsequently became included in written Gospel records is another matter altogether. The different evangelists no doubt received the oral tradition from more than one source, and made use of it according to the particular circumstances in which they were writing; so − as with most other 'parallel' passages − the descriptive language is varied. With the passage of time, however, the interpretation of this imagery, in which the Spirit is metaphorically 'a dove', plainly got out of hand. What is indicated by it is not any bodily likeness (however appealing that became to some medieval artists) but the *gentleness* (and perhaps *innocency* cf. Mt 10.16) of the Spirit's descent. Certainly there is a contrast in Luke's writing between the Spirit's calm response to Jesus' prayer and the emphatic gale that engulfed the apostles on the day of Pentecost [Acts 2.1-4]. We are reminded that in Hebrew, whereas *ruach* is God's mighty wind, *nephesh* is his 'breath' − such as Jesus himself bestowed on his disciples gathered in Jerusalem on Easter evening:

When he had said this, he breathed on them, and said to them, 'Receive the Holy Spirit'. [Jn 20.22]

The 'dovelike' movement of the Holy Spirit would thus seem to be the Father's way of confirming his Son's expression of humility. There is no reason to interpret the occasion, as some commentators have in time past, as God's *adoption* of Jesus as his Son (in theological language, 'an adoptionist christology', as contrasted with the Nicene Creed's presentation of Jesus as '*eternally* begotten' of the Father): rather, it endorsed the inner meaning of Jesus' Sonship, already known from his tenderest years, that he now fully appreciated after years of prayerful reflection upon the sacred scriptures.

Jesus' public ministry

Although Jesus' public ministry had been thus launched, a key issue inevitably arose concerning the overlapping role of John the Baptist: would the latter, for example, now retire gracefully from the scene altogether, assuming he did indeed recognise Jesus as 'the one who is mightier than I' [Mk 1.7]? It may be that Jesus was already aware of much displeasure directed against John by the public authorities, and had timed his visit accordingly – while popular acclaim was at its height, and before John's anticipated (?) arrest.

Here it should not be forgotten that these were troubled times. In the 1st century there were a number of individuals who claimed a messianic role, or who might be seen in that light, most of whom (according to the Jewish writer Josephus, the chief source of historical information about this period of Judaean life) were seen as a threat by the ruling elite. Among them were opportunists such as Judas, son of Hezekiah (based at Sepphoris in Galilee), Simon (in Peraea) and a shepherd called Athrongaeus, 'whose hopes were based on his physical strength and contempt of death':

> He set a crown on his own head, but continued for a considerable time to raid the country with his brothers... they were harrassing all Judaea with their brigandage.

Sometimes these insurrections were responses to provocations by the Romans themselves; for example, the census 'when Quirinius was governor of Syria' [Lk 2.2] which was regarded as a direct challenge to God's own sovereignty; or the occasion when Pilate 'secretly and under cover conveyed to Jerusalem the [graven] images of Caesar' which certainly defiled the sanctity of the holy city. Claimants to the throne were not necessarily setting themselves up as 'Messiahs', but the general instability so engendered no doubt contributed to heightened messianic expectations.

Josephus mentions other figures who may have been perceived by some as messianic because of the prophetic mantle that they wore. These are found in his later work *Antiquities of the Jews*. There was, for example, Theudas [cf. Acts 5.36], who in the end was executed. He writes too of John the Baptist:

Herod, who feared lest the great influence John had over the people might put it into his power and inclination to raise a rebellion (for they seemed ready to do anything he should advise), thought it best, by putting him to death, to prevent any mischief he might cause.

John's recorded location in the Jordan valley, not far from Qumran, makes it likely that he had some awareness of Essene teachings, which in several scrolls refer to a messianic being. However, a debate continues as to the Messiah's envisaged role, about which there is no apparent consistency: is he projected as a war leader, a prophet, a teacher of God's law, a ruler of the new Israel, a priest – or as God's agent would he be *sui generis*? John does not seem to identify any particular charism in his 'mightier' successor other than a baptism of Spirit and of 'fire'. Whether his preaching actually stirred up hopes of popular insurrection seems unlikely, but it was not long after his encounter with Jesus that he was arrested and imprisoned [Mk 1.14 cf. Matt 4.12; Lk 3.20], and like Theudas also put to death. The pretext for his execution was his apparent criticism of Herod's marriage to Herodias [Mk 6.17ff; Mt 14.3; Lk 3.19-20 – who adds '*and for all the evil things that Herod had done*']. Such outspoken comments would doubtless have been regarded as seditious and threatening; but, in fact, Mark seems to have been misled by popular rumour about Herod's family affairs (which were otherwise than he portrays), and may have misrepresented the circumstances of John's arrest. Josephus's assessment that it was a political attempt to suppress an obviously popular movement seems more likely.

After Jesus' baptism 'the Spirit immediately drove him out into the wilderness' [Mk 1.12]. This provided time for further close communion with his Father and for reflection on the challenges lying ahead. The 'forty' days mentioned is not necessarily an exact count. In the Old Testament 'forty' is symbolic for a time of 'testing', as in the days and nights of rainfall that brought about the great flood [Gen 7.4], the years spent by the Israelite 'refugees' wandering in the Sinai peninsula, or the period of Elijah's retreat on Mount Horeb [1 Kgs 19]. Such examples remind us that the 'wilderness' could also be a place of refuge, and Jesus may have waited there until 'after John was arrested' [Mk 1.14 cf. Mt 4.12] in order to keep his own coming ministry quite separate from John's in the public mind.

On the other hand, Mark may have omitted a good deal of detail, for in the Fourth Gospel there are several early verses in which Jesus has already recruited his own disciples and begun baptising *before* John was put in prison [Jn 3.22-23; 4.1]: such details may have been included because of questions the evangelist was trying to answer about the origins of specifically *Christian* baptism? But John the Baptist's continuing activity [cf. Acts 19.1-4] leaves one wondering whether this had become somehow supportive of Jesus – or whether it indicated a degree of doubt about 'he who comes after me'? There is at least a useful clue here that Jesus may have moved up to Galilee from Judaea because he was not yet ready to face the inevitable onslaught from the strict Pharisaic party, who were now aware that he was 'making and baptising more disciples than John'. He had much work (of preaching and healing) to accomplish first. He also appreciated that it was religious opponents, rather than political figures, who would pose the greatest threat [cf. Jn 7.1, 30ff; 8.59; 10.31]; so, despite the seat of Herod's tetrarchy being at Tiberias, he clearly felt safer in the north.

Discrepancies between the Gospels leave us far from clear what Jesus' movements were after his baptism, and for how long his ministry actually lasted. But then none of the evangelists were intent upon writing his biography with chronological exactitude; rather, their task was to select and present coherently the mainly oral tradition that came to them. So Mark offers us a 'pilgrimage' that begins with Jesus in his native territory of Galilee, and ends with the events in Jerusalem that culminated in his death and resurrection; whereas John's schema depicts him going more than once to Jerusalem for a festival (which had after all been his long-standing custom), and then back to Galilee (and sometimes Samaria) again. The impression we therefore gain from Mark is of a shorter ministry, perhaps little more than a year, contrasted with about three years in John's reckoning – a more plausible figure.

Yet, although John, who writes later, has recourse to stories and sayings not found in the Synoptic Gospels which may be historically well-founded, it should not be assumed that John is invariably the most factually 'reliable' Gospel. What he records often carries symbolic themes linking the narrative together, or reminding us of important ideas drawn from the Jewish tradition. For example, the 'days' referred to in his opening chapters seem to follow the patterns of revelation described in Exodus 19:

And the Lord said to Moses, 'Lo, I am coming to you in a thick cloud, that the people may hear when I speak with you, and may also believe you for ever.' Then Moses told the words of the people to the Lord. And the Lord said to Moses, 'Go to the people and consecrate them today and tomorrow, and let them wash their garments, and be ready by the third day; for on the third day the Lord will come down upon Mount Sinai in the sight of all the people.'

Much can be drawn out of this – including its subsequent fulfilment on the 'third day' known as Easter – but we note here just the conclusion of the story of the wedding at Cana, which also happened on the third day:

This, the first of his signs, Jesus did at Cana in Galilee, and manifested his glory; and his disciples believed in him.

A quick glance at any map of the Holy Land must surely dispel any idea that John's 'days' of chapters 2 and 3 are to be taken literally. Galilee is at the very least *several* days' walk from John the Baptist's location by the Jordan, reminding us that gospel itineraries are usually there to serve literary and theological purposes before anything else.

Indeed, despite their differences, what the four evangelists share in common is far more important. The Gospels were written as *testimony* to Jesus, and to his centrality in the life of Christian believers. The necessary selectivity of appropriate material and the purpose behind it are made most explicit in John's gospel:

Now Jesus did many other signs in the presence of the disciples, which are not written in this book; but these are written that you may believe that Jesus is the Christ, the Son of God, and that believing you may have life in his name. [Jn 20.30-31]

Similar aims and methods are implicit in the other Gospels, which all begin in some way by introducing the reader to *who* Jesus was, and end with testimony to his *continuing life* [Lk 24.51] or *presence* [Mt 28.20]. The picture is somewhat clouded in Mark's case, since the ending of his Gospel is uncertain. It is arguable that Mark's intent was actually to point ahead to a more glorious meeting with the risen Lord who always 'goes before you'.

Go, tell his disciples and Peter that he is going before you to Galilee; there you will see him, as he told you. [Mk 16.7]

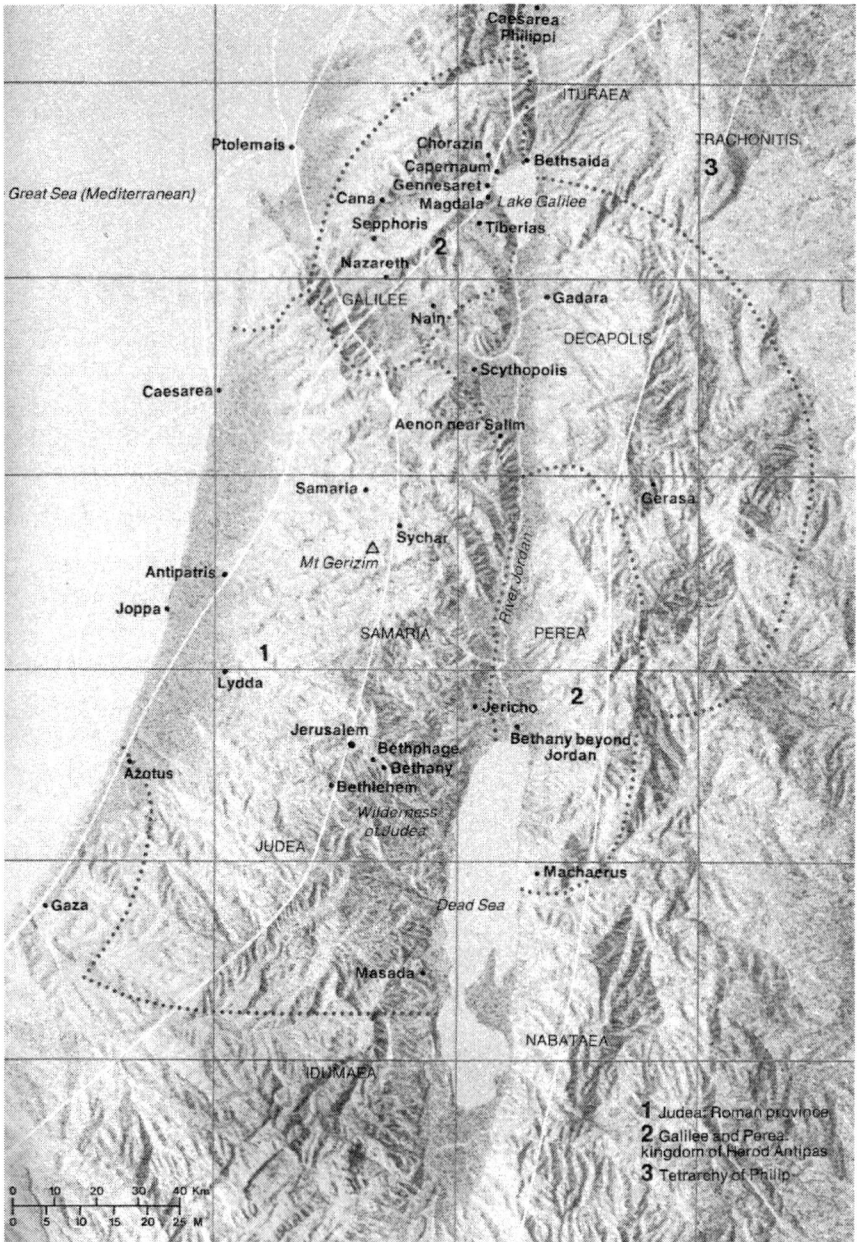

Caesarea
Philippi

ITURAEA

TRACHONITIS

3

Ptolemais

Great Sea (Mediterranean)

Chorazin
Capernaum • Bethsaida
Gennesaret
Cana • Magdala Lake Galilee
Sepphoris • Tiberias

2

Nazareth

GALILEE

Nain •

• Gadara

DECAPOLIS

• Scythopolis

Caesarea •

Aenon near Salim

Samaria •

Gerasa

Sychar

Mt Gerizim △

River Jordan

Antipatris •

SAMARIA

PEREA

Joppa •

1

Lydda •

2

• Jericho

Jerusalem •
• Bethphage
• Bethany

• Bethany beyond
Jordan

Azotus

• Bethlehem

Wilderness
of Judea

JUDEA

• Gaza

• Machaerus

Dead Sea

Masada •

NABATAEA

IDUMAEA

1 Judea: Roman province
2 Galilee and Perea:
kingdom of Herod Antipas
3 Tetrarchy of Philip

0 10 20 30 40 Km
0 5 10 15 20 25 M

Map of the Holy Land

316

Manifesting his glory

The suggestion here is that Jesus' self-awareness began at an early age and that his understanding of the divine mission yet to be accomplished deepened through years of prayer and scriptural reflection. It is surely no accident that, in Luke's Gospel, Jesus begins his ministry by preaching about the fulfilment of a text in Isaiah. Among all the Hebrew scrolls, this seems to have held the key to how he interpreted his coming role. It has sometimes been called the 'fifth Gospel' because, as Jerome once expressed it, the life of the Messiah is recounted in such a way as to make one think the prophet 'is telling the story of what has already happened rather than what is still to come.' The book of Isaiah is actually quoted in the New Testament more than any other book of the Hebrew scriptures apart from the Psalms: the fundamental reason for this is surely that this was the book that gave most guidance to Jesus during his so-called 'hidden years'.

It will be helpful to offer a brief survey of Isaiah's message. Although we now recognise historical development within the book as a whole, there are important common themes throughout, focusing on concepts such as God's holiness, and his desire for righteousness and faith, for peace and justice. Ritual purity and cultic practices are not enough in themselves, and indeed are condemned if they take the place of social justice [1.11-17; 58] or humility [66.1-4]. The Temple plays only a minor role in the visions of a new Jerusalem, and in those passages where it is mentioned, the emphasis is on opening its doors to foreigners [56.3-8] and to the nations of the world [2.2-4; 66.18-21].

Visions of a new age often highlight an individual champion of justice and righteousness. This includes the passage quoted by Jesus in his 'manifesto' at Nazareth:

> The Spirit of the Lord is upon me, because he has anointed me to preach good news to the poor. He has sent me to proclaim release to the captives and recovering of sight to the blind, to set at liberty those who are oppressed, to proclaim the acceptable year of the Lord. [Lk 4.18-19 cf. Isa 61.1-4]

This prophetic model seems to underlie two other texts, in which he is described as 'the servant of the Lord' [49.1-6; 50.4-9], though in each case the reference may include Israel as an entity. But above all there is the celebrated 'suffering servant' passage, which seems to speak of an individual who heals and redeems by vicarious suffering [52.13-53.12]. It expresses confidence in the power of God to heal wounds and to forgive sins. The servant himself is not identified in Isaiah's text, which draws on traditional Jewish ideas such as the scapegoat ritual [53.4, 6, 12] and hints at the figure of Moses, who offered to die for his people [Exod. 32.32]. A reminder of God's past graciousness is found in the occasional use of wilderness motifs [e.g. 43.19-21; 48.21; 55.12-13].

The idea of 'service' is certainly suggested in Jesus' use of the term 'Son of man'. This phrase occurs repeatedly throughout the book of Ezekiel, where the prophet is addressed in this way; but it is used in one text in Isaiah as well:

> Thus says the Lord: 'Keep justice, and do righteousness, for soon my salvation will come, and my deliverance be revealed. Blessed is the man who does this, and the son of man who holds it fast.' [Isa 56.1-2]

Here the stress shifts from the phrase itself to the hastening of God's salvation by the implementation of his will. As that overworked modern cliché suggests, 'walking the talk' is an essential element in God's mission.

So it was that Jesus saw how his Sonship of the Father could fittingly be expressed, not just in the unpretentious phrase 'Son of man', but in a ministry of 'Isaianic' self-offering. The radiance of his divine glory was only to be found in the self-authenticating testimony of his love and compassion for others. St Paul explained this to the Philippians in words that may have been in use already as an early Christian hymn:

> [Christ Jesus], though he was in the form of God, did not count equality with God a thing to be grasped, but emptied himself, taking the form of a servant, being born in the likeness of men. And being found in human form he humbled himself and became obedient unto death, even death on a cross. [Phil 2.6-8]

A wall painting in St Albans Abbey

It is also Paul, in letters that of course pre-date the Gospels, who offers an alternative version of the 'Son of man' periphrasis used by Jesus. Adam, he writes to the Romans, was 'a type of the one who was to come' [Rom 5.14]: hence Jesus may be described as 'the new Adam'. In fact, addressing the Church in Corinth Paul uses the phrase 'the last Adam':

> For as in Adam all die, so also in Christ shall all be made alive… Thus it is written, 'The first man Adam became a living being'; the last Adam became a life-giving spirit. [1 Cor 15. 22, 45]

> Christ as the new or last Adam enables Christians themselves to attain 'to mature manhood, to the measure of the stature of the fulness of Christ' [Eph 4.13].

In subsequent writings of the early Fathers, it was above all St Irenaeus who elaborated such teaching, particularly in his well-known line that Christ 'became what we are, that he might bring us to be even what he is himself'. More specifically, again in his *Against Heresies*, Irenaeus sets out the basis of what later became known as 'recapitulation' theology:

Therefore does the Lord profess himself to be the Son of man, comprising in himself that original man out of whom the woman was fashioned, in order that, as our species went down to death through a vanquished man, so we may ascend to life again through a victorious one; and as through a man death received the palm [of victory] against us, so again by a man we may receive the palm against death.

In perhaps simpler terms, one might explain Christ as the true exemplar of how God intended us to live as human beings, created in his own image and likeness [Gen 1.26], which in effect means therefore 'the man for others'. This is not a reduction to some form of humanism (such as the merely 'social' gospel), so long as we recall Irenaeus' important qualification:

The glory of God is man fully alive, *and the life of man is the vision of God.*

Here we must return to the person of Jesus, whose life was given in compassionate service to bring hope and healing to others. Is it indeed possible to glimpse in his life a manifestation of divine glory? This was St John's claim, expressed in the prologue of his Gospel:

And the Word became flesh and dwelt among us, full of grace and truth; we have beheld his glory, glory as of the only Son from the Father. [Jn 1.14]

No manner of drawing comparisons, and no form of reasoning, can bring us to the core of Christian faith in Jesus as *Lord*. When Simon Peter professed him as 'the Christ, the Son of the living God', Jesus observed:

Flesh and blood has not revealed this to you, but my Father who is in heaven. [Mt 16.17]

Of course, specific teachings of Jesus (which resonated with an aura of 'authority'), his miracles and acts of kindness, his personal disposition, the apparent resonances of his life with scriptural prophecies, his readiness to die for others and to forgive those who ill-treated him, and then his amazing resurrection, all contributed to people's perception of him. But even their combined weight could not 'prove' or infallibly reveal

320

the secret of who he truly was. This is illustrated by the fact that at one point 'many of his disciples drew back and no longer went about with him' [Jn 6.66] and that at the last he was betrayed by Judas Iscariot. More striking though is the story of the future apostle Paul, who began as a fanatical and determined opponent of the new Christian movement – and no doubt knew much of Jesus' own record – yet who turned dramatically to faith on the Damascus road. It was not religious logic that prompted this, but a personal revelation.

My yoke is easy, and my burden is light

Those who 'beheld' the fullness of divine 'grace and truth' in Jesus revered his teachings, which were not just spoken but frequently exemplified in his manner of life and his dealings with those he encountered. Paul is one of our earliest witnesses to the Church's intention to remain loyal to 'the Lord'. In his first letter to the Corinthians he addresses some of the questions that concern them, about which they had written. The whole of chapter 7 is devoted to marriage issues, and Paul's response is to start by considering the Lord's own guidance: 'I give charge – not I, but the Lord'; 'To the rest I say, not the Lord'; 'Concerning the unmarried, I have no command of the Lord, but I give my opinion as one who by the Lord's mercy is trustworthy.' At the end of this chapter he suggests that his personal advice is trustworthy, since 'I think that I have the Spirit of God.'

And it is certainly life in the Spirit that Paul commends. There were obviously many Christians who, like himself, came from a Jewish background, where religious teachings had developed over the years and by the 1st century gave detailed rulings about many aspects of life. How far were these rulings still important? In his letter to the Romans especially Paul offers a broad discussion of their pros and cons, but his conclusion is that 'in Christ Jesus' there is now a 'law of the Spirit of life' [Rom 8.2]:

Now we are discharged from the law, dead to that which held us captive, so that we serve not under the old written code but in the new life of the Spirit. [Rom 7.6]

This adheres closely to what Jesus himself had taught:

At that time Jesus declared, 'I thank thee, Father, Lord of heaven and earth, that thou hast hidden these things from the wise and understanding and revealed them to babes; yea, Father, for such was thy gracious will. All things have been delivered to me by my Father; and no one knows the Son except the Father, and no one knows the Father except the Son and any one to whom the Son chooses to reveal him. Come to me, all who labour and are heavy laden, and I will give you rest. Take my yoke upon you, and learn from me; for I am gentle and lowly in heart, and you will find rest for your souls. For my yoke is easy, and my burden is light.' [Mt 11.25-30]

The implied contrast here is with those who, like the Pharisees, 'bind heavy burdens, hard to bear, and lay them on men's shoulders' [Mt 23.4]. Jesus emphasises that his way is truly the Father's intention, in a passage where (unusually for a Synoptic Gospel) he speaks of his intimate relationship with the Father. We are reminded of the so-called 'farewell discourses' in the Fourth Gospel, where Jesus explains to those whose 'learning curve' is now sufficiently advanced:

The words that I say to you I do not speak on my own authority; but the Father who dwells in me does his works. [Jn 14.10]

A further comparison may be made between the two Gospels: the 'burden' mentioned by Matthew is elaborated in John's text: the disciples are 'to love one another', to follow Jesus' example of 'washing one another's feet', and to witness faithfully to him despite persecution.

We should also note an important rider concerning Jesus' teaching:

I have yet many things to say to you, but you cannot bear them now. When the Spirit of truth comes, he will guide you into all the truth; for he will not speak on his own authority, but whatever he hears he will speak, and he will declare to you the things that are to come. He will glorify me, for he will take what is mine and declare it to you. [Jn 16.12-15]

The 'many things' yet to be understood would no doubt include the wisdom of those (like St Paul) who may be judged to have 'the mind of Christ' [1 Cor 2.16]. It rests with the faithful to discern whether such teachings are distinct from 'the wisdom of this age' and focus truly on 'Jesus Christ and him crucified' [1 Cor 2.2]. Interpretation of his existing words, but also of the values he implemented in his own practice, certainly belongs to the Church's future agenda – and in fact had already begun when the Gospels were written down, since they themselves embody the fruits of Christian reflection over several decades.[10]

The Church has plainly had to face many new issues since the time of our Lord, and much guidance has emerged over the centuries. The danger is that what is relevant for one set of circumstances may be too rigidly retained even when the context has changed significantly. This is where Jesus' flexibility needs to be brought to mind. His concern was to bring liberty to the oppressed and to reach out to those who were marginalised, even if in so doing he appeared to transgress Jewish codes of behaviour. He was accused of being 'a glutton and a drunkard, a friend of tax collectors and sinners', which elicited the challenging comment, 'Yet wisdom is justified by her deeds' [Mt 11.19]. And in response to the accusation that his disciples had broken the Sabbath, he memorably replied:

The Sabbath was made for man, not man for the Sabbath. [Mk 2.27]

Jesus was also aware that God's highest hopes and expectations are not necessarily fulfilled immediately. Human weaknesses and limitations may mean that we fail to realise God's true purposes; but we are not abandoned when we stumble. Three different examples from the Gospels spring to mind, as Jesus relates to people with varying degrees of 'acceptability':

- By the time Jesus sits down to eat the Last Supper with his disciples, it is already in Judas Iscariot's mind to betray him. Yet he is not expelled, but shares the meal with them all. Jesus even (in Matthew and Mark, but not in Luke or John) accepts his false kiss in the garden afterwards.

- Jesus requests a drink of water from the woman of Samaria, who has had five husbands already and is now living with another man

---

[10] When Paul was accused of being an 'inferior' apostle by Christians in Corinth, his appeal was to 'the things that show my weakness' [2 Cor 11.30]. Not least were his physical sufferings, so that he claimed to carry even in his body 'the death of Jesus' in order for the life of Jesus to be visibly manifested [2 Cor 4.10–11]. His final plea to any Galatians who might still dispute his teaching was the same: 'Henceforth let no man trouble me; *for I bear on my body the marks of Jesus*' [Gal 6.17]. It was of course such marks still carried in Jesus' hands and side that enabled 'doubting Thomas' to recognise his risen Lord [Jn 20.27–28].

altogether. He tells her that, if she had asked him, 'he would have given you living water' [Jn 4.10].

- Peter, who had earlier denied knowing Jesus, nevertheless professes love (*agape*) for him when they meet later by the Sea of Tiberias. He repeats this claim, and is 'grieved' to be asked again. Jesus accepts his final response as perhaps more honest: Peter now restates his love as *philia* – affection, less demanding than the commitment implied in *agape*. Yet in the end he too would come 'to glorify God' by the manner of his death [Jn 21.19].

A remaining enigma

We need to recall that the inherited oral traditions used by the different evangelists were not all the same. They developed in a variety of contexts over differing lengths of time. Some issues may have mattered more or less to individual Christian communities, which may therefore be reflected in the details or phraseology of particular *pericopes* or sayings, as well as in the significance attached to them. Material found in one Gospel may be wholly omitted in another, or found in a remarkably variant form. The influence of Old Testament passages may differ from one Gospel to another, and of course each evangelist structured his Gospel in order to communicate as best he could with the particular audience for whom he was writing.

We have already noted Jesus' frequent use of the phrase 'Son of man' as his preferred way of speaking about himself. In most instances in the Gospels it is clearly not a messianic title, but this seems to change in later chapters of the Synoptic Gospels where the end times are discussed and the *parousia* is prophesied:

> Then will appear the sign of the Son of man in heaven, and then all the tribes of the earth will mourn, and they will see the Son of man coming on the clouds of heaven with power and great glory; and he will send out his angels with a loud trumpet call, and they will gather his elect from the four winds, from one end of heaven to another. [Mt 24.30-31]

The imagery seems to be taken directly from the book of Daniel:

> I saw in the night visions, and behold, with the clouds of heaven there came one like a son of man, and he came to the Ancient of Days and was presented before him. And to him was given dominion and glory and

kingdom, that all peoples, nations, and languages should serve him; his dominion is an everlasting dominion, which shall not pass away, and his kingdom one that shall not be destroyed. [Dan 7.13-14]

Yet is all this consistent with the temptations that Jesus rejected earlier?

The devil took him to the holy city, and set him on the pinnacle of the temple, and said to him, 'If you are the Son of God, throw yourself down; for it is written, He will give his angels charge of you.' ... Again, the devil took him to a very high mountain, and showed him all the kingdoms of the world and the glory of them... [Mt 4.5-6, 8]

It is almost as if Jesus' time of humble service on earth as 'Son of man' was subsequently considered (in some, but not all, circles) to have been ineffective; and so a 'second coming' with *power* and *great glory*, together with a company of *angels* – adjuncts that were deemed inappropriate at his first coming – is still necessary for God's kingdom to be fully established.

Of course, we are in the realm of imagery here, reassuring us that God's final victory is not in doubt. The early Church certainly needed to be reminded that the sacrifices of the faithful would not be in vain; so could it be that, when the Hebrew scriptures were scrutinised for messages of hope, the occurrence of the phrase 'Son of man' in Daniel was understood as referring to Jesus, prophesying the climax both of his story and of the world's; then, instead of remaining a poetic description of the End, a more literal version became embedded in the tradition and eventually in the (Synoptic) Gospels? Christian teaching about the Lord's coming clearly arose at a fairly early stage, since Paul instructs the Thessalonians in similar terms well before the Gospels were composed. It was, he says, '*by the word of the Lord* that we who are alive, who are left until the coming of the Lord, shall not precede those who have fallen asleep.' His account continues as vividly as the Synoptic writings:

The Lord himself will descend from heaven with a cry of command, with the archangel's call, and with the sound of the trumpet of God. [1 Thess 4.16]

The point, however, is that virtually none of this language occurs in John's Gospel. So the question arises: apart from speaking to his disciples of troubled times ahead, and therefore of their need to stand firm and if necessary to take up their own crosses (a warning found variously in all the Gospels), did Jesus also predict a 'second coming' in such apocalyptic language? How much of the latter was *by the word of the Lord*, given that the Fourth Gospel presents a rather different future? In his farewell discourses Jesus announces that he is 'going to the Father' [Jn 16.10, 28] and will be seen no more. 'The Counsellor' (the Holy Spirit) will then be present 'for ever' with his disciples and will bring all his teaching to their remembrance. He himself will 'prepare a place' for them, indicating that 'he will *come again* and will take you to myself, that where I am you may be also' [Jn 14.3].

The manner of his coming is left unspecified in this Fourth Gospel: will it be a corporate or a personal visitation? C.K. Barrett suggests the following in his *Commentary*:

> The primary reference... is to the eschatological advent of Jesus, or at any rate to his coming to the individual disciple at his death. But the ensuing discourse... shows clearly that John's thought of the advent is by no means exhausted in the older Synoptic notion of the parousia. The communion of Jesus with his disciples, their mutual indwelling, is not deferred till the last day, or even to the day of a disciple's death.

Indeed, it is in this Gospel that we find a strong emphasis upon *eternal* life:

> God so loved the world that he gave his only Son, that whoever believes in him should not perish but have eternal life. [Jn 3.16]

> Whoever lives and believes in me shall never die. [Jn 11.26]

It is worth noting too Jesus' exchange with the crowd before Jesus' final Passover in Jerusalem:

> '*Now* is the judgment of this world, *now* shall the ruler of this world be cast out; and I, when I am lifted up from the earth, will draw all men to myself.' He said this to show by what death he was to die. The crowd answered him, 'We have heard from the law that the Christ remains for ever. How can you say that the Son of man must be lifted up? Who is this Son of man?' [Jn 12.31-34]

For John, the supreme moment of judgment is his Cross, which is simultaneously the revelation of his glory. It is a baffling idea to those (maybe even among the apostolic communities) who have not fully absorbed Jesus' stress upon messianic service, and his understanding that as the incarnate Son of the Father he fulfils this role most perfectly in his self-offering as 'Son of man'.

If, however, we argue that within the New Testament a mature appreciation of Jesus' teaching about what the future holds is expressed better among later writings such as the Fourth Gospel, we should also be aware that a vast literature exists that includes many other proposals. The nature of the *parousia* is, one may safely say, as much an unresolved issue for us as it was for the early Church and for every generation of Christians ever since. It has become even more perplexing with the relatively recent growth in scientific understanding of the universe, which sees the prospect of life on earth quite differently from how it was regarded two thousand years ago. However, the phrase found in the Apocalypse, 'a new heaven and a new earth' [Apoc 21.1 cf. 2 Pet 3.13; Isa 65.17; 66.22], surely points us beyond biblical literalism to a deeper spiritual understanding of what God has in store for our world.

The suggestion that later strands of the New Testament may be more helpful than apparently earlier texts in coming to understand Jesus' teaching may sound surprising, given that historians tend to give weight to the more 'original'. In science, of course, the reverse is usually true – newer theories that leave fewer unexplained observations come to supplant less satisfactory hypotheses. But with religious writings, and especially with prophetic material, something similar often happens. Many of the Hebrew scriptures were subsequently reworked and recontextualised according to changing circumstances and developing insights; hence we may be misled into thinking (for example) that Genesis, which has definite theological priority, is the first book of the Old Testament ever to be written. Likewise in the Qur'an the idea of 'abrogation', whereby later revelations make some earlier verses obsolete, is firmly expressed in the text itself. This has led to serious disputes of interpretation, in the absence of unanimity about which verses are over-written. Nevertheless, divine revelation is a form of communication, requiring therefore its expression in language that – as far as possible – conveys its real meaning. This can well emerge gradually, under the guidance of the Holy Spirit [Jn 16.13]. It is not that Christians thereby 'abrogate' any Gospel sayings, but rather come to understand them better.

The key can often be to avoid reading 'difficult' texts in isolation (*'meaning'*, we were taught at Oxford by G.B. Caird, *'equals text plus context')* – so the 'Son of man' sayings have been read here alongside each other. Their context can be widened further by recalling that Jesus' future coming is not confined to the Last Day. The Gospels testify that he will be present under the forms of bread and wine in the Eucharist ('where two or three are gathered in my name'), anticipating the heavenly banquet – and prompting Jesus' disciples to live the new heavenly life even now. For what they do in acts of compassionate love (which is the keynote of heavenly existence) 'to one of the least of these my brethren' [Mt 25.40], is done to the Lord himself.

So we may conclude with the evocative title of the profoundly moving book *The God who Comes*, written by that Little Brother of Charles de Foucauld, Carlo Carretto. His closing words are also mine:

> He comes for the last time to break through the veil of my limits and to introduce me – with all his people which is the Church – into his invisible kingdom of light, life, and love. In order to hurry that day, from now on I am taking for myself the most beautiful prayer, expressed in the last words of Revelation and placed like a seal on revealed things: 'Come Lord Jesus'. How I embrace as mine the joyful hope contained in the reply 'Yes, I am coming soon.' Amen.

THE END

Rejoice in the Lord always
again I will say
Rejoice

I heard what seemed like the
voice of a great multitude
in heaven

The figure from KuNgoni Craft Centre in Malawi is carved from a single piece of wood.

He represents for us, not just one jubilant individual, but the whole company of saints.

et erat fenum & fal
nec luna ut lucceret in
luminauit eum & lux erat
est agnus